# INTERNATIONAL LAW

## Challenges of new global events

**1st Edition**

**Global**South
P R E S S

Copyright © 2015 by

**Wilson Almeida**

For more information, please contact info@globalsouthpress.com
or go to http://www.globalsouthpress.com/

Book design by **Héctor Guzmán**

# INTERNATIONAL LAW
## Challenges of new global events

ALMEIDA, Wilson
ISBN: 978-1-943350-17-9
International Law. Challenges of new global events
United States, GlobalSouth Press Inc. 2015, p. 292
Includes Bibliographical references and Index
1. Law - International Law. 2. International relations
3. International Studies

4

**Raising**South
P R E S S

## Editorial Board:

# Content

12

## PREFACE

Writing a book is always a lot of effort, but when the effort is shared with others, it decreases as much as your partners are responsible and competent. That's what happened in this research paper entitled "International Law: the Challenges of the New Global Events". We had many researchers of all levels, including Law and International Relations graduates; experimented researchers in the level of Post-graduate Professors, most of them at Catholic University of Brasilia and course coordinators and Professors of public and private universities participated as well. Many colleagues were excited and willing to contribute their thinking to understand the "New Global Events".

The chapters are composed of topics such as "South American regional integration: the gas of an approaching instrument", which discusses South American integration from the perspective of production and gas consumption; and "Brazil-China Cooperation in building sustainable energy infrastructure", dealing with important and recent cooperation between Brazil and China in the context of sustainable energy and infrastructure in the subcontinent.

There are topics like "Transnational organized crime in post-cold war: an analysis of drug trafficking and money laundering", analyzing a very important phenomenon in "New global events" such as international organized crime. We also deal with "Domestic and foreign impacts to the international mega-events: the case of Brazil and the preparations for world cup 2014" which reinforces the belief that the mega events bring important results for the host countries.

Other papers, such as "Foreign policy and security: development and impact of the Brazilian Defense Policy during Lula da Silva's administration" deal with an emphasis on foreign policy and national defense. Continuing with the challenges of the new global events, "The internationalization of Brazilian fashion industry under the perspective of knowledge" shows how Brazil has advanced in regards to the fashion industry.

There is the case of topics such as "The role of Institutions on the economic development of the Americas during the political emancipation" that have a historical nature and are very relevant. There is also a topic on "International law of protection in case of disaster response" and one that brings up a very current problem, which is "The tax consciousness of an instrument to combat tax avoidance and tax evasion".

"New strategic alliances to Taiwan: important partnerships in the world increasingly driven by economic and technological interests" is a chapter that providers understanding to a new moment for Taiwan in this "New global event" that may be the growth of China and the regional rivalry with the USA. There is a chapter which deals with the "polluter pays principle and its effectiveness in the scope of international environmental law" noting that these principles define new international regimes in law.

"Creation of a new statutory framework in Brazil for voluntary partnerships between the public administration and civil society organizations, members of third sector" is a long title to describe the importance of the third sector in the context of the new global events of this century. And, last but not least, "The right to die. The Appropriate forum for end-of-life decision making: courts and clinical", which deals with an important issue of our time, the right of each individual to die.

It can be accurately inferred that the above texts deal with some of the most important issues of the twenty-first century, the reader is invited to travel through these, which are the New Global Events that defy international law today.

Brasilia, October 2015

Wilson Almeida

16

# SOUTH AMERICAN REGIONAL INTEGRATION: GAS AS AN APPROACHING INSTRUMENT

Wilson Almeida[1]
Ivan Dib[2]
Christian Klein[3]

## INTRODUCTION

The relationship between Brazil and the other countries of the Southern Cone should be analyzed particularly from the relations between Brazil and Argentina, given that these countries represent the main axis of South American regional politics, which are the leading ones in Mercosur.

The International relations between Brazil and Argentina are conflicted in regards to the international projection of the two countries. Both have sought to undertake greater participation in the multilateral forums and international negotiations and to occupy a prominent position in the UN - United Nations - and in the WTO - World Trade Organization. The quest for a leadership position by Brazil makes the relations between the two countries more tense. Another divergent point refers to "the macroeconomic policies adopted by the two countries, which within Mercosur may imply in competitive disadvantages in terms of trade" (TELES; CANEDO, 2006, p. 3).

Nevertheless, there are converging points regarding foreign policy of the two countries, especially regarding the defense of democratic stability in the region and the bilateral cooperation.

> Brazilians and Argentinians share responsibilities for the preservation of democratic regimes and security of South American countries, as well as cooperating in the spheres of health and education, among others. (TELES; CANEDO, 2006, p. 3).

---

1 Professor at Catholic University of Brasilia.
2 Analist of International Relations
3 Professor at Catholic University of Brasilia.

If the international relations between Brazil and Argentina reveal divergent and convergent points, the relations between Brazil and Argentina with Paraguay and Uruguay are fading. These last two countries have expressed their dissatisfaction with the "meager results that the integration process has brought to their economies." (TELES; CANEDO, 2006, p. 4). For this reason, representatives of both Paraguay and Uruguay have been seeking the right to conclude free trade treaties with countries outside Mercosur.

> Another source of discontent from Paraguay and Uruguay would be the result of so-called 'bilateralism' that Argentina and Brazil would practice, according to which countries would maintain the affairs of Mercosur between them, bringing them to the negotiating table only when the agreements were already consummated.
>
> [...]
>
> As it does not receive the proper attention from their main partners, in this case Brazil and Argentina, Paraguay seeks to strengthen its relations with countries outside of the region, which represents a strong threat to South American integration and the objectives of regional leadership from Brazil. (TELES; CANEDO, 2006, p. 4).

A relationship in South America that keeps affinities both in the political and in the economic field is the relationship between Brazil and Chile. Chile has the most stable economy in South America, which makes it very attractive to neighboring states. For this reason, Brazil has sought to enhance its commercial transactions with this country, with the objective to reach higher gains and to straighten bilateral relations.

In the political sphere, as one of the objectives of regional integration in Brazil is the preservation of democracy. The consolidation of democracy in Chile is a crucial factor for the strengthening of ties between the two countries.

> In addition, Chile has shown constant support Brazilian initiatives, both at the regional and the global levels. Support for the creation of the South American Community of Nations and the Brazilian ambition to occupy a permanent seat in the Security Council of the United Nations are evidence of this fact. (TELES, CANEDO, 2006, p. 5).

Another point to be considered is the relationship between Brazil and the countries that make up the Andean Community of Nations - CAN - (Bolivia, Colombia, Ecuador and Peru). The Andean Community of Nations - CAN presents difficulties in meeting their goals of integration since its inception in 1969. These difficulties are, in short, due to internal political conflicts and differences between trade policies of its members.

With regard to relations between Brazil and Bolivia, Brazil is the main consumer of Bolivian gas and soybeans. These products account for nearly half of all exports from Bolivia. However, Bolivia's decision to nationalize its natural gas fields and oil has generated tension in the relationship between the two countries.

Despite of the fact that the investments of Brazil in Bolivia represent about 20% of Bolivia's GDP, Bolivia states that:

> Natural gas should not be exported under the current conditions. The laws of hydrocarbons (oil and gas) should be modified first, so that the Bolivian State receives 50% and not 18% of taxes, as currently collected by the oil companies that exploit them. (TELES; CANEDO, 2006, p. 6).

Conflicts between Brazil and Bolivia impair both countries. Affecting Brazilian interests once that, "24 million cubic meters of Bolivian gas are consumed in Brazil at a ratio of 80%, in power generation of industrial enterprises, in the supply of the vehicle fleet powered by Natural Gas (NGV), and thermoelectric as well"(TELES.; Canedo, 2006, p. 6)

Bolivian interests, in turn, are affected in the extent that their decisions can drive away prospective foreign investments, besides the political uneasiness suffered by the international level, resulting in loses of its market share in its exports.

Regarding Venezuela, it should be stressed that the country is no longer part of Andean Community of Nations - CAN in 2006, arguing that the integration efforts that drove the group found themselves mitigated by the decision of Colombia and Peru to sign free-trade treaties with the United States.

With Chávez, Venezuela began to exert great regional influence, making high investments based on raising the price of oil. Thus, the Brazilian strategy in South America comes into tension with dollars earned from the fossil fuel that Hugo Chavez used to influence the region with.

Thus, the international politics of Brazil in South America finds obstacles in Venezuela's "petro-activity" and the personalist regime of Hugo Chávez that does not hide its aspiration to lead alliances in the subcontinent.

We can thus conclude that the exit of Venezuela from the Andean Community of Nations - CAN and the nationalization of hydrocarbons by Bolivia represented an obstacle at first to the South American regional integration.

> With the abandonment of Venezuela in the block, Bolivia clearly aligned to Venezuela, while Ecuador adopted a more neutral policy, but still defending the process of regional integration. At the same time it left the Andean block, Venezuela has criticized Mercosur, noting that if there is no social change, the block will have the same order of CAN.

> This situation sparked fears in the governments of Brazil and Argentina, which until then, were excited about the possible entry of Venezuela into MERCOSUR.

> [...]

> Thus, the output of Venezuela to CAN threatens the viability of the two blocks of integration of South America, as well as the design driven by Brazil, a regional leader in South America. (TELES, CANEDO, 2006, p. 7).

Nevertheless, since July 31, 2012 Venezuela became part of Mercosur, expanding the Economic Block created in 1991, demonstrating thereby a clear interest in the Regional Integration and consequent economic, political and social development of the block's country members. With the formalization of Venezuela's participation:

> Mercosur entered a new stage (...), relying on a population of 270 million inhabitants and a GDP of around $ 3 trillion, which represents about 83% of South America's GDP and 70% of population of South America. (...) Mercosur becomes a leading global producer of food and minerals. (BRASIL, 2012).

## THEORETICAL FRAMEWORK OF REGIONAL COOPERATION

To understand the phenomenon of regional integration, it is of high importance to understand the theories of coordination and cooperation.

Richardson (1994, apud. VILAS BOAS, 2004) explains the coordination from concepts about industrial organization, applicable as an analogy to the formation of regional blocks. Coordination is nothing more than "intra-firm" balanced organization with market transactions. Thus, applying this concept to regional integration, countries would be like islands "of coordination and planning in a sea of market relations" (RICHARDSON, 1994 apud VILAS BOAS, 2004, p. 13). However,

Businesses operate, in most cases, through a cooperation network formed by its subsidiaries and affiliates interrelated and performing transactions through agreements and subcontracts that distort the dichotomy between companies and via market transactions.

[...]

Negotiations between countries may be comparable to some extent, such as bilateral relations governed by contracts, to the extent that they also have coordination mechanisms as incentives, decision rights allocation, provisions that aim to give credibility to the commitments and others. However, it should be noted that, despite some similarities, relations between nations cannot and should not be reduced to bilateral business relations governed by contracts.

[...]

Anyway, the comparison of trade between nations with relations between companies is valid in that it highlights the role of coordination and the search for stability in the relationship between the parties. [...] The coordination can facilitate the convergence of the strategies of the parties, or at least reduce the discrepancy of shares in searches of interests of each one. (VILAS BOAS, 2004, p 14-15).

Thus, *mutatis mutandis*, we can say that the process of Regional integration is like cooperative activities of a company, which relate to other businesses, balancing and minimizing their particular interests, in order to achieve the common goals of cooperative enterprises.

Applying these concepts to international relations, analogically, it can be stated that, in the regional integration process, States should act in a cooperative manner, balancing national interests with those of other countries, aiming at the realization of common interests in the region. Highlighting, however, that in the occurrence of coordination and cooperation, there is no assignment of any portion of the autonomy or sovereignty of the State.

For a better theoretical understanding of the regional integration process, we must keep in mind two other theories: the Economic Theory of Integration and the Political Theory of Integration, which will be the subject of upcoming topics.

## ECONOMIC THEORY OF INTEGRATION

After World War II, international economic integration began to be studied as an autonomous branch. During World War II, it became clear that "isolationism" should give way to another economic model that led States to a "freer trade through international institutions that promote not only the abolition of barriers, but also a better balance between countries "(Pinto, 2004, p. 2).

From 1950, the term economic integration was renamed "the voluntary process of growing interdependence of separate economies"(PINTO, 2004, p. 2).

Even though Gregory and Haberler had published, in 1921 and in 1936, respectively, about precursor studies on customs unions, the first author to systematize the study of international economic integration was Jacob Viner, with the work on customs unions published in 1950.

> Before the work of Viner, economic analysis of integration based on the theory of comparative advantage leading to it, regional agreements were held as beneficial for both countries as members and for non-members and that such agreements produced many of the consequences of global trade liberalization. (PINTO, 2004, p. 2).

The "economic integration" is subdivided into "sectoral integration" and "general integration. "This" sectoral integration "is one that covers only certain sectors of economic activity, while the "general integration" is one that covers all economic sectors. An example of sectoral integration is the European Coal and Steel Community - ECSC, which covers only coal and steel products. The Southern Common Market - MERCOSUR, in turn, is an example of general integration.

Economic integration can take various levels, according to Pinto (2004), namely: national integration, regional integration and universal integration. The national integration concerns the integration of the various regions of the same country. Regional integration refers to the gathering of various countries in an economic block. And Universal integration occurs when all countries come together in a single economic block. Regarding the deepening, according to Balassa (1980 apud MARIANO, 1995, p. 18), economic integration can be classified as:

a) Free Trade Area: assumes the complete extinction of tariffs between the countries, members keeping full sovereignty in relation to third countries.

b) Customs Union: is the expansion of the free-trade zone by eliminating tariffs and other measures seen as barriers to trade, the creation of a common external tariff of the member countries in relation to others. Furthermore, this type of integration requires some delegation of sovereignty. It is a gradual process, initiated by a common agenda for the creation of equal rates for all.

c) Common Market: Assumes all that was mentioned above, plus the free movement of capital goods and production factors. A level of homogeneity and common law requires some type of supranationalism, requiring some institutionalization. Trading is very complex and requires for its formation, coordination and macroeconomic policies allowing a limited unification of those.

d) Economic Union: is all of the above, plus the unification of the macroeconomic policies of countries, because the differences between them are problematic and require solving (reaching this means coming to a complete economic integration) The economic union tends to dilute the economic identity of nations and could result in integration policy where countries would become parts of a larger state.

By this classification, Pinto (2004) still adds monetary union and the Economic and Monetary union. According to the author:

> The monetary union entails the replacement of the currencies of participating countries for a common currency to all of them, as is the case of the euro relative to the most integrated in the European Union countries.

> The economic and monetary union characterized by the existence of several states, concerted economic policy, a single currency and a common central bank, which holds the power to issue of currency. (PINTO, 2004, p. 4).

Economists, according to Gilpin (2001 apud PINTO, 2004), analyze the Economic integration from the point of view of the resulting consequences. Already, political scientists seek to analyze the causes of economic and political integration, the latter being the object of study of the following topic.

## POLITICAL THEORY OF INTEGRATION

Unlike the relations of coordination and cooperation, which does not imply a reduction or loss of autonomy or sovereignty to the States, the relations of integration always imply flexing the portion of sovereignty by the countries involved. Moreover, the process of integration presupposes the practice of aimed policies to enable this association.

Economic integration theories seek to explain the causes of the integration process, while political theories seek to explain the phenomenon of integration itself.

The main political theories about the process of regional integration are, according to Pinto (2004), federalism, functionalism, neo-functionalism, neo-institutionalism and the inter-governmentalism.

Federalism is defined as the process of political integration, in which an institution, or a set of institutions are created, for which States transfer voluntarily sovereignty.

However, Gilpin (2001) notes that the Federalist theory does not have a decisive impact on the matter of integration, since there are reduced cases of success.

With so many theoretical differences, two new theories have emerged about the integration policy that sought to synthesize what their predecessors defended: the theory of neo-institutionalism and the theory of inter-governmentalism.

Neo-institutionalism emphasizes the need to create "International institutions to solve market failures, economic problems and also problems arising from the economic and political integration "(Pinto, 2004, p. 19).

> For neo-institutionalists, international institutions promote cooperation and create incentives for states to resolve their disputes. These theories echoed the opinions of political elites, which widely accept the neo-institutionalists explanations of participants' interest in cooperating in the regional context in which institutions are seen as organized rules, codes of conduct and structures that provide significant gains to solve problems collectively (Coleman, 1998 apud PINTO, 2004, p. 19).

Regarding the theory of inter-governmentalism, Gilpin (2001) argues that this is the most significant theory about political and economic integration, since it considers the economic interests as the driving force of regional integration, which, to highlight the importance of regional institutions, assigns a central role to national governments.

Although these theories try to explain the process of political integration, none of them is able to exhaust the topic, once it is a process, that integration is constantly changing and improving.

# REGIONAL INTEGRATION AND THE STRENGTH OF THE GAS

In the context of regional integration, energy, whose scope is the search for "socio-economic growth of all stakeholders, promoting a better utilization of the value in the chain energy sector" stands out an important way (OXILIA; FAGA, 2006, p. 5).

Energy is the key factor for economic and social growth of a country and is equally correct to say that energy drives the development of a region, since it promotes the development of each country belonging to certain regional block.

According to Vilas Boas (2004), access to energy is a prerequisite not only for economic growth but also to achieve greater equity in society.

Considering that economic growth and social equity cause increased energy consumption, the Southern Cone countries (region composed of Brazil, Argentina, Paraguay and Uruguay, plus Chile and Bolivia as associate members) have turned to the discussion about the energetic integration of the region. Among the various forms of energy, one has excelled in the scenery of the Southern Cone: natural gas. According to Vilas Boas (2004, p 20.):

> In the Southern Cone, the growth in energy supply is directly related to the increased supply of natural gas. Both by increasing the end use of natural gas in the industrial, commercial, residential and vehicular segments as primarily for its use in thermoelectric generation.

The gas integration has proved key to the regional integration of energy in the southern cone, and the rapid growth of natural gas demanded in the southern cone makes it important to analyze the aspects of this industry and those involved in the integration process.

According to Vilas Boas (2004), coordination and cooperation are the most efficient ways to implement the integration, especially in the gas energy sector in the Southern Cone, because they allow better planning and predictability of demand, stability of rules, most allocative efficiency of resources and lower political risk.

Specifically meaningful to natural gas is its production chain, in order to be able to understand the difficulties in the integration of an energy field. This fact will be the subject of study in the next section of this paper

The chain production of natural gas is divided into up-stream, which is actually getting the product, and down-stream, which is the use of natural gas as a feedstock. The levels of down-stream are exploration, production and natural gas processing. "The production covers the rise of natural gas reservoir, the primary processing in the field, separating water - gas-condensate - oil and finally the transportation to the storage base." (Martins, 2006, p 6). The down-stream activities are related from product supply to final consumers:

> However, their connections are more extensive, once the mentioned activities using large number of complex and specific equipment (platforms, pipelines, refining and processing equipment) and specialized services (engineering, automation, consulting, construction, maintenance, security, and others).

To define exploration, it is the phase of evaluation of the probability of occurrence of natural gas in a given geological formation, studying the gas potential of a geographic region, geology, drilling of exploratory wells and commercial feasibility of geological formation or field.

Exploitation in turn, involves the commercial activities that allow the operation of the wells. It includes drilling, completion and re-complementation of the wells, placement of sealing heads, valves, remote commands, pumping units, injection and reinjection and other accessories that will enable the production of natural gas within safety standards.

The production comprises the steps of rising natural gas, primary processing, separation "water - gas-condensate - oil and transportation to the base storage or treatment facility" (Martins, 2008, p. 6).

The processing of natural gas refers to all activities conducted after production.

> In the primary processing performed in the field, the heavy fractions are removed from the natural associated gas, so as to enable its compression to the nearest processing station, where they will be recovered and separated from the net waste gas to be transported or to stored hydrocarbons.

The transportation of natural gas can occur in two ways: through pipelines or in the form of liquefied or compressed gas. Storage is in disabled formations or those specially constructed for this purpose.

The activities of down-stream, after the distribution of natural gas, are related to product supply to end users.

Next, the supply chain of natural gas in the Southern Cone region will be analyzed with emphasis on Argentina, Bolivia and Brazil, countries where the production is concentrated in natural gas.

Furthermore, we will analyze the natural gas reserves in Brazil, as well as its importance and its impact on the regional integration process. And finally a historical overview of the energy integration process in the European Union will be presented, aiming to elucidate the difficulties and aims of this integration.

## THE SOUTHERN CONE AND THE ENERGY INTEGRATION

The production chain of natural gas in the Southern Cone focuses on Argentina, Bolivia and Brazil. Currently, Paraguay and Uruguay do not have large reserves of natural gas or have any demand for this energy source.

Bolivia has relatively limited reserves. However, domestic consumption of fuel is very small. Thus, most of the production is exported or reinjected into the fields. Argentina on the other hand has ample reserves, which are sufficient to cover relatively large domestic demand and meet foreign markets needs. (OLIVEIRA; ARAÚJO, 2012). Argentina is also the owner of the most developed natural gas industry in the Southern Cone region. Brazil, and Bolivia, has limited natural gas reserves, however, there is an expectation of significant growth of these reserves.

Argentina and Bolivia are potential suppliers of natural gas to Brazil, where demand for natural gas has increased. This gas supply, as seen, occurs mainly through pipelines, as we will see in the topics: Brazil - Bolivia Gas Pipeline and Argentina - Brazil Pipeline.

## BRAZIL - BOLIVIA GAS PIPELINE

The first negotiations between the Brazilian and Bolivian governments about the energy policy took place in 1992 under the government of Collor. However, the mobilizations for the construction of a gas pipeline between the two countries were interrupted by the institutional crisis of the Collor administration and the consequent impeachment. Later, in the presence of Itamar Franco, who had Fernando Henrique Cardoso as the Minister of Foreign Affairs, the process of pipeline construction was resumed.

Petrobras, who at the time was not as influential, took the leadership of the project, becoming its main promoter and financier. The construction of the Bolivia- Brazil – Gasobol pipeline started in 1990, in which we two billion dollars where invested for its construction (Barufi, et al., 2006).

In 1999, Gasobol started commercial operations: 3,150 kilometers long, with a capacity to transport 30 million cubic meters of natural gas per day (Barufi, et al., 2006).

"The pipeline has contributed to a substantial diversification of the Brazilian matrix of importation of energetic goods, collaborating with increasing energy security of the country "(Barufi, et al., 2006, p. 190).

Once Brazil's dependence on Bolivian gas had become a growing concern. Petrobras saw itself pressed to gradually replace the dependence on Bolivian gas for greater domestic production of natural gas.

"The explanation for this concern is related to the rapid growth of the Brazilian market for gas (although much below potential) and the fact that the Bolivian gas accounted for a significant share of this market "(Barufi, et al., 2006, p. 190-191).

> In 2004, about 54% of all gas sold, excluding Petrobras' own uses, was imported, Bolivia being the main supplier. In physical terms, the Bolivian imports represent more than 80% of the gas sold in São Paulo, Mato Grosso do Sul and the entire southern region of the country.
>
> [...]
>
> This situation leaves the country vulnerable to various political instabilities that have shaken countries in South America and troubled trade, particularly sensitive to losses in the gas area. Therefore, since 2005, even before the nationalization of the Bolivian reserves, the debate has widened towards Brazil diversification of its sources of gas supply. (Barufi, et al., 2006, p. 191-192).

In order to reduce Brazil's dependence on Bolivian gas two strategies were adopted: a) the performance of new import projects, seeking to integrate new areas of supply, so as to reduce Bolivian lead; b) investment by Petrobras in natural gas production in the Basin of Campos, Santos and Espirito Santo.

However, imports of Bolivian gas should be analyzed beyond strictly energy interest. The Gasobol is a reference axis for investment and creation of new productive activities for the two countries: Brazil and Bolivia. Nowadays, Brazil is the first trading partner of Bolivia and is considered by the country as a prime source of investment and promising market consumer of its mineral wealth and energy inputs (Barufi, et al., 2006)

## ARGENTINA – BRAZIL GAS PIPELINE

Brazil has studied with Argentinian state companies *Yacimientos Petrolíferos Fiscales* - YPF and *Gas Del State*, the possibility of integration and technical-economic cooperation in the natural gas sector, especially regarding the possibility of import of Argentinian natural gas to Rio Grande do Sul (RODRIGUES, 1989).

In July 1986, the Integration and the Economic Cooperation Agreement was signed by Brazil and Argentina, which involves several areas of interest, each with specific protocols. Protocol No. 8, which was about the energy sector, beyond the possibility of joint action among countries in the petroleum industry, established the studies on the import of Argentinian natural gas to Brazil.

Since 1989, BRASPETRO, a subsidiary of Petrobras, operates in Argentina in the energy sector. Thus, this company started with some Brazilian private companies, "to participate in the expansion of the collection system and to program gas transfer, with installation and construction of treatment plants and pipelines in Argentina." (RODRIGUES, 1989, p. 2)

The import of Argentinian gas to Brazil was made possible after the signing of the Economic Cooperation and Integration Agreement. Previously, some projects had already been considered, as Roberts points out (1989, p 4.):

> (...) It is worth remembering that included is the implementation of a pipeline to transport about 10 million m³ / day for the market of São Paulo, with approximately 2,300 km long and is 1.450km in Argentinian territory and 860km on the Brazilian side. This pipeline would have on Home Field of Duran, Province of Salta, in Northern Argentina, and Brazil entering in through Foz do Iguaçu, and was then directed to São Paulo. Total investments were valued at $ 1.6 billion. However the discovery of large natural gas reserves associated in the Campos Basin and the prospects for gas production in the Santos Basin showed the impossibility of importing Argentinian natural gas in the region of São Paulo, at least within a medium-term vision.

With this, Brazil and Argentina began to consider the possibility of importing Argentinian gas to Rio Grande do Sul. However, studies conducted under the Protocol 8 showed two difficulties to build a pipeline linking San Jeronimo Sud, in Argentina, to Porto Alegre: the demand for natural gas was very small and there was a significant difference between the price offered by Argentina and feasible price for the Brazilian market.

The political side repeatedly expressed by their "Presidents to promote the integration of the two countries through an energy vector" led, however, to be given to further studies" (RODRIGUES, 1989, p 4.) aiming to analyze other market possibilities, in order to consume more gas (from 2 to 2.5 million m³ / day), ensuring the economic viability of importing.

## RESERVES OF NATURAL GAS IN BRAZIL

Gas reserves are discovered natural gas resources commercially recoverable. According to Martins (2008, p. 10th) reservations can be classified on:

- Proven Reserves - are those who, based on the analysis of geological and engineering data commercially recover estimates with a high degree of certainty;

- Probable Reserves - are those whose analysis of geological data and engineering indicate greater uncertainty in their recovery when compared to estimates of proven reserves;

- Possible Reserves - are those whose analysis of geological data and engineering indicates greater uncertainty in their recovery when compared to estimates of probable reserves;

- Total Reserves - represents the sum of proven, probable and possible reserves.

In Brazil, between 1994 and 2005, the number of proven reserves increased by 54%. This increase is related primarily to research in the area, aimed at reducing the dependence on oil (Martins, 2008). The proven reserves of natural gas in Brazil in 2005 totaled 306 billion cubic meters.

The main findings of natural gas reserves in Brazil occurred in the Campos Basin - "Sedimentary basin where the largest concentration of giant fields of the country lies, such as Albacora, Marlin and Roncador" and the Solimões Basin - "sedimentary basin which hosts the Polo Urucú, where much of the gas is reinjected, and the deposit of Jurua, still without commercial application". New reserves were also found in the State of Espírito Santo (Espírito Santo Basin), a region that has been highlighted as the second largest source of oil and gas in the country. (MARTINS, 2008, p 11)

These findings positively influence Brazil to foster the process of energy integration in the Southern Cone, since the country is strengthened in the domestic market and can move on to discussing their entry into the international market, not only as consumers but also as a natural gas supplier.

The transportation and distribution of natural gas are marked by Natural monopoly. Natural monopoly occurs when certain industrial activity is concentrated in a single firm, with no competition with other companies in the same industry market.

The sub-activity, which "arises from organizational advantages of concentration of production in a single firm, in other words, reducing transaction costs" (VILAS BOAS, 2004, p 31), is what enables the natural monopoly. Regarding the sub-activity and their reflections in earnings of the company, Church and Mansell explain (1997 apud VILAS BOAS, 2004, p 31-32.):

> The costs of expansion of facilities can be minimized if they are significant and infrequent. The optimal expansion strategy is that which maximizes profit trade-off between, on one hand, the reduction the cost of major constructions/ installations at once, and secondly, increases in maintenance costs due to idle capacity (while demand is still not sufficient to occupy the whole capacity increase). In general, the gains are larger when expansions undertaken by a single firm, for costs related to the coordination of a group of firms seeking the optimal expansion are considerable. They are also tied to the operation of pipeline less complex networks and with single operator gains. Besides the fact that the construction of a network by a single firm is more likely to achieve the optimal configuration

The transportation and distribution of natural gas have specific characteristics that link the decision making processes and investments to the natural monopoly model.

Regarding the supply of natural gas contracts, these should be long-term, in view of the "indivisibility of equipment, the long period time required to build and maturing investments and high sunk costs associated with the difficulty of storage." these factors offer incentives for vertical integration, form of integration through which the States unite on a multinational level.

The marketing of natural gas, unlike transport and distribution, encourages competitiveness, since it can be efficiently carried out by various companies in the same market. In the competitive organization, there is the search of several advantages (quality, cost, speed, innovation and flexibility) over competitors.

The supplier of natural gas in the competitive markets, adds to the natural gas chain "efficiency, competition and liquidity" (RODRIGUES, 2003 apud VILAS BOAS, 2004, p. 32). Efficiency means doing right things and smarter with less effort and better use of resources. Competition, in turn, refers to the position of a market in which traders act independently in relation to consumers, seeking to reach their goals, as profit or sales through different instruments (price, quality, etc.). Liquidity is the ability of the asset to be converted into cash quickly and with little loss of value, so it can be used in transactions (BARBOSA, 2010).

The competitiveness in a market contributes to the balance of the system, because the profit comes from the arbitrage possibilities of values. Moreover, "the trading companies often provide services such as risk mitigation" (VILAS BOAS, 2004, p 33). Thus:

> A trader can get a lower price when buying large volumes of a producer, achieving greater security of supply by diversifying their sources and increasing the efficiency of a contract by selling to consumers with seasonality and peak distinct consumption.

However, not always will competition have potential competitive activity. Therefore, in many countries, the step of commercialization of natural gas requires special attention from regulators. This is because the exploration, production and marketing of natural gas are constituent parts of a larger chain, which comprises the transportation and distribution of naturally monopolistic activities. Therefore, it is necessary to integrate the production chain of natural gas, which usually occurs through vertical integration.

## NATURAL GAS INDUSTRY IN BRAZIL

The natural gas industry in Brazil has a low market share on energy. The consumption of gas in Brazil is reduced compared to the consumption of "mature markets" (LAUREANO, 2002, p. 32).

The modernization of the natural gas industry in Brazil is a current process. "Until recently, the low level of reserves and a basic transport infrastructure are still in development which has characterized the industry. No clear or specific regulations were in place for the Natural Gas Industry" (LAUREANO, 2002, p. 31)

The changes being implemented in the Brazilian natural gas industry are due to recent discoveries of reserves, both in Brazil and throughout South America, linked to reforms in the electric power industry, which increased production being related to increased consumption of natural gas.

In addition, the Brazilian gas industry historically marked by the monopoly of the State is opening up to competition, favoring the growth of the sector along with the expansion of the pipeline network.

As per Laureano (2002, p 31.):

> The Brazilian energy reform focuses on growth convergence between the gas and electric industries, mainly to route the electricity supply crisis. However, this goal has major barriers in the country, given to the descpivel development of both industries in Brazil. Although the present electricity market has relative maturity, especially in the Southeast, the gas market is still incipient.

Conclusively, one realizes that this new policy has modified the strategies of energy companies, which have sought integration as means of establishing the market.

In this sense, Ghirardi (2008, www.diplo.org.br) says:

> The possibility to integrate the natural gas industry offers advantages. Countries in the region seek to take advantage of the complementarity between supply and demand, the financing capacity and technological capability. There is need for investment in various sectors of the industry, to explore and expand the reserve base and production, how to build transportation networks to take the product from the fields to the consumer centers, or to build local urban distribution centers. The construction of a network of regional gas trade can indeed be an effective tool for the development of the countries of the regional block.

Especially in the Southern Cone region, integration of the natural gas industry has become an excellent strategy for the development of the region, as will be discussed in the next section of this study.

The human being has always been in contact with some form of energy. However, in earlier times, man saw energy as something inherent to the natural environment.

Fire was one of the primary sources of energy with which man had contact with, and when he had mastered the technique of making fire, this source of energy had become part of their everyday life, whether for the purpose of space heating (cave) or in improving their food. Since then, the search for energy sources has become critical to maintaining quality of life.

During the Industrial Revolution, with the creation of the steam engine, the search for energy sources had gained greater amplitude. "The burning of coal supplied energy to move a lot of machines that would be made over the coming years." (BORGES, 2010, p. 5).

Currently, there is no sector of society that is free from energy dependence. The economy of a country always has, directly or indirectly, from some form of energy.

The present scenario of globalization imposes upon states, requiring them to be self-sufficient in some source of "distinct energy from oil, which constitutes the major energy source even from a fossil and pollutant fuel."(Borges, 2010, p.7). This ensures self-sufficiency to the State security in the face of possible energy crises that may occur due to high dependence on fossil fuel oil, on which the overwhelming majority of economies are based.

Thus, the search for alternative sources of energy, especially the energy produced from natural gas has gained strength in the Southern Cone. The region has invested especially in the natural gas industry, with the goal of expanding the energy mix of the region, to ensure good levels of growth and economic development and ensure its energy security

It should be noted that "to say that a nation has energy security is synonymous with guarantee of freedom, independence and, consequently, self-determination". (BORGES, 2010, p. 7).

The big question that curtails energy integration is reconciling with the following factors:

> Security of energy supply, reduction of energy dependence of national states and the mitigation of impacts of climate change caused by greenhouse gases, especially from the burning of fossil fuels. (Queiroz, 2010 www.infopetro. wordpress.com).

The compatibility of these factors is extremely complex, which highlights the growing importance of the binomial Energy-Technology in the process of finding solutions (QUEIROZ; 2012).

In this sense, it is clear that, on an international level, there should be an expansion of the degree of interdependence of national energy policies. This interdependence is important as in the production process, the growth of a region directly influences the growth of the regions with which it interrelates. In the national level, States should seek a significant share in the international energy scene and it should carry institutional arrangements, regulatory devices and energy policy instruments different from those used in the past and to adequate to the new objectives. (QUEIROZ; 2012).

Thus, we can conclude that there is, in the Southern Cone region, an energy dependence between states, since the energy sources in the region are unevenly distributed.

Despite the differences, there is a strong interdependence, as the expansion and development of any of the States of the Southern Cone necessarily leads to the expansion and development of other States with which they interrelate. The import of natural gas, for example, within the Southern Cone is essential to produce the supply of import markets. Furthermore, this import is also fundamental to the composition of Gross Domestic Product - GDP of exporting countries.

Among the various sources of energy explored in the Southern Cone region, the one which presents greater potential for energy integration is natural gas.

A great potential for economic growth exists in the Southern Cone from the set of labeled interconnection of natural gas. Furthermore, this interconnection is a strong opportunity for the region to migrate from a dependence on oil for an energy independence based on natural gas, favoring a "matrix model of the future which focuses on renewable energy "(CORRAL, 2009, p. 1).

There is, however, a need for countries in the region to coordinate their international policies and their legal systems, because although there are clear conditions of supply and demand in the region to enhance the integration; the lack of coordination of these factors causes a shock in the relationship between countries and causes distrust in potential investors.

Thus, there is a balance between the external policies of countries in the region and the "unification" of understanding between their legal systems, countries can benefit from a closer relationship and therefore more conducive to energy integration. Accordingly, such countries may receive foreign investment, providing energy and regional integration, with all the benefits therein.

## GAS INTEGRATION IN THE SOUTHERN CONE

With the increasing demand for fuel "natural gas" on the global scenarios, the Southern Cone countries have an opportunity to develop such a resource related industry in the region, so as to fit within the international market, once that they are in possession of large reserves.

Energy integration, especially the gas integration in the Southern Cone, may be driving regional integration in South America. Aiming to elucidate these claims, the reserves of the region and in the world, the flow gas trends within the Southern Cone and the transportation infrastructure of the natural gas in the Southern Cone will be explored. The historical and recent developments in the gas integration in the Southern Cone will be analyzed, along with the contribution of gas integration in the Southern Cone for the development of regional integration in South America and, finally, energy integration, through natural gas, as enabler of the South American regional integration.

Russia owns 30.5% of the proven gas reserves of the world, and the remaining reserves are distributed as follows: the Middle Eastern countries have, in addition, 36% of total proved reserves, Europe has 8.6%, Southeast Asia and Australia have 8.1%, Africa has 7.6%, North America has 4.6% and South America and Central America have 4.5% (VILAS BOAS, 2004).

In this context, it is noteworthy that North America, which in 1992 had 6.8% of total world proven gas reserves, had a 24% drop in their natural gas reserves, being in a state of impending deficit supply of natural gas. Concomitantly, South America and Central America, which in 1992 had 3.9% of total world proven gas reserves, had a 33% increase in its reserves, making it therefore possible to become exporters of natural gas to North America (VILAS BOAS, 2004).

There are projects for natural gas terminals on the east and west coasts of the United States of America and Mexico, in order to ensure the supply of the growing demand for natural gas in the country.

> This prospect is viewed with great concern by the American authorities. The important role of natural gas in the energy matrix of the USA, which in 2002 accounted for 27% of primary energy consumption in this country, reflects the dangers of a lack of gas. VILAS BOAS, 2004, p. 59).

In the Southern Cone, in turn, the scenario is different. The reserves of the region are sufficient to meet the demand for natural gas for years. Despite the reservations of the region representing only 4.5% of total world proven gas reserves, Bolivia's reserves grew at a rate of 9.2% p.a., Brazilian grew at a rate of 3.1% p.a., and Argentina grew at a rate of 0.2% p.a.

Chile has a small volume of natural gas, and its reserves are in hard to reach places. Now, Paraguay and Uruguay do not have natural gas reserves whatsoever. (VILAS BOAS, 2004).

The potential growth of the Bolivian and Brazilian proven gas reserves is significant, considering the proven and possible reserves (VILAS BOAS, 2004). The development of reserves in the Santos Basin should triple the proven reserves of Brazil, increasing the position of the Southern Cone for proven gas reserves. "Another factor that points to a large potential for reserve growth in the region is the short time in which the basins were really explored" (VILAS BOAS, 2004, p. 62), particularly in Bolivia and Brazil, where investments in the gas industry are recent.

> In short, the natural gas reserves in the Southern Cone had considerable growth in recent years and, as a consequence of the dynamics of reserve growth and production in countries in the region, the reserve/production ratio has increased in Bolivia and Brazil and declined in Argentina, where the reserve/production ratio increased from 21.6 years in 1992 to 16 years in 2002.

> Aiming to better present the dynamics of natural gas within the Southern Cone region, in the following topic the flow of the early exploration of natural gas in the region will be explored to indicate the possible change of these flows as a result of newly discovered natural gas reserves.

Historically, due to the layout of natural gas reserves and according to the consumer market, Bolivia and Argentina have always been the leading exporter of natural gas in the Southern Cone, while Brazil, Chile and Uruguay were the importers of fuel. Paraguay does not import natural gas, because it has no demand, either produces or exports, because it has no reserves on its territory, and were therefore outside of the natural gas market in the Southern Cone. However, due to newly discovered natural gas reserves in Brazil, highlighting the Santos Basin, there may be a change of the gas flows in the Southern Cone. These reserves can reduce Brazil's dependence on Bolivian and Argentinian gas. Furthermore, there are no forecasts of large growths in the Argentinian gas industry nor any new discoveries of gas reserves. Thus, the demands of Chile and Argentina itself should be enough to consume the entire supply of Argentinian gas.

It is noteworthy that all caution is necessary in this type of analysis, given the uncertainties and historical surprises inherited to the activity of exploitation of hydrocarbon reserves. Anyway, even though risky, a conclusion of all this new framework may be that the trade flow should change with greater allocation from the Argentinian reserves to the domestic and Chilean markets (reducing the expectation of export to Brazil). In this scenarios, Brazil is closer to its self-sufficiency [sic]; as well as Bolivia with significant availability of reserves. (VILAS BOAS, 2004, p. 66).

With this, we can conclude that the natural gas reserves in the Southern Cone region should be sufficient to meet gas demand in the region for decades. Furthermore, the wide availability of natural gas in Bolivia may the subject of a project to export natural gas to North America and Mexico.

The new dynamics of natural gas trade in the Southern Cone makes the gas integration of the region even more necessary. Firstly, because of the not yet exploited complementary potential among energy markets and, secondly, due to the need to interconnect borders to export gas to other regions. That is because Bolivia is the country with the greatest potential for gas exports, and its geographical position does not facilitate the export flows, which should be made via Brazil (with the expansion of Gasbol to the Brazilian coast, from where the gas would be transported by ships) or via Chile (with the expansion of the transportation infrastructure between the two countries until the arrival of the gas to the Chilean coast).

Based on these needs, the next point of this study aims to highlight the transportation infrastructure of natural gas in the Southern Cone.

The main vehicle of natural gas in the Southern Cone is the pipeline network that runs through the region. But despite the growth of the pipeline network and its development in recent years, it is still in its "infancy", compared to the pipeline network in developed markets and its insufficiency to provide the implementation of an integrated gas market in the region.

Bolivia has three export pipelines: one for Argentina and two in Brazil (Gasbol and Lateral Cuiabá). The Gasbol is the leading international gas pipeline in the Southern Cone because it integrates the largest holder of natural gas reserves, Bolivia, the largest consumer market in the region, and Brazil.

Argentina has a network of pipelines to ship its products abroad, which links to Chile, Brazil and Uruguay.

The Gasandres pipeline is responsible for transporting the gas to the Argentinian Metropolitan Region of Santiago, Chile. The Del Pacifico pipeline is the main means of transportation of Argentinian gas to the southern Chile, also having three other pipelines that export gas from Argentina to the Chilean Methanex, mainly a company of methanol.

The TGM is the leading Argentinian gas pipeline to Porto Alegre, Brazil. A draft of this interconnection pipeline with Gasbol is a pipeline linking Bolivia to Brazil. However, this project is being reassessed due to recent discoveries of gas reserves in the Santos Basin region and the prospects for the reserves of Argentina, as already discussed.

The network of pipelines between Argentina and Uruguay consists of two main pipelines: the Cruz Del Sur leading Argentinian gas to Montevideo, and the Gasoducto Del Litoral, leading Argentinian gas to Paysandú.

## CONCLUSION

According to the theories of Ernst Haas and Deutsch, regional integration is a process that, from a political point of view, requires that tending States promote the integration from the transfer portion of their sovereignty, and, under a social point of view, induces sense of community from trusted institutions meeting the expectations of a society.

The history of the South American continent and its cultural and linguistic proximity gave rise to a conception of unity in the region. However, the actual process of integration of the region is recent and still ongoing.

In Latin America, the process of regional integration has arisen as well, in response to the globalization process, as a response to the colonial period, in which the continent suffered the European exploration and later from the US.

The integration process on the continent began with the Treaty of Montevideo in 1980, which created the ALADI- Latin American Integration Association. In 1985, the creation of the Free Trade Area of South America – ALCSA was proposed. In 1986, the Uruguay Round of negotiations was held in GATT sphere, whose aim was to search for less discriminatory practices and international trade liberalization. Brazil and Argentina signed in 1988, the Treaty of Integration, Cooperation and Development, in order to form a free trade zone. In 1991, they signed the Treaty of Asuncion, where Mercosur, which was supplemented in 1994, made the decisions adopted in Buenos Aires and Ouro Preto.

The intensification of the regional integration process in South America was promoted from the decrease in performance of the respective States in the economy, as well as from the reduction of barriers to free trade. Internally countries, with such intensification took off mainly from the macroeconomic adjustment processes. Mercosur was born precisely in this historical and political context, and its creation was therefore marked by the block insertion attempt at a liberal global economy. In addition, the block sought to settle breaking with the old dependency paradigm related to the developed countries.

The possibility of regional integration should be analyzed in the light of the economic potential that can be boosted and the weaknesses that may justify this integration. In this respect, there is no way to ignore the energy wealth, especially the gas energy, existing in South America, especially in the region recognized as the Southern Cone.

Currently, the major driver for regional integration in the Southern Cone is natural gas. The great discoveries of natural gas reserves in the region during the 90s, rising oil prices and the rapid growth of demand for natural gas in the world put gas integration in the Southern Cone in the center of discussions for regional integration. The region holds 4.5% of all the worlds proven gas reserves, having sufficient reserves to meet the demand in the region and part of the external demand.

The weakness justifying regional integration in the Southern Cone is the unequal distribution of its energy sources. In the case of natural gas, for example, fuel reserves are concentrated in Bolivia, Argentina and Brazil, while Chile, Uruguay and Paraguay have no reservations in their territory or are in inaccessible places. However, these differences are also a booster for integration, since the expansion and the development of any of the States of the region will lead to the expansion and the development of other States with which they relate to.

With all these favorable factors, the gas integration of the region should already be an established reality. However, other factors, such as lack of maturity of the industries and commerce and the inconsistency between the legal standards, are still obstacles to the effective integration process.

Although there are clear conditions that favor the gas integration of the region, there is a need for countries in the region to coordinate their international policies and their legal systems since lack of coordination of these factors causes a stir in the relationship between these countries and causes distrust of possible investors.

Currently, the Southern Cone countries are working on reforms, with emphasis on modernization and harmonization of their regulatory frameworks, aiming to facilitate regional integration. In this process, the Southern Cone has sought guidance from the consolidated integration process by the European Union, where the objectives were pursued from the pre-planning that sought a share of the international market with fair prices, with a balanced competitiveness with security energy and aimed at protecting the environment.

Countries in the region, whilst pursuing these goals, have sought to modernize its energy industries. The modernization of the natural gas industry in the region is a recent process and is due to recent discoveries of reserves.

In the Southern Cone, all the effort that has been undertaken on energy integration, particularly of gas integration, aims to achieve regional integration of South America. The idea is that gas integration could go to other sectors, branching out into a process of spill-over. Thus, the Southern Cone seeks regional integration in South America in the topic of gas, which allows the inclusion and the best positioning of developing economies in the global economy, promoting political and social development of the region.

# REFERENCES:

ALMEIDA, Paulo Roberto de. **O Brasil de o processo de formação de blocos econômicos: conceito e história, com aplicação aos casos do Mercosul e da Alca.** Disponível em: <http://www.pralmeida.org/05DocsPRA/1091BrBlocosEconomicos. pdf>. Acesso em: 22 out. 2012.

ALMEIDA, Wilson. **Mercosul: efeitos da integração assimétrica.** Goiânia: Deescubra, 2003.

BARBOSA, Heitor Monteiro. **A análise de demonstrativos financeiros como ferramenta para tomada de decisão nas micro e pequenas empresas.** Disponível em: <http://www.faer.edu.br/revistafaer/artigos/edicao2/heitor.pdf>. Acesso em: 4 dez. 2012.

BARUFI, Clara Bonomi; SANTOS, Edmilson Moutinho dos; IDE, Cristiane Reis. **Auto-suficiência energética e desenvolvimento: o comércio de gás natural entre Brasil e Bolívia.** São Paulo: Cadernos PROLAM/USP, 2006.

BAUMANN, Renato; MUSSI, Carlos. **Mercosul: então e agora.** Disponível em: <http://www.cepal.org/cgi-bin/getProd.asp?xml=/publicaciones/xml/1/24531/ P24531.xml&xsl=/brasil/tpl-p/p9f.xsl&base=/brasil/tpl/top-bottom.xsl >. Acesso em: 25 out. 2012.

BORGES, Marco Aurélio dos Santos. **Direito fundamental do acesso à energia na era da globalização.** Disponível em: <http://apps.unibrasil.com.br/revista/index. php/ direito/article/viewFile/424/345>. Acesso em: 25 nov. 2012.

BRASIL. **CALC.** Disponível em: <http://www.itamaraty.gov.br/temas/america-do-sul-e-integracao-regional/calc>. Aceso em: 30 set. 2012.

CARNEIRO, Ricardo. **Globalização e integração regional.** Disponível em: <http://www.iececon.net/arquivos/publicacoes_16_2930536019.pdf >. Acesso em: 30 set. 2012.

CORRAL, Amalia del Carmen Casas de lãs Peñas del. **A integração energética na América do Sul: instrumentos jurídicos e institucionais para projetos gasíferos sub-regionais.** Disponível em: 65<http://www.portalabpg.org.br/PDPetro/5/ publicacoes/repositorio/trabalhos/31982009.38.3.2.pdf>. Acesso em: 25 nov. 2012.

COSTA, Wanderley Messias da. **O Brasil e a América do Sul: cenários geopolíticos e os desafios da integração.** Disponível em: <http://www.geo.uel.br/didatico/omar/brasil_america_sul.pdf>. Acesso em: 30 set. 2012.

FALEIRO, Sandro N. **A pesquisa científica.** Disponível em: <ensino.univates.br/~snf/mettecn/Cap3_Pesquisa_científica.ppt>. Acesso em: 13 set. 2011.

FELLET, João. **Sem Paraguai, Mercosul oficializa entrada da Venezuela.** Disponível em: <http://www.bbc.co.uk/portuguese/noticias/2012/07/120731_mercosul_venezuela_jf.shtml>. Acesso em: 5 dez. 2012.

FERNANDES, Flávio; SANTOS, Edmilson Moutinho dos. **Situação de oferta e demanda de gás natural no Cone Sul.** Disponível em: <http://www.bgfconsultoria.com.br/pag/documents/Gas_Summit_ppt.pdf>. Acesso em: 30 set. 2012.

FERREIRA, Rafael da Costa. **Vantagens e desvantagens da integração regional.** Disponível em: <http://www.ldcinf.com.br/site/information/texto/artigos/1.htm>. Acesso em: 25 nov. 2012.

FERREIRA, Thiago José Milet Cavalcanti. **As etapas do processo de integração regional.** Disponível em: <http://jus.com.br/revista/texto/12833/as-etapas-do-processo-de-integracao-regional/2 >. Acesso em: 30 set. 2012.

GHIRARDI, André. **Gás natural na América do Sul: do conflito à integração possível.** Disponível em: <http://diplo.org.br/2008-01,a2109>. Acesso em: 7 nov. 2012.

GOLDEMBERG, José. **Energia e desenvolvimento.** Disponível em: <http://www.scielo.br/scielo.php?script=sci_arttext&pid=S0103-40141998000200002>. Acesso em: 30 set. 2012.

GOMES, Cristiana. **Globalização.** Disponível em: <http://www.infoescola.com/geografia/globalizacao/>. Acesso em: 24 out. 2012. 66.

HOLANDA, Francisco Mauro Brasil de. **O gás natural no Mercosul: uma perspectiva brasileira.** Brasília: FUNAG, 2001.

HURRELL, Andrew. **Os blocos regionais nas Américas.** Disponível em: <http://www.anpocs.org.br/portal/publicacoes/rbcs_00_22/rbcs22_06.htm >. Acesso em: 25 out. 2012.

IANNI, Octavio. **Globalização: novo paradigma das ciências sociais.** Estud. av. v. 8. n.21. Maio/Agosto. São Paulo, 1994.

JUNG, Carlos Fernando. **Metodologia científica: ênfase em pesquisa tecnológica.** 3. ed. rev. ampl. Disponível em: <http://www.mecanica.ufrgs.br/promec/alunos/download/metodolo.pdf>. Acesso em: 13 set. 2011.

LAUREANO, Fernanda Helena Garcia Cobas. **A indústria de gás natural no Brasil e a viabilização de seu desenvolvimento.** Defesa em: 2002. 64 folhas. Monografia do curso de graduação em Economia – Universidade Federal do Rio de Janeiro, Rio de Janeiro, 2002.

MARCOVITCH, Jacques. **Integração energética na América Latina.** Revista Brasileira de Energia, Itajubá, v. 1. nº. 3, p. 1-8, 1990.

MARIANO, Karina L. P. **O neoliberal institucionalismo: um modelo teórico para a integração regional.** Disponível em: <http://www.cedec.org.br/files_pdf/CAD50.pdf>. Acesso em: 04 out. 2012.

MARIANO, Marcelo Passini; MARIANO, Karina L. Pasquariello. **As teorias de integração regional e os Estados subnacionais.** Disponível em: <https://docs.google.com/viewer?a=v&pid=sites&srcid=ZGVmYXVsdGRvbWFpbnx0ZXh0b3NkZXBvbGl0aWNhaW50ZXJuYWNpb25hbHxneDoyN2hbHhneDozOGI4Yzc5NWNlOGFkZTll&pli=1 >. Acesso em: 25 out. 2012.

MARTINS, Maria Paula. **Setor de gás natural no Brasil.** Rio de Janeiro: Seminário Internacional – Reestruturação e regulação do setor de energia elétrica e gás natural, 2008.

MELLO, Eduardo Reis de. **Spill-over vertical: o papel dos entes federados rumo à integração.** Disponível em: <www.inpri.com.br/img/artigos/4.doc>. Acesso em: 04 out. 2012. 67

MERCOSUL. **Quais são os Estados parte e os Estados associados que compõem o MERCOSUL?** Disponível em: <http://www.mercosur.int/msweb/portal%20intermediario/es/faqs.html#2>. Acesso em: 28 set. 2012.

MORESI, Eduardo. **Metodologia da pesquisa.** Disponível em: <http://www.inf.ufes.br/~falbo/files/MetodologiaPesquisa-Moresi2003.pdf> . Acesso em: 28 nov. 2012.

NEVES, José Luis. **Pesquisa qualitativa – características, usos e possibilidades.** Disponível em: <http://www.ead.fea.usp.br/cad-pesq/arquivos/c03-art06.pdf>. Acesso em: 13 set. 2011.

OLIVEIRA, Adilson de; ARAÚJC, Márcio Silva de. **A importação brasileira de gás natural no contexto do Mercosul.** Disponível em: <http://www.rep.org.br/pdf/60-2.pdf >. Acesso em: 30 set. 2012.

OXILIA, Victorio; FAGÁ, Murilo Werneck. **As motivações para a integração energética na América do Sul com base no gás natural.** Petro & Química, Ano XXX, n° 289. São Paulo: Valete Editora, 2006.

PINTO, MS. **As teorias da integração regional.** Disponível em:<http://repositorium. sdum.uminho.pt/bitstream/1822/866/2/Cap%20I_1.1%20-%201.2%20-%201.3_. pdf>. Acesso em: 18 out. 2012.

QUEIROZ, Hugo. **A inexorável interdependência das políticas energéticas nacionais.** Disponível em: <http://infopetro.wordpress.com/2010/08/30/a-inexoravel-interdependencia-das-politicas-energeticas-nacionais/>. Acesso em: 25 nov. 2012.

RODRIGUES, Cid. **A viabilidade do gasoduto no contexto da integração Brasil – Argentina.** Disponível em: <http://revistas.fee.tche.br/index.php/indicadores/article/viewFile/177/388 >. Acesso em: 7 nov. 2012.

S.A. **Entrada da Venezuela no Mercosul tem significado histórico, afirma presidenta Dilma.** Disponível em: <http://blog.planalto.gov.br/entrada-da-venezuela-no-mercosul-tem-significado-historico-afirma-dilma/>. Acesso em: 4 dez. 2012.

S.A. **Relatório sobre integração regional na América do Sul: histórias e perspectivas.** Disponível em: <http://www.ibase.br/pt/wp-content/uploads/2011/06/relat%C3%B3rio-final-int.-am%C3%A9rica-do-sul.pdf>. Acesso em: 18 nov. 2012. 68 S.A. **Venezuela ultrapassa Arábia Saudita em reservas de petróleo, diz OPEP.** Disponível em: <http://g1.globo.com/economia/noticia/2011/07/venezuela-ultrapassa-arabia-saudita-em-reservas-de-petroleo-diz-opep.html>. Acesso em: 21 nov. 2012.

SALLES, Cláudio J. D. **Integração energética: teoria e prática.** Disponível em: <http://congressoemfoco.uol.com.br/opiniao/forum/integracao-energetica-teoria-e-pratica/>. Acesso em: 24 out. 2012.

SÃO PAULO. **Petróleo e gás natural.** Disponível em: <http://www.investe.sp.gov. br/setores/petroleo-gas >. Acesso em: 30 set. 2012.

SCHIFF, Maurice; WINTERS, L. Alan. **Regional integration and development.** Disponível em: <http://books.google.com. br/books?printsec=frontcover&vid=LCCN2002074094&redir_esc=y#v=onepage&q&f=false>. Acesso em: 28 set. 2012.

TELES, Ana Flávia Lima; CANÊDO, Sílvia Helena Guilherme. **Brasil e o contexto sul-americano.** Disponível em: <www.pucminas.br/.../CNO_ARQ_NOTIC20060607100520.pdf>. Acesso em: 23 out. 2012.

UNIÃO EUROPEIA. Disponível em: <http://europa.eu/about-eu/countries/index_pt.htm>. Acesso em: 4 dez. 2012.

VIANA, André Rego; BARROS, Pedro Silva; CALIXTRE, André Bojikian. **Governança global e integração da América do sul.** Disponível em: <http://www. ipea.gov.br/portal/images/stories/PDFs/livros/livros/livro_governancaglobal.pdf>. Acesso em: 04 out. 2012.

VIEIRA, George; FRANÇA, Rafael de. **Integração regional na América do Sul.** Disponível em: <http://pt.scribd.com/doc/36125968/Integracao-Regional-na-America-do-Sul >. Acesso em: 30 set. 2012.

VIGEVANI, Tullo; FAVARON, Gustavo de Mauro; RAMANZINI JÚNIOR, Haroldo; CORREIA, Rodrigo Alves. **O papel da integração regional para o Brasil: universalismo, soberania e percepção das elites.** Disponível em: <http://www. scielo.br/pdf/rbpi/v51n1/a01v51n1.pdf>. Acesso em: 18 out. 2012.

VILAS BOAS, Marina Vilela. **Integração gasífera no Cone Sul: uma análise das motivações dos diferentes agentes envolvidos.** Defesa em 2004. 129 folhas. 69 Tese de Mestrado do Curso de Pós-Graduação em Ciências e Planejamento Energético – Universidade Federal do Rio de Janeiro, Rio de Janeiro, 2004.

VILELA, Maria Estela Moreira. **Métodos e técnicas de estudo.** Disponível em: <http://famanet.br/pdf/cursos/semipre/metodos_tecnicas_estudo_md3.pdf>. Acesso em: 13 set. 2011.

VIVIANE, Katia. **Blocos econômicos.**<www.cesg.kit.net/trabalhos/ trab_blocos. PDF>. Acesso em: 23 out. 2012

# BRAZIL-CHINA COOPERATION IN BUILDING SUSTAINABLE ENERGY INFRASTRUCTURE

Riod B.Ayoub[4]
Wilson Almeida[5]

## INTRODUCTION
### The Brazilian Energy Matrix

Brazil is a privileged country regarding its ability to generate energy. With its large territory, its land is cut by the largest rivers in the world, capable of producing electricity through hydroelectric power plants. It has more than 7,000 km of coastline with great potential for wind power generation in addition to using tidal power. It has equatorial climate with sun shining throughout the year in all regions of its vast territory, to favor high emissions of sunlight, raw material for solar energy production; it has large mineral reserves as; oil, mineral coal and natural gas. It has still great farmlands for productions of sugar cane to extract ethanol from and to promote the reforested wood cultivation to use in thermoelectric power plants. All that makes it a giant in an energy power that will bring guaranteed development in the decades that approach in a sustainable manner, respecting the healthy environment acquiring technologies that will provide the ability to generate clean, renewable energy.

In the past century the world energy production has grown progressively in part by the industrialization that caused the urban exodus in almost all regions of the planet.

Our country was no different. In the 1930s and 1940s Brazil had a mostly rural population and witnessed the following ones a large increase in population that migrated to the centers with industrialization as a major factor. Later, however in the twentieth century there was a need to generate power in a way that was less aggressive to the environment , replacing the wood consumption of that time, brought by large amount of wood in the green continent and the lack of technology and environmental policies.

---

4 Lawyer, engineer, master's degree in law from the Catholic University of Brasília (UCB).
5 Professor at Catholic University of Brasília.

But it was after World War II when the constant population increased, reaching in 1970 the 90 million mark of Brazilian inhabitants, in which the energy matrix began to suffer most effective changes, since new technologies were applied for building hydroelectric power plants and energy transmission to the cities that were formed.

The construction of these power plants moved from our rivers' water occurred during the military regime that ruled the country as part of the national development plan enhancements, idealized by ministers John Paulo dos Reis Velloso and Mario Henrique Simonsen, who had the replacement of the old energy matrix as a focus.

In search of new energy sources, Brazil's step in the decade; was the Proálcool, the federal program that stimulated sugarcane planting for the ethanol production which was used in thousands of cars as a way to reduce pollution emitted by fossil fuels and make dependence on oil imports less difficult.

The significant increase of energy consumption in Brazil has always been verified due to the great development in various economic sectors; primary, secondary and tertiary.

Company data from the Energy Research Company (ERC) realized that in the 1970s', the primary energy demand was 70 million toe (tons of oil equivalent) and in the 2000s', with a 170 million population, energy demand almost tripled, reaching 190 million toe.

The following table, provided by Electronic Library Online (Scientifc) *apud* EPE, shows the national energy matrix evolution between the 1970s' and 2000s's as well as the forecast for the 2030s';

## Evolution of the Energy Supply Structure
Brazil- 1970-2030

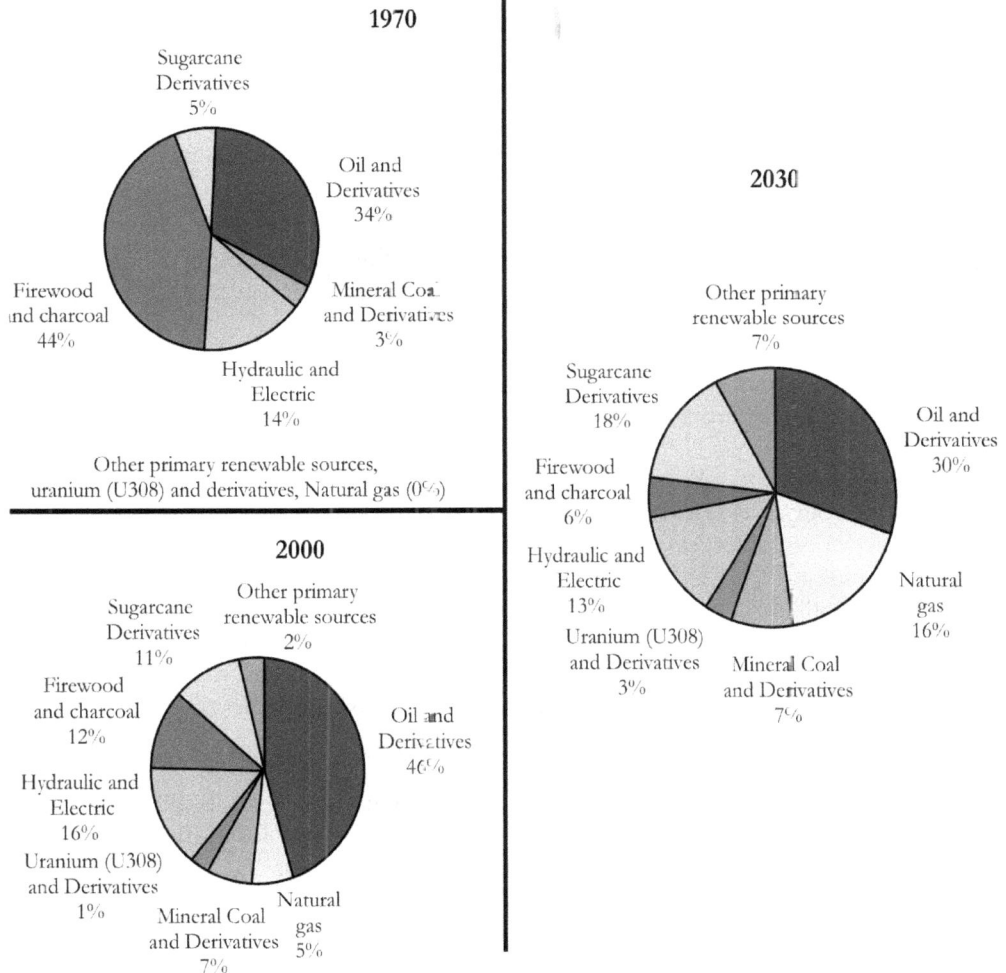

### 1970

Sugarcane Derivatives 5%

Oil and Derivatives 34%

Firewood and charcoal 44%

Mineral Coal and Derivatives 3%

Hydraulic and Electric 14%

Other primary renewable sources, uranium (U308) and derivatives, Natural gas (0%)

### 2000

Sugarcane Derivatives 11%

Other primary renewable sources 2%

Firewood and charcoal 12%

Hydraulic and Electric 16%

Uranium (U308) and Derivatives 1%

Mineral Coal and Derivatives 7%

Natural gas 5%

Oil and Derivatives 46%

### 2030

Other primary renewable sources 7%

Sugarcane Derivatives 18%

Oil and Derivatives 30%

Firewood and charcoal 6%

Hydraulic and Electric 13%

Natural gas 16%

Uranium (U308) and Derivatives 3%

Mineral Coal and Derivatives 7%

Our energy matrix currently represents one of the most renewable in the world. We still depend heavily on oil, because most of our means of transport use fossil fuel.

However, the energy that keeps our industries and cities is derived mostly from clean sources such as; hydro, biomass, wind and solar, representing a percentage higher than 45% of the energy produced in our country.

We have reached this level because of the largest hydroelectric power plant of the world; Itaipu, Belo Monte, São Luiz do Tapajós, Tucuruí, St. Anthony, Ilha Solteira, Jirau, Xingó, Paulo Afonso, Tres Marias and Boa Esperança, among others that overcome thousands and account for around more than 90% of the electricity consumed in all our country, due to the existence of a vast territory with many rivers of plateau source, and good national rainfall, and worldwide it is one of the largest hydraulic potential countries, surpassed only by Russia and by China, which has increased energy production in recent years from the renewable matrix, especially hydraulic, the construction of the giant Três Gargantas hydroelectric power plant being a good example.

We still have the energy produced by thermoelectric power plants, nuclear power plants and so called alternative energies: wind and solar.

As for fossil fuels, Brazil already produces oil in sufficient quantities for domestic consumption, but does not have refineries in quantity to refine the heaviest type that is derived from our reserves, which depends on oil imports.

With the pre-salt discovery and the construction of new refineries we can achieve in self-sufficiency in the petroleum fuel industry and transport base elements in our country the near future, since we do not have a modern rail network moved by electricity, which has timidly emerged recently in urban transport of people in large cities, such as the subway.

However if we do not practice a serious policy in the coming years towards clean and renewable energy sources, we will have to use more and more fossil fuels. This is the understanding of the National Energy Plan 2050 (PNE 2050);

> According to the National Energy Plan of the Ministry of Mines and Energy (PNE 2050 - MME) we will have to make a transition to thermoelectricity, natural gas, coal and nuclear since the national hydroelectric potential will not support the demand by the year 2050.

New hydroelectric power plants should be built, especially in the Amazon region; wind power must be increased using our coasts' potential; solar energy will have a significant advance taking advantage of the incidence on our areas of one of the largest solar radiations in the planet, adopting new technologies and mainly through cooperation agreements, particularly with China, deploying a plant in our territory, modern solar panels, which will lower the costs and make this form of energy, one of which is more developed in the next five years.

Furthermore, the National Electric Energy Agency (ANEEL) approved a revolutionary ordinance that allows consumers to be energy producers, beginning the age of micro and mini-generation in Brazil, a trading system with credits storage possibility.

One aspect that should be noted is the fact that Brazil will save energy, so that in the near future undesirable shortages are not embitter. The population will have to be educated to consume less energy; equipment improvement will have to be encouraged as for the quality used in industry and households, as well as the automotive vehicles, making them cleaner and more economical; improving urban mobility to avoid unnecessary spending on transport, in short; taking measures that can reduce the need for power consumption.

In one way or in another, Brazil has to be looking for a way to take advantage of its energetic potential to guarantee sustainable development, without importing energy, mainly improving its energetic matrix to start to use renewable energies again, without polluting energies and their cause impacts, assuring a healthy environment to a present and future generation, in order to predict the Federal Constitution of Brazil in its art. 225.

To achieve those objectives, it is necessary that the institutions responsible for the energy production in our country adopt effective planning and programs, deep studies about productive demand and capacity allied to the new technologies and incentives, minimizing costs and noticing nature conservation instead of attacking it, always emphasizing the use of the clean energy matrix at our disposal.

Programs will be listed which seek goals of improving the energy matrix in search of a sustainable production as the Incentive Program for Alternative Sources of Electric Energy (PROINFA), the Electricity Conservation Program (PROCEL), the National Rational Use of Oil and Natural Gas Program (CONCEPT), the Brazilian Labeling Program, the energy Efficiency Law, the National Biodiesel and Ethanol Program, and funding encouragement for the generation towards alternative energy.

Surely we trace the paths achieve planned in the near future with an expansion of the quality energy supply, that current legislation and global ecological conscience require.

We cannot neglect the knowledge of the existing energy structure in our country, which will not be able to generate enough energy for the next thirty years. Demonstration of this has already taken place these days, where due to climate change, we witness scarcity of rains which influences energy production, resulting in blackouts.

However the expansion of energy supply according to EPE, for the period 2005-30 may exceed twice the current installed capacity in all segments all, depending on the seriousness of priorities in the electricity sector.

The EPE, through its ten-year plan for energy expansion in 2023 states that the percentage of hydro energy in the energy matrix will rise from the current 86 GW to 121 GW in 2023. Of the 77.2 GW scheduled to be installed between 2013 and 2023, 45% are hydroelectric, 26% wind, 9% comes from biomass and 5% from solar sources. In other words 85% of the expansion will come from renewable sources and as of 2050 they will not be enough and more thermal energy will be required (natural gas, nuclear and coal).

The relevance and projection of the Brazilian energy matrix are represented by the chart below, provided by EPE;

**Electric Matrix 2009 (ME- med)**        **Electric Matrix 2030(ME- med)**

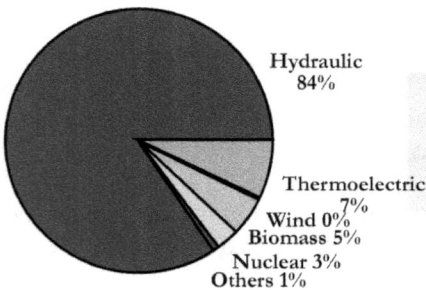

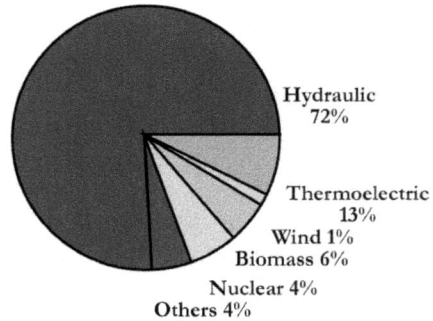

Source: EPE - Energy National Balance 2010, Decennial Energy Plan 2011-2020 and Energy National Plan 2030

This data shows that Brazil is on the right track. It has one of the lowest power consumption rates per capita, due to our tropical climate, knowledge on how to program demonstrates the balanced use of the renewable and clean sources of energy, avoiding the use of fossil energy, always with a holistic view of the problems and needs in the electricity sector to ensure sustainable development for present and future generations.

## Solar Energy in Brazil

Since the nineteenth century solar energy is studied, but it was only in the last century that it has been used in water heating for American homes and satellites. In Brazil, solar power had its first moments when used in photovoltaic panels in rural areas to power boreholes and lighting in small scale with high cost, which rarely justified the investment.

Solar energy is and has always been promising when we see that, coming from the sun, it is present every day in almost every corner of the planet, it is in a position to generate clean energy without harming the environment.

To get solar energy there are two commonly used ways: the first through photovoltaic panels with direct conversion into electricity and the second, for solar thermal energy through flat collectors that heat water.

Conducted surveys show that solar radiation in Brazil ranges from 8 to 22 MJ / m2 during the day with the best average comparable regions of the world.

As the Vitae Civillis data; Brazil receives solar energy into its territory in the order of 1013 annual MWh which corresponds to an average of 50,000 times the annual electricity consumption. However, it is one of the least exploited sources in our country wasting energy potential available in all our regions, particularly in the northeast

According to the useful energy balance published by the Ministry of Mines and Energy (MME); a significant energy portion generated in Brazil is consumed as heat, process and direct heating, as well as domestic heating bath water, consuming billion KW/h that could be supplied with solar energy through solar heaters .

Solar energy can improve the quality of the national energy matrix for being clean and renewable, besides avoiding distribution expenses as it is a form of distributed energy and low maintenance.

The sun provides us with solar radiation serving for energy production at no cost. It is fundamental to providing access to energy for the poorest families, needing only investment in equipment becomes more accessible every day, adding the privileged geographical conditions in Brazil that will soon become one of the world leaders in production of solar energy, the energy of the future.

Interesting data gathered from the second edition of The Brazilian Power Industry and Sustainability, made by NGOs claim that Brazil has solar capacity to meet 10% of its demand for light, enabling only 5% of the urbanized area in the country.

Surely, we're getting a new age in energy production where every individual, without the need for state intervention can generate their own energy through an inexhaustible, clean and renewable source. that is solar radiation. The maintenance of this system is minimal and the initial investment becomes less costly every day, with a unique cost advantage because there is no need to pay for a solar energy bill, coupled with the fact that the capture system has a great useful life cycle.

Some disadvantages are being overcome every day as the incidence of high import taxes on solar panels, particularly with exemptions and installation of high-tech factories in our territory; as per the future construction in partnership with China for a solar panel factory in the city of Campinas, state of São Paulo, according to the agreement signed between the two countries in May 2015.

According to EPE, Brazil has currently about 20 MW installed capacity of solar photovoltaic generation, the vast majority (99% according to IEA, 2011) for service to isolated and remote systems especially in situations where the extent of the distribution network does not appear economically feasible.

As a new resolution of rules of No. 482 of April 17, 2012, ANEEL could revolutionize the production of solar energy, which presents therefore, rules for micro and mini-generation related to distribution systems. In a direct way the compensation system is set to encourage the use of solar energy in the country by consumers, as it allows the generation of all or part of their demand, which can be through solar panels that connect to the distribution network, in the energy trading regime.

Solar technology is the most suited for this new resolution rules in view of the solar potential which is available and any resident can use their roofs and an open area for the installation of photovoltaic panels to produce electricity at the same time that clean energy will be produced while contributing to the preservation of a sustainable environment.

Another important point of this type of generation is the connection into the power net without needing new transmission lines which require costs and environmental damage.

Certainly, power generation is not for sale, but an exchange that will generate consumer credit is, which is usable within three years, meaning lower costs in their consumption of traditional electricity since there is a need to consume energy in the evening hours, which is when the owned generation system is flawed due to the absence of solar radiation.

This measure taken by the Brazilian government is a major breakthrough for changing the national energy matrix, which will from now be an effective, inexpensive tool and accessible to all levels of society especially in the energy chain where the cheapening of solar energy equipment production is present and can have whole cities interconnected by a traditional electricity grid in an Eco-energy production revolution.

Several developed countries have already adopted the technology of using environmentally friendly cities in the construction of its covered building roofs with photovoltaic cells producing solar energy as is the case of France, where a law was created requiring certain sectors to use green roofs or solar panels; Germany and Israel; have China as a leading supplier of this technology, which has in recent years emerged as the largest manufacturer of solar panels in the world.

> The example we have is the company Solar Holdings Co. Ltd. (NOW), one of the largest manufacturers of solar energy products with high performance in the world announced that the Israeli Parliament (Kenesset) used the VF NOW modules in its energy project solar roofing installing 1,500 photovoltaic panels that produce 10% of all electric energy needed for the building.

Today the cost of MW/h of electricity produced by solar panels is still very expensive, higher than the amount produced by hydroelectric plants and their distribution systems, which is due in much the lack of incentives given by the government to provide, mainly research and the creation of laws that make the use of this energy source mandatory, which would increase demand and the price reduction of the system for the benefit of nature.

We know that solar energy is intermittent and needs to address its flaws, especially at night, in order to work connected with the conventional electrical system in use in our country, derived from hydropower, which greatly softens the consumption and the creation of new power plants. Even though they provide clean energy sources, they cause environmental impact when they are built.

Information from the Globe News Portal (G1) states that over the course of a year, each square meter of Brazil receives 1900 kWh of energy from the sun on average. This is an average efficiency of 100%, assuming that photovoltaic panels can produce 10 kWh of energy per year per square meter of panels.

The Research Center of Electricity (CEPEL) dates back to the 1990s performing activities in the photovoltaic energy sector to rural electrification in several states, an efficient solar home model is shown as follows;

**Efficient solar house- source: CEPEL**

Brazil is rich in solar energy and possesses silicon deposits, raw materials for making solar panels, which can certainly increase the use of solar energy in the coming years and in partnership with the energy generated by hydroelectric, provide a cleaner power source for future generations.

## The legislation

The Brazilian Constitution in its art. 225 clearly states that: everyone has the right to an ecologically balanced environment, which makes it the State's obligation to encourage research and to use forms of energy that less attack the environment. Solar energy is an example of what can be adopted by all to impose effective measures for this clean and abundant energy to ensure sustainability as per the Constitution.

Legislation linked to environmental energy production sector is still very tenuous, deserving the drafting of laws that will make the use of solar energy mandatory in buildings, therefore promoting greater environmental awareness in search of change in our energy mix.

Nowadays, there are laws that provide implementation of solar heating systems, as well as the general use of energy and its regulations.

One of the important goals in the development of solar energy in Brazil came from ANEEL's initiative through a normative resolution No. 482 of April 17, 2012, which sets forth the overall conditions for access of micro and mini-generation using electricity distribution systems: the power compensation system, among other provisions.

This resolution allows the production of solar energy in a consumer unit, which is connected to standard power grid. The level of compensation for the excess solar energy produced is passed on to the network whose uses can compensate the energy that will subsequently be required by the concessionaire.

This really is a great stimulus for expansion of solar power systems in the country, which should significantly increase the production of this energy in the coming years.

By Law 10,438/2002 the Incentive Program for Alternative Sources of Electric Energy (PROINFA) was created, in order to promote diversification of the Brazilian energy matrix and search for alternatives to increase security in the electric power supply, besides allowing the appreciation of characteristics, as well as regional and local potential.

Bill n°. 630/03, authored by Congressman Roberto Gouveia, amending art. 1 of Law n°. 8,001, of March 13, 1990, was presented to establish a special fund to finance research and promote the production of electrical and thermal energy from solar and wind power, and other measures.

Authored by Congressman Julio Campos, Bill No. 4529/2012 establishes incentives for the use of solar energy, which greatly resembles the rules of ANEEL Resolution 482/2012.

There is also Bill n°. 317/2013, which exempts from taxes to import equipment and components for generation of electrical solar sources.

Changes are already occurring as in the city of Recife, where Municipal law 18,112 / 2015 enacted on 13/04 was created, provides for the planting vegetation on buildings roofs over four stories to avoid the effect of heat.

Some Brazilian cities already have laws regulating the application of solar cells in buildings to supply water heating systems, such as Law 14.459 of the state of São Paulo, which provides for the installation of water heating systems in new buildings that were regulated by Decree 49,148; as well as in Rio de Janeiro and Porto Alegre.

Bill n°. 1859/2011 by Congressman Peter Uczai is underway which provides incentives for the use of solar energy, giving new wording to Art. 82 of law n° 11,977 from July 7 2009, that requires the installation of water heating systems by solar energy in dwellings financed with Housing Financial System resources.

We find this bill to be a change in the context of the rules, which was already included in the deployment of the demand for water heating systems by solar energy in public housing.

There is also interest from the state, as well as from locals to promote the use of solar energy, as in Bill n° 072 of the city of Manaus (AM), establishing incentives program for the use of solar energy; Bill 161 of the city of Vitória (ES), which fosters the development of alternative sources of energy programs; Bill n° 64 of Belo Horizonte (MG), establishing the mandatory installation of water heating systems by solar energy in new buildings in the Belo Horizonte city; Bill n° 0086.1, which provides for the water heating systems by solar energy in buildings in the state of Santa Catarina.

In the state of Goias Bill n°. 292 was approved, which created the state policy to encourage the use of solar energy, which deserves to be followed by other states of the federation, so that we can increase the installation of new sources of renewable and clean energy in our country, so that along with the energy produced by hydropower, we can rely less and less on fossil energy sources.

We note that our legal system moves to establish rules intended to require the use of solar energy in all urban and rural properties by sharing with the network of power utilities, looking to take advantage of solar radiation and contribute to building a clean and sustainable energy matrix, ensuring future supply.

## The Cooperation Agreement Brazil – China

On May 19th, 2015, Brazil and China signed the 2015-2021 Joint Action Plan called: JOINT STATEMENT BETWEEN THE GOVERNMENT OF THE FEDERAL REPUBLIC OF BRAZIL AND THE GOVERNMENT OF THE PEOPLE'S REPUBLIC OF CHINA TO VISIT THE PRIME MINISTER STATE COUNCIL, Li Keqiang, which among various issues emphasized on;

13. The two Heads of Government agreed on the high potential for cooperation in the fields of energy and mining. They reaffirmed the importance attached to the partnership between Brazilian and Chinese companies to develop oil fields, particularly the field of Libra. They also welcomed the partnerships for the construction and operation of power transmission lines in Brazil. They reiterated their commitment to intensify cooperation in mining, including the areas of geological research, exploration, integrated sustainable use and exploitation of mineral resources. They agreed on the high potential of bilateral cooperation in clean energy sources, renewable and efficient, to promote sustainable development, especially in the wind power and solar sectors. Committed to stimulate the integration of productive chains of the two countries in these segments and to promote technological joint development in the energy area.

14. By emphasizing the importance of the knowledge of economy as a key element for equitable and sustainable development, the two leaders stressed the progress made in bilateral cooperation in science, technology and innovation, in particular through the Brazil-China Center for Climate Change and Innovative Technologies for Energy; the Brazil-China Center for Research and Innovation in Nanotechnology; and the Brazil-China Center for Biotechnology, among other research and development initiatives set between the two countries. Welcomed the holding of the Second High-Level Dialogue on Science, Technology and Innovation, to be held in Brasilia on June 19th, 2015, as well as the IV Meeting of the Subcommittee on Science, Technology and Innovation of China-Brazil High Level Commission Coordination and Coordination (High-level Committee). They expressed appreciation of the intention to sign the Memorandum of Understanding between the Ministry of Science, Technology and Innovation of Brazil and the Ministry of Science and Technology of China on Bilateral Cooperation between Science Parks. They highlighted the importance of the involvement of companies, research centers, universities and government agencies in bilateral initiatives in C, T & I and industrial cooperation to promote socioeconomic development and well-being of the people of both countries. They stressed the importance of China-Latin America cooperation in Science, Technology and Innovation.

In the context of the visit, among signing several bilateral acts, there is the cooperation agreement in 321MW in wind power projects in Brazil.

Through friendly consultations, the two sides agreed on several points in particular:

Article 6 - the cooperation agreement in the area of energy and mining which provides various ways to enhance the production of clean energy;

1. Both parties agree on the great potential for cooperation between the two countries in energy and mining area.

2. Under the Energy Subcommittee and Mining High-level Committee, the two parties will further facilitate the exchange of information, promote the implementation of cooperation projects in the area of energy and mining, monitor the implementation of projects and facilitate bilateral investment and as the joint development of technologies.

3. The two sides will strengthen cooperation in oil and natural gas, including on issues related to trade, exploration and development, financing, engineering services and equipment, in order to facilitate the development of Chinese companies operating in Brazil and partnerships with Brazilian companies. The two sides will also cooperate to promote mutual investments in the production chain of oil and gas.

4. The two sides will strengthen cooperation in the areas of electricity generation, exchange insights on technology and joint technological development and facilitate cooperation in energy transmission technologies and construction projects.

5. Both Parties shall cooperate in energy efficiency, smart grids and the development of new sources of energy, especially renewable sources (wind, solar, hydroelectric, biofuels and biomass).

6. The two sides will cooperate in nuclear energy, including through the organization of technical seminars on the subject.

7. The two sides will step up cooperation and the development of partnerships in biofuels, with a view to consolidating their role as energy commodities and to spread its production and international use.

8. The two parties agree to expand cooperation between Brazilian and Chinese companies in the mining sector; encourage bilateral investments and joint investments in third countries; and promote the necessary investments in infrastructure to enable economic exploitation of mineral resources and trade in mineral products.

9. The two parts will pay particular attention to the joint development and processing of minerals such as iron, aluminum, nickel, copper, potassium, phosphate, rare earth and charcoal. The two parties agree, therefore, to facilitate bilateral investments, including investments in infrastructure to support exports to China, as well as the value-adding process to the production and local processing.

10. The two sides will exchange views on energy issues and mining, especially on public policy, long-term planning methodologies, conservation efforts and joint development of new technologies.

11. The two sides will promote meetings and business fora on trade and investment in the energy and mining sectors in both countries.

12. The two parties identify areas for the creation of clusters to promote Chinese technologies in Brazil, China and Brazil technologies.

The Chinese government's announcement of cooperation package that provides for the signing of 35 agreements for investment in various sectors of infrastructure and the Brazilian economy turning around US $ 53 billion, including in clean energy production area with emphasis on the solar energy, came in good time.

The Chinese interest in financial cooperation shows that Brazil is a country that has the potential to develop unprecedentedly, when possessed of an interesting domestic consumer market as well as features that support commodity exports; it has the latest technology in various industries like aerospace and food production; energy potential has mostly clean, renewable energy; all this, combined with the security and stability that prevail to justify investment as significant values.

In fact, Chinese investment could boost the Brazilian economy in the present time of crisis increasing trade through Brazilian, Chinese and transnational companies installed, mainly by having the intention to build a transoceanic highway that will lower the cost of products that Brazil can provide, which are of vital importance to the sustainable growth of the Chinese.

In the energy sector exchange of information, the implementation of cooperation and facilitating bilateral investment projects, and the development of new technologies especially in regard to clean and renewable energy sources, especially solar and wind, takes place.

There is no doubt of the Chinese ability to innovate when it comes on clean and renewable energy production; having developed technologies that will give Brazil important breakthroughs, especially in the solar energy production area, leading the possibility of increasing the energy matrix national with significant participation of clean energy provided by the sun in the short term, consolidating it as one of the cleanest and renewable on the planet to ensure sustainable development.

## Construction of a Photovoltaic Panels Factory in Brazil

The coming of the Chinese Prime Minister Li Keqiang in May 2015 in Brazil led to the signing of several bilateral acts with the Brazilian government, especially in the energy sector. Among the signed agreements the agreement between the Brazilian Agency for Export and Investment Promotion (APEX-BRAZIL) and the Chinese group BYD energy for construction of a plant to be installed in Campinas (SP) is highlighted, whose goal is to produce about 400MW of solar panels per year, with an investment of around US $150 million.

The signing of this cooperation agreement with China was a major step toward changing the national energy matrix for the exchange of technologies and investments in the energy sector, particularly on clean and renewable energy, the country can, in record time, achieve sustainability as desired.

It was also planned to build a research center and development of solar energy, electric vehicles, batteries, etc.

The APEX-BRAZIL Brazilian Company supports foreign companies on market information, locations for plant installation and mainly government dialogue at all three levels: federal, state and city, which had exemplary participation in the conclusion of this agreement which enabled Chinese investments as the construction of the factory of solar elements, demonstrating alignment with the organs in the national electricity sector.

The BYD Group energy by 2017 intends to invest R$1 billion in Brazil. For the director of government relations at BYD Brazil, Adalberto Maluf, investment in solar panels inaugurates a new phase of clean energy. "We will bring the latest technology, called double glass, photovoltaic solar panels that will mean more efficiency and durability compared to conventional panels. As a result, clean and decentralized generation will be increasingly competitive in Brazil."

Another important factory installed in Brazil by the Chinese, who invested about R$100 million, was the construction of an electric bus factory, representing a breakthrough to change the energy matrix of means of transportation used in the country based on fossil fuels, for electricity that can be produced by clean, renewable sources.

The Brazil-China Cooperation has developed in the way it strengthens the economy of both countries especially Brazil which increments the contents of its exports to the largest consumer market on the planet as well as sharing technologies that lead, in the near future, to reach an array for totally clean, renewable energy with increasing solar energy production.

The senior vice president of BYD, Stella Li says that the group plans to invest a billion dollars in Brazil until 2017 and said; "I believe that our commitment to technology and innovation in everything we do, will bring to the Brazilian alternative renewable energy to meet future challenges, and live a healthier and more fulfilling life".

## CONCLUSION

Solar energy has emerged as more affordable alternative to ensure the supply of clean, renewable energy in the near future in our country.

Brazil has been seriously dealing with the issue of energy through a policy of the Ministry of Mines and Energy and instituting programs, studies and strategies to facilitate the generation of the practice of green energy technology partnerships, including those with China, such as mass production of photovoltaic cells.

The National Plan on Climate Change provides for an increase in the share of renewable energy sources and clean, the use of biofuels and reducing consumption as a way to achieve sustainability. For such claims the expansion of hydroelectric, wind and solar generation is necessary.

The Incentive Program to Alternative Sources of Electric Energy (PROINFA) plays an important role in this change especially when it aims to increase the production of solar energy in urban and rural areas to ensure the future supply of electricity.

Certainly the policies and techniques adopted in the growth of solar energy production in Brazil will ensure in the near future, the formation of a matrix sustained by interconnected hydroelectric power producing solar power sources, ensuring the supply of clean, and renewable energy making the country an example sustainability.

# REFERENCES

1.http://www.scielo.br/scielo.php?pid=S010133002007000300003&script=sci_arttext. Accessed 03/10/2015

2. https://www.ambienteenergia.com.br/index.php/2014/12/segundo-relatorio-ate-3.2050-matriz-energetica-brasil-devera-ser-diversificada/25086. Accessed 03/10/2015

3.http://www.mma.gov.br/clima/energia/energias-renovaveis/energia-solar

4.http://www.energiabrasil.gov.br/BEN/BalancoEnergiaUtil.pdf)

5.http://www.autossustentavel.com/2013/08/beneficios-energia-solar-brasil.html. Accessed 03/10/2015.

6.http://www.epe.gov.br/geracao/Documents/Estudos_23/NT_EnergiaSolar_2012.pdf. Accessed 03/10/2015

7.http://www.prnewswire.com/news-releases/projeto-solar-do-parlamento-israelense-adota-modulos-da-ja-solar-498866091.html. Accessed 03/10/2014

8. http://g1.globo.com/Noticias/Ciencia Accessed 03/10/2015

9.http://www.cepel.br/ Accessed 03/10/2015

10. Constituição Federal/1988

11.resolução normativa nº 482/2012 da ANEEL

12.http://www.itamaraty.gov.br/index.php?lang=pt-BR Accessed 03/10/2015

13.http://ciclovivo.com.br/noticia/china-vai-instalar-primeira-fabrica-de-paineis-solares-no-brasil. Accessed 03/10/2014

14.http://www.mma.gov.br/estruturas/smcq_climaticas/_arquivos/plano_nacional_mudanca_clima.pdf. Accessed 05/10/2015

# TRANSNATIONAL ORGANIZED CRIME IN POST-COLD WAR:
## AN ANALYSIS OF DRUG TRAFFICKING AND MONEY LAUNDERING (1990-2012)

Eduardo Júnio de Souza França
Fábio Albergaria

## INTRODUCTION

With the end of the Cold War, the international system has seen a range of changes and transformations. These changes made the world increasingly interconnected due to the overcoming national borders, the advancement of communication, transportation, technology and the increase in global trade and financial flows. These transformations have brought enormous benefits to humanity, however they have collaborated to the evolution of transnational organized crime.

Currently considered one of the greatest threats to human security, transnational organized crime is a huge global problem that presents itself as a real threat to the political, economic, social and cultural development of society and therefore to international security.

The transnational organized crime has several comprehensive modalities, however, for the purposes of this study, we sought to focus on two of its manifestations: illicit drug trafficking and money laundering.

So the first part of this study is responsible for raising the concept of transnational organized crime and its two forms of manifestation. Then the second part will analyze the characteristics of transnational organized crime and its organizational structure. Finally, the third part is more empirical, seeking to describe and analyze the mechanisms of cooperation that states have adopted to fight transnational organized crime.

## CONCEPT OF TRANSNATIONAL ORGANIZED CRIME AND FORMS OF ACTION.

### Transnational Organized Crime

"The practice of crime is as old as humanity itself." An affirmation by Castells (1999) states that the crime is not a new phenomenon, unlike this, Castells shows that since its existence, mankind has to live with the problem of crime. Vladimir Aras (S / D) points out that in the history of mankind there have always been groups of more or less organized criminals, who gathered their forces to achieve common goals of territorial control and economic power, often using violence and corruption.

With the intense changes of the world after the Cold War, agents of organized crime have changed their ways. They began to act increasingly organized and structured, with more transnational impact (PEREIRA, 2010, p.08).

The advent of globalization accompanied by technological change, the spread of democracy and the economy have had a fundamental role in the evolution of organized crime, to the extent that the entire apparatus developed for the formal economy and for legitimate capitalist exchanges was appropriate for criminal schemes around the globe, thus prior crimes committed only in the domestic sphere of nations began to be committed in a transnational plain facilitated by the new global economy (ARAS, S / D, P.03).

This scenario has posed a striking and difficult challenge for most modern societies, particularly for those who are governed, at least theoretically, by democratic governments and/or framed by free market economies. International criminal networks have shown great agility to take advantage of opportunities worldwide, emerging from the extraordinary changes in politics, in business, in technology and communications. Thus, according to Naim (2006, p.35):

> The new environment offers advantages to criminal organizations, who are able to respond and adapt quickly to new opportunities, allowing constant location, tactics, means and mechanism changes to earn as much money as possible (Naim, 2006, p.35).

Note that crime, then, as a phenomenon inherent to society, kept pace with population and technological development of the society in which it is inserted, while modernizing itself as well. In this sense, one can define organized crime as a phenomenon because it follows the changing trends of the national and international markets (WERNER, 2009).

However, the definition of organized crime is an arduous task for the lack of a concrete definition and no consensus on its definition. Mendroni (2009) points out that there is the presence of several definitions with similar points, but distinct from general content.

During most of the twentieth century, crime was seen by governments as a matter of domestic jurisdiction, relating to public safety and not to national or international security (PEREIRA, 2011, p.21). This led to greater theoretical difficulty to deal with the issue, which is the definition of organized crime. Nowadays, there is no concrete definition for "organized crime", and in fact there are ideological debates related to these issues (Araujo, 2010).

Many countries are seeking to define organized crime using the term given by the Palermo Convention, for fundamental legal framework, which is:

> **(A) "Organized criminal group"** *shall mean a structured group of three or more persons, existing for a period of time and acting in concert with the aim of committing one or more serious crimes or offences established in accordance with this Convention, in order to, directly or indirectly, obtain the financial benefit or other materials;*

> **(C) "Structured group"** *shall mean a group that is not randomly formed for the immediate commission of an offense and that does not need to have formally defined roles for its members, continuity of its membership or a developed structure;*

Another highlight is the definition of William Werner (2009) that classifies the organized crime from three perspectives: (1) the political perspective where organized crime is the result of a weak state structure; (2) social, which through cultural and social elements as factors in the development of transnational organized crime; (3) and economic, which develops due to the demand for illicit goods and services.

Transnational organized crime, therefore, can be understood as that which causes offense to at least two countries, covering legal, political, economic and social aspects, seeing reputable criminal organizations as a hierarchically stable and pre structured group with pre-arranged norms, dedicated the practice of illegal activities with the goal of raising funds.

*Drug Trafficking*

A striking feature of criminal organizations is specialization. There are those who work in drug trafficking; others who engage in the trafficking of firearms; some who specialize in smuggling of organs and endangered species. There are still those who act solely in the financial and economic fields (ARAS, S / D, P.02). According to UNODC the three most profitable activities in transnational organized crime are drug trafficking, arms trafficking and human trafficking.

Drug trafficking is the most lucrative type of crime in the world, higher even than the national income of many countries (WERNER, 2009, p.13). The UN registers the drug trafficking in more than 150 countries around the world, represented nearly in all of its member countries. It recognizes that it is physically difficult to quantify with any precision because it is an economy that operates in an obscure manner. The UNODC estimates that this market will move more than 400 billion dollars per year.

We know that today's drug trafficking operates on a global scale comprised of countless criminal organizations and its production originates, in general, in failed states and developing countries and their consumption made largely in rich countries (PEREIRA, 2010).

However, despite its expansion starting in 1970, it was as from the 90s' that a remarkable growth in the drug trafficking industry was observed, increasing the number of countries that stepped into the illegal circuit, which transformed the economics and politics of many of these countries. It can be assumed that in failed states, where the governments are weak, the power of trafficking enters the highest echelons of national institutions and social organization.

Castells (1999) quotes five characteristics for understanding drug trafficking. The basis of this phenomena is demand and supply driven, with the consumer boom and the popularization of the drug, especially in the developed capitalist countries like the United States and Western European countries.

The second feature is the internationalization and the division of labor in the production process. An example is the Andean region, which for years has specialized in the cultivation of coca leaves.

The third characteristic is "the essence of all the drug industry as a component in the system of money laundering", which will be explained later.

A fourth characteristic is the use of violence to ensure the interests of traffic and transactions. Trafficking is not just capital, as it also has private armies with extremely modern weaponry.

The last feature concerns corruption because the dealers need to corrupt and/or intimidate local and national authorities, such as judges, politicians, police, customs, businessmen, journalists and others. This control practiced by traffickers is more effective in failed states. Drug trafficking not only generates income; but the consequence of its operation undermines all the inherent mechanisms in standards and safety. This is because organized crime encourages corruption in public agencies to ensure the interests of trafficking.

*Money Laundering*

In the opinion of COAF, money laundering is the process or act by which the criminal conducts various commercial or financial transactions to incorporate resources in the economy that have originated from unlawful acts or are somehow connected to them, eliminating the evidence of its origin.

Therefore, money laundering is the method in which the criminal organization processes financial gains from illegal activities, seeking to disguise them as lawfully obtained. Therefore, it is possible to say that all criminal organizations practice money laundering (MENDRONI, 2009, p.25).

This process, according to COAF, involves and is explained in three steps: Placement, Layering and Integration. In the placement process, the launderer seeks to insert the money obtained illegally in the economic system, i.e., the criminal agent puts money into a legitimate financial institution, usually through small deposits or small asset purchases, in order to hinder monitoring of banks.

The second phase is blind, also called stratification. It is the most complex stage of money laundering, because, after the insertion in the financial market, the illicit assets must be disconnected from their source, so the values are fractional and moved to hinder tracking by the financial authorities.

In the last stage, Integration, money is reinstated to formal economy legitimately. It is usually made in the form of investments in local companies, where the criminal has profit sharing. Thus, with the continuous reinvestment of illegal money in the market for a transformation of illegitimate aspect in legitimate succession (Lamb, 2009), Barros (apud ARAS, S / D) points out that:

> In the second stage of the money laundering process dissimulation is practiced, also known as phase control or stratification, which corresponds to the accumulation of investments that aim to make up the accounting trail of the proceeds of the predicate offense. At this stage of the criminal action, the conduct is of various successive operations and economic-financial transactions, including the so-called "tax havens", made with the use of sophisticated means and purpose of disguising illicit origin of dirty money, and then many bank accounts, diversified investments, etc. are used involving the participation of individuals and companies engaged in camouflaging illicit assets. It's unfolding in this superposition of transactions that the cycle is basically effective washing, behold, it is inherent in concealing the ultimate goal of structuring illicit profits with new appearance of lawful assets.

It is observed that the crime of money laundering is an international threat, as the criminal agents are enabled with a way to fund their illicit activities. On the other hand, one has to consider that almost every criminal organization merges with unlawful-lawful activities (MENDRONI, 2009). Experts estimate that about $500 billion of illicit money - about 2% of global GDP - annually circulate in the economy. [1]

## CHARACTERISTICS OF TRANSNATIONAL ORGANIZED CRIME, AND THEIR ORGANIZATIONAL STRUCTURE - "MODUS OPERANDI"

### Features Transnational Organized Crime

For a better understanding of the organizational structure of transnational organized crime, as well as its *modus operandi,* analysis of its characteristics is necessary. So Mingardi (1998 apud LIMA, 2005) highlights that no single model of organized crime exists and at least two distinct types can be seen: the traditional business and organized crime. The author also shows how central features of organized crime: (a) existence of a definite hierarchy; (B) a forecast of profit, operating income, hence the result of a model with traces of capitalist enterprise; (C) symbiosis with the state last reason of subsistence and longevity of organized crime.

Giraldo and Trikunas (2007 apud WERNER, 2009, p.88) highlight three visions for the analysis of organized crime, which may be competitive or co-exist with each other:

a) **Hierarchy:** classic model of studies about the mobs and other manifestations of traditional organized crime,

b) **Networks:** approach which uses the sociological instrumental, from the way of the formation of criminal networks and their intersubjective articulations, and;

c) **Market:** approach based on the markets where the illicit goods and services develop, impacting the formal economy.

We note, therefore, that organizational structures vary in different hierarchical methods. In this sense, Werner (2009) identifies two key characteristics of the organizational forms of organized crime: an associative (linked to hierarchy and networks) and the other market (linked to economic activity that aims to profit). Thus, transnational organized crime can be defined as a strategic association of individuals, where the goal is to obtain unlawful gains.

*Defining the Nature of the Illicit: From Rigid Overcoming Hierarchical Organization Performance in the form of networks.*

The debate around crime for several decades has been monopolized by the concept of hierarchy, which gave a totalitarian character of their leaders. Thus, the hierarchy was initially identified as the main feature of organized crime, being used as an analysis tool to traditional criminal groups.

However, the influence of a more dynamic, increasingly global and characterized by an incredible technological development, society brought the assimilation of these transformations to transnational organized crime and overturned the notion of monopoly control of criminal organizations through the hierarchy.

With the strengthening of organized crime around the world, especially drug trafficking, as from 1990, crime criminal organizations perfected their *modus operandi,* acquiring a more complex and transnational nature. Thus, they began to operate as true businesses with criminal objectives, working in corporate molds and exploring criminal activities like a legitimate enterprise (OLIVEIRA, 2005).

In this regard, a study developed by the Office on Drugs and Crime United Nations is noteworthy, where information of forty groups of transnational organized crime was collected from operations in sixteen countries that allowed the identification of five different kinds of hierarchical structures of criminal networks, described in the chart below:

**Table 1:** Hierarchical Structure and Characteristics of Criminal Organizations

| | |
|---|---|
| | **REGIONAL HIERARCHY:** is the most sophisticated form of hierarchy, having the following characteristics:<br><br>• Rigid lines of command starting from a center;<br><br>• Relative autonomy to regional components;<br><br>• Multiple activities |
| | **HIERARCHY OR GROUPED IN CORE:**<br><br>• Set of criminal groups that have established a control system;<br><br>• Central command with several peripherally hierarchies is rich;<br><br>• Orders starting from the central core to the peripheral organizations, which have a high degree of autonomy |

| | CENTRAL GROUP: |
|---|---|
| | • Center is relatively rigid and well organized but unstructured; <br><br> • Limited number of participants (20 individuals or less); <br><br> • Low social bond or ethnic identity |
| | **CRIMINAL NETWORK:** <br><br> • Defined by individuals who engage in illicit activities by volatile alliances; <br><br> • Is formed around key individuals; <br><br> • Filiations to criminal groups isn't necessary; <br><br> • Loyalty and union are essential for the maintenance of the network; <br><br> • Reform of the network after a key individual quits. |

**Source: United Nations, Pilot Research, 2002 p.39-44 2**

The first model mentioned by the study is the standard hierarchy. This is the way that traditionally characterized organized crime. Leadership is exercised by a single leader, responsible of making and maintaining command. Power is centralized on a person. Strict discipline is kept among the group. The union is based on the social ties of ethnic and cultural identity.

The second model is highlighted in the regional hierarchy. This form has more dynamism than the first. The nuclei of regional action enjoy some autonomy in decision making. However, there is a control center, from where the commands come. The recommendations of the core may void any initiative of local groups. This structure resembles the franchise business, where there is transfer of percentages of earnings to the central command.

The third model is identified or grouped in the core hierarchy. Here there is also a central command group. This relates to the other and the other with each other, having a high degree of autonomy. The performance of the core group is to solve possible disputes between the peripheral groups and optimize resources. It is observed that its structure is similar to an umbrella, where the central core connects with each peripheral nucleus and these, with each other.

The fourth model identified is the core group. In this, the number of persons involved is relatively small, usually not more than 20 individuals. Core activities are managed around a periphery. In it groups are arrayed according to those who will practice a criminal activity. Central Chiefs perform their tasks according to their specialties.

Finally, the pilot search identifies the network structure. Unlike previous groups, there is no central hierarchy that holds the powers of centralized command. The network is comprised of individuals who engage in the activity by volatile bonds. There is no need for affiliation to the criminal group, just individuals that have the skills that are demanded. This type of binding is looser and complicates the tracking of actions and identification of authors by state authorities. When the authorities identifies a suspect, the network immediately vanishes and subsequently reorganizes around other individuals (WERNER, 2009).

Castells (2000, p.498) states that we must understand the imminence of networks from the development of contemporary capitalism, as Castells points out that:

> Networks are appropriate instruments for a capitalist economy based on innovation, globalization, and decentralized concentration; to work, workers and companies focused on flexibility and adaptability; to a culture of continuous deconstruction and reconstruction; a policy for the instant processing of new values and public moods; and a social organization aimed.

Even as the author cited, the prominence of formats in networks is comprehensive and are the main form of organization of a contemporary society. Thus, Castells (2003) points out that the success and expansion of transnational crime in the 90s was due to the versatility and flexibility of organizations. The author then points out that the formation of networks is their *standard modus operandi*, both internally, i.e., in each criminal organization, and internationally, at the level of other criminal organizations. These, in turn, will be constructed according to the interests of criminal groups and, in order to facilitate their practice internationally.

In this sense, it is important to note that the form of hierarchical organization will be slowing down in the exact measure in which the actions of state hamper the operations of criminals (WERNER, 2009, p.99). Thus, the new arrangements in networks seek compromise the identification of criminal leaders and combat organized by state authorities.

However, we note that changes in the modus operandi of organized crime is due to two factors already mentioned earlier: *globalization,* which means, technological and communications advances, the growth of transnational flow of people, goods and capital and; *weakening* of the *state,* represented in the political changes that occurred in the closed economies and authoritarian regimes, along with the anxiety caused to the end of the Cold War (WERNER, 2009).

Nowadays the power in networked organizations is widespread and its exercise is effected through cores of command. This feature facilitates the performance of the organization, allowing it to be in different time zones and locations. Thus, participation in networks provide leadership and criminal associations at a level of cooperation and distancing, and reducing their vulnerability in the face of actions of state confrontation. Then we observe that organizations start to bear a level of sophistication and deception that hinders its combat (WERNER, 2009).

*Fuzzy Networks for Economic Performance*

According to Oliveira (2005) transnational crime is of a business nature, characterized as a systematic and similar venture as a well-directed economic activity, approaching a corporation, given the impersonality of the organization, which leads us to think about transnational crime from the point of view of their performance in the markets.

Currently, organized crime is present in the business world, sports, entertainment and information. Its capital is connected in real time to intangible futures and derivatives market in major real estate transactions, among other leading sectors of the formal economy (LIMA , 2005).

The organization of diffuse networks of economic performance has been the most common organizational structure of international criminal groups. The mode of action network is characterized by a pervasive hierarchy, different to the traditionally known hierarchy. This mode mounts a criminal network of high proportions and breaking national boundaries, becoming a complex web of vast performance. In this sense Werner (2009, p.105) states that:

The acting perspective of transnational organized crime can be attributed to the inexorable logic of the market, in place of sophistication or corporate reach of large organizations, there is currently a trend of a large number of small entrepreneurs who identify the demands, create appropriate offers for the illegal demanded goods and services, and interacting through the diffuse and fluid networks, aiming to hinder identification and making activities virtually impossible to trace.

Thus, the model structure in networks, diffused action is more advantageous to transnational organized crime, since it is able to collect and analyze information and can quickly adapt to crime-fighting strategies used by state authorities, as well as learning from the experience. She fits the goals of the group, the flexibility of the market and the political dynamics of government institutions.

In this sense, Castells (2003, p.240) complements stating that: "The great mobility and extreme flexibility of networks allows them to get rid of national regulations and strict procedures for cooperation between police from different countries."

Therefore, the structures are an expansive network format. Soon, a social structure based on networks is an open and highly dynamic, susceptible innovation system without threats to their balance (Castells, 2000). Thus, the diffusing networks that connect illegally in space are becoming wider, increasing its joints and hampering their fight.

## INSTRUMENTS OF INTERNATIONAL COOPERATION IN THE FIGHT AGAINST TRANSNATIONAL ORGANIZED CRIME

Transnational crime is a threat that practically affects all nations directly and/or indirectly and has had its rise facilitated internationally with the end of the Cold War.

Globalization, too, was critical to the advancement of organized crime around the world. However, the process of globalization can be analyzed from several perspectives, all of them related to the transformation of domestic spaces in global arenas. Thus, themes that were previously structured under a strictly national viewpoint spend worldwide, deeply modifying the dynamics of economic, financial, social and informational relationships (SAADI; BEZERRA cited JUSTICE, 2012).

Therefore, international cooperation operates, as per the scenario described above: as a logical response to violations caused by the interaction of the countries in creating mechanisms to suppress the development of transnational organized crime (Medeiros, 2009).

*Mechanisms to Combat Transnational Organized Crime*

According to UNODC estimates, transnational crime moves about two to three percent of world's economic output annually (WERNER, 2009). No doubt the phenomenon of globalization and the process of deregulation of markets has facilitated the spread of crime, and has now increasingly become of transnational character and a threat to democratic institutions and organizational structures of states, as well as a challenge to the international legal order (SANDRONI, S / D).

The fight against transnational organized crime is important for States and the international society. In this context, one sees the need to establish a global agreement and enhance international cooperation in an attempt to obstruct the criminal activities. Therefore, the cooperation is an indispensable tool in this fight, both in bilateral relations between states as multilaterally in international bodies like the United Nations, the European Union and Mercosur. (SANDRONI, S / D, MEDEIROS, 2009). In this sense Medeiros (2009, p.64 notes that:

> Besides the actions of police, financial and strategic intelligence that should guide public policies to combat major criminal conglomerates, some others have been shown effective for this purpose of cooperation.

As discussed previously, transnational organized crime has changed its hierarchical structure, replacing a rigid hierarchy by acting in networks, dispersing its activities, planning and logistics in various continents, seeking thereby to confuse the used state legal systems to combat transnational crime and its manifestations. Therefore, as strange as it may seem, the fact that each country has its own legislation on organized crime hinders the fight against this global threat. Then it is evident that the state alone is insufficient in the fight against this evil, because transnational crime is a problem that transcends national borders (SANDRONI, S / D).

Thus, according to the UNODC, it is necessary to adopt effective regional responses to contain illicit activities and the efforts of States in the implementation of an international legal instrument.

*Main Instruments of International Cooperation in Combating Transnational Organized Crime*

It is observed that the international context and the treatment of security issues have changed over time, especially with the end of the Cold War, with the emergence of new security threats targeted at different sectors of the military, for example, the political, social, economic and environmental spheres (WERNER, 2009).

Naim (2006) elaborates that the leaders of the twenty-first century should keep in mind that technology alone is not enough to combat illicit trade. Thus, agencies around the world need to unite in an effort to promote global action that can confront this threat that is equally global. In this sense, international cooperation becomes imperative in the fight against transnational organized crime.

Thus, one cannot lose sight of the existence of multiple levels of "cooperation." On the one hand, internal cooperation, the righteous and the police, on the other hand cooperation on an international level. We note, therefore, the need for cooperation between the institutions of security, both in internal states, as well as externally. Therefore, in this context regional and supranational institutions play a noticeable role in the integration and cooperation of security agencies (SALVADOR, 2009; WERNER, 2009).

It is worth noting that the current process of globalization pressured states to cooperate with the international community, where an act of refusal of a State to cooperate in the repression of transnational crime may result in the qualification of the country internationally as not reliable (SALVADOR, 2009, p .122).

## United Nations Office on Drugs and Crime:

Resulting from increased activity of organized crime in the international arena, the UN, observing the magnitude of the problem, created a specialized agency in 1997 on the subject - the United Nations Office on Drugs and Crime (United Nations Office on Drugs and Crime - UNODC) - which aims to give support and infrastructure to countries interested in combating organized crime. The UNODC currently has approximately 21 offices worldwide and is operating in over 150 countries. [3]

The work of the UNODC focuses on three areas of action: prevention, protection and criminalization. In the field of prevention, UNODC works with governments, in order to create campaigns to be aired on radio and TV, as well as the distributing of flyers and seeking partnerships to increase public awareness about the threat of transnational organized crime.

In the field of protection, UNODC cooperates with countries to promote training for police, prosecutors, judges and prosecutors. Finally, UNODC seeks to strengthen justice systems of countries to which the greatest number of criminals are to be tried. [4] In this sense, it follows an illustrative picture of the work of UNODC, and cooperation in combating transnational crime.

We observe, therefore, that the UNODC cooperates with a network of regional and international institutions, which allows thorough exchange of experiences. Thus, these programs assist countries in the development, ratification and implementation of Conventions and additional protocols such as the Palermo Convention, and to promote the application of internationally recognized principles in areas such as mutual legal assistance and extradition (Rabelo, 2007).

> As the author cited, the prominence of formats in networks is comprehensive and are the main form of organization of contemporary society. Thus, Castells (2003) points out that the success and expansion of transnational crime in the 90s is due to the versatility and flexibility of their organization. The author then points out that the formation of networks is their *standard modus operandi,* both internally, i.e., in criminal organizations, and internationally, at the level of other criminal organizations. These, in turn, will be constructed according to the interests of criminal groups and in order to facilitate their international practice.

In this sense, it is important to note that the form of hierarchical organization will be slowing down in the exact measure in which the actions of state hamper the operations of criminals (WERNER, 2009, p.99). Thus, the new arrangements in networks seek to compromise the identification of criminal leaders and combat organized crime by state authorities.

However, we note that changes in the modus operandi of organized crime is due to two factors already mentioned earlier: *globalization,* which means, advances in technology and communications, the growth of the transnational flow of people, goods and capital and *weakening* the *state,* represented in the political changes that occurred in the closed economies and authoritarian regimes, along with the anxiety caused by the end of the Cold War (WERNER, 2009)

Nowadays, the power in networked organizations is widespread and exercise is affected through core command. This feature facilitates the performance of the organization, allowing it to be the same in different time zones and locations. Thus, participation in networks provide leadership and criminal associations a level of cooperation and distancing, and reduce their vulnerability in the face of actions of state confrontation. Then we observe that organizations start to bear a level of sophistication and deception that hinders its combat (WERNER, 2009).

*Fuzzy Networks for Economic Performance*

According to Oliveira (2005) transnational crime is of a business nature, characterized as a systematic and similar venture as a well-directed economic activity, approaching a corporation, given the impersonality of the organization which leads us to think about transnational crime from the point of view of their performance in the markets.

Currently organized crime is present in the business world, sports, entertainment and information. Its capital is connected in real time to intangible futures market and derivatives market in major real estate transactions, among other leading sectors of the formal economy (LIMA , 2005).

The organization of diffuse networks of economic performance has been the most common organizational structure of international criminal groups. The network actions are characterized by a pervasive hierarchy, different to the traditionally known hierarchy. This mode mounts a criminal network of high proportions and that breaks national boundaries, becoming a complex web of vast performance. In this sense Werner (2009, p.105) states that:

> The acting perspective of transnational organized crime can be attributed to the inexorable logic of the market, in place of sophistication or corporate reach of large organizations, there is currently a trend of a large number of small entrepreneurs who identify the demands, create appropriate offers for the illegal goods and services demand, and interact through the diffuse and fluid networks, aiming to hinder identification and virtually impossible to trace the activities developed.

Thus, the model structure in networks diffuse action is more advantageous to transnational organized crime, since it is able to collect and analyze information and can adapt quickly to crime-fighting strategies used by state authorities, as well as learn from the experience. The goals of the group are met, the flexibility of the market and the political dynamics of government institutions.

In this sense, Castells (2003, p.240) complements stating that: "The great mobility and extreme flexibility of networks allows them to get rid of national regulations and strict procedures for cooperation between police from different countries."

Therefore, the structures are expansive from network format. Soon, a social structure based on networks is an open and highly dynamic, susceptible innovation system without threats to their balance (Castells, 2000). Thus, the diffuse networks that connect illegally in space are becoming wider, increasing joints and hampering its fight.

## INSTRUMENTS OF INTERNATIONAL COOPERATION IN THE FIGHT AGAINST TRANSNATIONAL ORGANIZED CRIME

Transnational crime is a threat that practically affects all nations directly and/or indirectly, and has had its rise internationally facilitated with the end of the Cold War.

Globalization, too, was critical to the advancement of organized crime around the world. However, the globalization process can be analyzed from several perspectives, all of them are related to the transformation of domestic spaces in global arenas. Thus, themes that were previously structured under a strictly national viewpoint deeply modify dynamics of economic, financial, social and informational relationships worldwide (SAADI; BEZERRA cited JUSTICE, 2012).

Therefore, international cooperation operates, with reference to the scenario described above, as a logical response to violations caused by the interaction of the countries in creating mechanisms to suppress the development of transnational organized crime (Medeiros, 2009).

*Mechanisms to Combat Transnational Organized Crime*

UNODC estimates that transnational crime moves about two to three percent of the world's economic output annually (WERNER, 2009). No doubt the phenomenon of globalization and the process of deregulation of markets has facilitated the spread of crime, now increasingly. as it has transnational character, becoming a threat to democratic institutions and organizational structures of states, as well as a challenge to the international legal order (SANDRONI, S / D).

The fight against transnational organized crime is important for States and the international society. In this context, one sees the need to establish a global agreement and enhance international cooperation in an attempt to obstruct criminal activities. Therefore cooperation is an indispensable tool in this fight, both in bilateral relations between states as well as multilaterally in international bodies like the United Nations, the European Union and Mercosur. (SANDRONI, S / D, MEDEIROS, 2009). In this sense Medeiros (2009, p.64) notes that:

Besides the actions of police, financial and strategic intelligence should guide public policies to combat major criminal conglomerates, some others have been shown effective for this purpose cooperation.

As discussed previously, transnational organized crime has changed its hierarchical structure, replacing a rigid hierarchy by acting in networks, dispersing its activities, planning and logistics in various continents, seeking thereby to confuse the state legal systems used to combat transnational crime and its manifestations. Therefore, as it may seem, the fact that each country has its own legislation on organized crime hinders the fight against this global threat. Then it is evident that the state alone is insufficient in the fight against this evil, because transnational crime is a problem that transcends national borders (SANDRONI, S / D).

Thus, according to UNODC, it is necessary to adopt effective regional responses to contain illicit activities and the efforts of States in the implementation of an international legal instrument.

*Main Instruments of International Cooperation in Combating Transnational Organized Crime*

In the international context, the treatment of security issues has changed over time, especially with the end of the Cold War, with the emergence of new security threats targeted at different sectors of the military, for example in the political, social, economic and environmental spheres (WERNER, 2009).

Naim (2006) elaborates that the leaders of the twenty-first century should keep in mind that technology alone is not enough to combat illicit trade. Thus, agencies around the world need to unite in an effort to promote global action that can confront this threat that is equally global. In this sense, international cooperation becomes imperative in the fight against transnational organized crime.

Thus, one cannot lose sight of the existence of multiple levels of "cooperation." On the one hand, internal cooperation, the righteous and the police, on the other hand, cooperation on the international level. We note, therefore, the need for cooperation between the institutions of security, both internal states, as externally. Therefore, in this context regional and supranational institutions play a noticeable role in the integration and cooperation of security agencies (SALVADOR, 2009; WERNER, 2009).

It is worth noting that the current process of globalization pressures states to cooperate with the international community, where an act of refusal of a State to cooperate in the repression of transnational crime may result in the qualifying the country as not reliable on an international level (SALVADOR, 2009, p .122).

United Nations Office on Drugs and Crime:

Resulting from increased activity of organized crime in the international arena, the UN observing the magnitude of the problem created a specialized agency on the subject in 1997- the United Nations Office on Drugs and Crime (United Nations Office on Drugs and Crime - UNODC) - which aims to give support and infrastructure  countries interested in combating organized crime. The UNODC currently has approximately 21 offices worldwide and operates in over 150 countries. [3]

The work of UNODC focuses on three areas of action: prevention, protection and criminalization. In the field of prevention, UNODC works with governments, in order to create campaigns to be aired on radio and TV as well as distributing flyers and seek partnerships to increase public awareness about the threat of transnational organized crime.

In the field of protection, UNODC cooperates with countries to promote training for police, prosecutors, judges and prosecutors. Finally, UNODC seeks to strengthen justice systems of countries, where the greatest number of criminals are to be tried.  In this sense, it follows an illustrative picture of the work of UNODC, and cooperation in combating transnational crime.

We observe, therefore, that the UNODC cooperates with a network of regional and international institutions, which allows a thorough exchange experience. Thus, these programs assist countries in the development, ratification and implementation of Conventions and additional protocols such as the Palermo Convention, to promote the application of internationally recognized principles in areas such as mutual legal assistance and extradition (Rabelo, 2007).

## Table 2: Breakdown of UNODC and Technical Assistance by Region

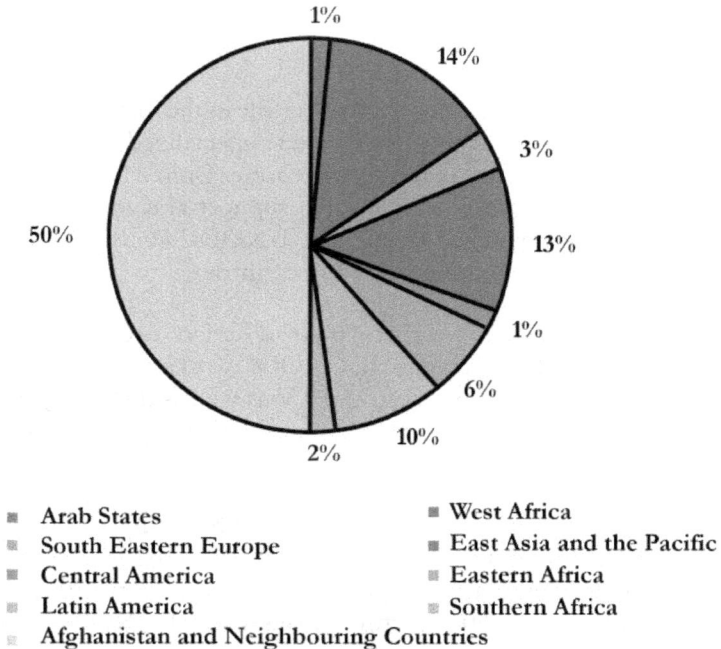

Pie chart values: 1%, 14%, 3%, 13%, 1%, 6%, 10%, 2%, 50%

Legend:

- Arab States
- South Eastern Europe
- Central America
- Latin America
- Afghanistan and Neighbouring Countries
- West Africa
- East Asia and the Pacific
- Eastern Africa
- Southern Africa

**Source: Action Against Transnational Organized Crime and Illicit Trafficking, Including Drug Trafficking (2011 - 2013) p.57**

### International Convention Against Trafficking in Drugs (1988):

The International Convention Against Drug Trafficking was held in Vienna in 1988 as an attempt to contain the spread of transnational crime.

It is observed that the International Convention Against Drug Trafficking initiated the movement to criminalize in most countries and the establishment of various international agencies to combat organized crime, not just drug trafficking (SALVADOR, 2009).

Thus, the Convention aimed to take action against illicit drug trafficking, but also materialized significant advances with regard to combating the crime of money laundering. Since established, by way of international cooperation, the obligation of each signatory country criminalizes and penalizes money laundering derived from drug trafficking (ALMEIDA, 2008, p.54).

## Palermo Convention:

The evolution in the form of organized crime act as an increasing transnational character, which led the United Nations, in 1998, through the General Assembly, to deliberate for drafting the UN Convention against Transnational Organized Crime, best known as the Palermo Convention (WERNER, 2009).

The Palermo Convention was held suggestively in the Sicilian city dominated by the *Cosa Nostra* Mafia and is seen as the main instrument to combat transnational crime (WERNER, 2009). The Convention has 147 signatures and 100 parties united [2], plus three additional protocols that target specific areas: *Additional Protocol against Transnational Organized Crime to Prevent, Suppress and Punish Trafficking of Persons, particularly Women and Children* ; *Protocol against the Smuggling of Migrants by Land, Sea and* ; *Protocol against the Illicit Manufacturing of and Trafficking in Firearms, their Parts and Components and Ammunition* .

According to researcher Dimitri Vlassis (apud SALDANHA, S / D, p.11), the Palermo Convention was organized in four steps: criminalization, international cooperation, technical cooperation and implementation. According to him:

> Criminalization concepts and forms of transnational crimes were defined in parts and technical cooperation was based on the subjects relating to the exchange of information, intelligence, training and funding of promotional activities against transnational crime programs. Finally, the implementation stage created a body called the Conference of the Parties, which is empowered to monitor, suggest changes, and facilitate the activities of information exchange; additionally serving as a forum for assistance for those countries least developed in the implementation of measures to combat transnational organized crime.

Therefore the Palermo Convention aims to promote cooperation to prevent and combat transnational organized crime. So many of the articles establish various mechanisms to classify crimes, defining new concepts related to transnational organized crime (JUSTICE, 2012).

Therefore, since promoting coordination and cooperation among states is shown as the main purpose of the Palermo Convention, greater standardization of national policies addressing this issue is provided. Soon, the Palermo Convention marked a breakthrough in the issue of combating transnational organized crime.

## The international Financial Action Task Force (FATF / GAFI)

As discussed previously, money laundering is essential to the maintenance and funding of transnational organized crime and their joints (Castells, 2001; Lamb, 2009; Naim, 2006).

Thus, the International Financial Action Group (Financial Action Task Force on Money Laudering - FATF) comes with the intention of creating rules to control criminal operations within the banking system in order to combat money laundering (ALMEIDA, 2008; ANSELMO, 2010).

The FATF aims to develop, review and promote policies to combat money laundering. The purpose of these policies, then, is to prevent the products of drug trafficking and other illicit crimes that are used in other illegal activities, impairing the lawful activities of the various countries (ALMEIDA, 2008).

In 1990 the FATF presented forty recommendation calls. As recommendations, they were not presented as mandatory but as suggested actions in criminal, financial and international cooperation (SALDANHA, S / D) framework.

It is noteworthy that despite the forty recommendations that were presented in 1990, they constantly undergo revisions aiming to upgrade them against the advances of transnational crime. The most recent update occurred in 2012 [6] , and was treated on the establishment of "anti-laundery" programs to be followed by member countries and designed for universal application, covering the legal, financial and international cooperation systems (SALVADOR, 2009).

Finally, Edson Pinto points out that despite the FATF / GAFI there has not been any international legitimacy to apply direct sanctions, countries are simple added to the "blacklist" as a penalty as there is a loss of credibility in the international community (cited SALVADOR , 2009, p.126).

*Analysis of Cooperation Mechanisms*

After having explained the main treaties and organizations that deal with transnational crime, we continue with a more empirical part of this study - the analysis of the efficiency and the results of these mechanisms.

States, since the end of the Cold War, were concerned with the advancement of transnational crime and sought means of cooperation to regulate their actions with the criminal actions.

In this context, we realize that the UN is one of the main instruments used by the State in combating transnational crime. In this regard, it is noteworthy that the UNODC office was created by the United Nations only to address issues about crime. It is noticed that UNODC has a fundamental role in breakthroughs to combating transnational crime, since this seeks to integrate its member countries, providing the exchange of knowledge and the exchange of information, and supporting infrastructure to interested countries that engage in combating transnational crime.

However, it is noted that states have difficulties in ratifying the treaties of cooperation in combating transnational crime. This is explained in the UN Convention against Transnational Organized Crime, which, despite having 147 signatory states, has nearly one third of treaties that have not been ratified by the Convention.

Below is a table, which summarizes the characteristics of cooperative actions in combating transnational crime by addressing its pros and cons.

Table 3: Summary of Cooperative Actions of the States.

| | YEAR | INSTRUMENTS OF COOPERATION | PROS | CONS |
|---|---|---|---|---|
| **1990 TO 2012** | 1990 | FATF | Suggested actions in the criminal financial and political context | Still do not have international legitimacy |
| | 1997 | UNODC | Provided technical assistance and infrastructure support to countries combating organized crime | The plan of action depended on the financial resources made available by the UN |
| | 2003 | United Nations Convention Against Transnational Organized Crime | Criminal classification in national law acts as participation in organized criminal groups, money laundering, corruption and obstruction of justice. Promote cooperation to prevent and combat transnational organized crime. | Despite being an important legal foundation on the subject, about one third of the signing States have not yet ratified. |

# CONCLUSION

After explaining and discussing transnational organized crime, which in recent decades has been expanding and has had greater visibility in the area of operation of organized crime, by transgressing national borders, organized crime has become a global actor, and therefore, a threat to the international security system.

Thus, the first part of this study defined as strategic transnational organized association of individuals those that operate in a decentralized manner and have as goal illicit gains crime, this includes several illegal modes and presents a threat to the environmental, economic, legal, military, political and social areas. Also it was demonstrated that drug trafficking is the most profitable type of illicit organized crime, while money laundering is responsible for bringing the illicit gains in the economy in a lawful manner and funding the advancement of transnational crime.

It was observed also that countries where state actions are weak become a safety zone for criminal organizations. Therefore, organized crime, through globalization, can expand its activities and became a threat to international society.

In the second part, it was observed that criminal organizations have overcome the traditional concept of hierarchical organizations, rising to associate strategically through network structures - in order to hinder their combat by the authorities and government institutions.

Finally, it became evident that the trend of penetration of criminal networks in governments and institutions, especially in *failed states,* may cause criminal organizations to control and influence the decision making process in the countries, furthermore in the markets and international politics either partially or totally. Thus, the supranational bodies play an important role in combating transnational organized crime. These are presented as an important forum for debate and provide valuable contributions of information networks to strengthen the relationship of the countries, and provide opportunities for knowledge sharing.

Therefore, measures to combat crime must be based on cooperation, not only between states but also between the new actors that become relevant in the contemporary international situation, such as NGOs and international organizations. Soon, more multilateralism and cooperation is necessary to combat the threat of transnational organized crime effectively.

# REFERENCES

ALMEIDA, Márcio J. M.. **A Atividade de Inteligência e o Direito no Combate ao Crime de Lavagem de Dinheiro.** 122 f. Tese (Mestrado) - UCB, Brasília, 2008.

ANSELMO, Márcio A.. O Ambiente Internacional do Combate à Lavagem de Dinheiro. **Revista de Informação Legislativa,** Brasília, v. 47, n. 188, p.357-371, 10 out. 2010. Disponível em: <http://www2.senado.gov.br/bdsf/bitstream/id/198729/1/000901859.pdf>. Acesso em: 22 set. 2012.

ARAS, Vladimir. **Lavagem de Dinheiro Trasnacional:** Crime de Competência Federal. Disponível em:<http://gtld.pgr.mpf.gov.br/lavagemdedinheiro/artigos/artigos-docs/competencia-ld-transnacional.pdf>. Acesso em: 20 set. 2012.

ARAS, Vladimir. **Lavagem de Dinheiro, Organizações Criminosas e o Conceito da Convenção de Palermo.** Disponível em<http://gtld.pgr.mpf.gov.br/artigos/artigos-docs/convencao-palermo.pdf>. Acesso em: 29 set. 2012.

*CASTELLS, Manuel.* **A** Era **da Informação**: economia, *sociedade* e cultura, vol. 3, São Paulo: Paz e terra, 1999.

CASTELLS, Manuel. **O Poder da Identidade.** Trad. Klaus Bradini. São Paulo: Editora Paz e Terra, 2002.

CEPIK, Marcos; BORBA, Pedro. Crime Organizado, Estado e Segurança Internacional. **Contexto Internacional,** Rio de Janeiro, v. 33, n. 2, p.375-399, jul/dez. 2011.

CORDEIRO, Marcelo D.. **Enfrentamento Integrado e Globalizado da Criminalidade Organizada Transnacional Estudo de Caso: Operação Oceânica.** 2009. 206 f. Tese (Mestrado) - Universidade Católica de Brasília, Brasília, 2009.

CRESSEY, Donald R.. G. **Theft of the Nation: The Stucture And Operations Of Organized Crime In America**, New York, 1969. Apud: WERNER, Guilherme Cunha. **O crime organizado e as redes criminosas:** presença e influência nas relações internacionais contemporâneas. 241 f. Tese (Doutorado) - Universidade de São Paulo, São Paulo, 2009.

GIRALDO, Jeane; TRINKUNAS, Harold. Transnational Crime. In Contemporary Security Studies. COLLINS, Alan (org.). Gran Bretanha. p. 346-366. Apud: WERNER, Guilherme Cunha. **O crime organizado e as redes criminosas:** presença e influência nas relações internacionais contemporâneas. 241 f. Tese (Doutorado) - Universidade de São Paulo, São Paulo, 2009.

JUSTIÇA. **Manual de Cooperação Jurídica Internacional e Recuperação de Ativos.** Brasília, 2012

MACHADO, Anderson F.. **Criminalidade Organizada Transnacional e a Globalização.** 2006. 180 f. Tese (Mestrado) - Universidade Católica de Brasília, Brasília, 2006.

MENDRONI, Marcelo B. **Crime organizado:** aspectos gerais e mecanismos legais. São Paulo, 2002.

NAÍM, Moisés. **Ilícito**: O ataque da pirataria, da lavagem de dinheiro e do tráfico à economia global, Rio de Janeiro, 2006.

ONU. **Action Against Transnational Organized Crime And Illicit Trafficking, Including Drug Trafficking (2011 – 2013).** Disponível em: <http://www.unodc. org/documents/commissions/WG-GOVandFiN/Thematic_Programme_on_ Organised_Crime_-_Final.pdf>. Acesso em: 20 maio 2013.

KEOHANE, Robert O.; NYE, Joseph S. **Power and Interdependence.** Nova York, 2001.

PROCÓPIO, Argemiro; VAZ, Alcides C.. O Brasil no Contexto do Narcotráfico Internacional. **Revista Brasileira de Política Internacional**, Brasília, v. 40, n. 1, jan/jun. 1997. Disponível em: <http://www.scielo.br/scielo.php?script=sci_ arttext&pid=S0034732919970001 0004&lng=pt&nrm=iso>. Acesso em: 20 set 2012.

RABELO, Carolina G.. Cooperação Jurídica Internacional e o Crime Organizado Transnacional. **Prisma Jurídico**, São Paulo, v. 6, n. , p.277-291, 01 jan. 2007.

REIS, Linda G.. **Produção de monografia:** da teoria a prática o método de educar pela pesquisa. Brasília: Senac, 2006.

SALDANHA, Katherinne. **Da Prevenção e Repressão à Lavagem de Dinheiro.** Disponível em: <http://www.ebs.edu.br/portal/wp-content/uploads/

Artigo-Katherine-Saldanha.pdf>. Acesso em: 20 set. 2012.

SALVADOR, Sérgio C. S.. **A Nova Ordem Global, O Crime Organizado e a Cooperação Jurídica Internacional em Matéria Penal.** 2009. 156 f. Tese (Mestrado) - Universidade Católica de Santos, Santos, 2009.

SANDRONI, Gabriela A.. **A Convenção de Palermo e o Crime Organizado Transnacional.** Brasília: s/d.

WERNER, Guilherme Cunha. **O crime organizado e as redes criminosas:** presença e influência nas relações internacionais contemporâneas. 241 f. Tese (Doutorado) - Universidade de São Paulo, São Paulo, 2009.

# DOMESTIC AND FOREIGN IMPACTS TO THE INTERNATIONAL MEGA-EVENTS: THE CASE OF BRAZIL AND THE PREPARATIONS FOR WORLD CUP 2014.

Eric Pinheiro
Ironildes Bueno

## INTRODUCTION

Globalization is a remarkable phenomenon and visible nowadays, but intensely dynamic and pluralistic, according to transformationalists. They argue that globalization has new ones changing the world order, but states still have major relevance in the global scenario. Perceived by changes in the international system, operated by the spread of institutions and organizations, is one way that society is positioning itself in relation to this new political space, providing indicators of civil societies in the process of internationalization (HELD, MCGREW, 2000; KECK, SIKKINK, 1998).

In this new globalized world, emerging countries become increasingly important, with their consumer markets mainly. As an emerging country, Brazil has great relevance in the world stage, holding the 7th world economy, according to The Economist (2013 apud JORNAL DO COMÉRCIO). With an estimated population of 190 million, the country has one of the most diverse cultures in the world. Internationally, the country gained a relatively significant image, both in cultural terms, as the political and economic aspects, especially during the 21st century.

Being a country with great tourism potential, its beautiful beaches and scenery, attracting many tourists from countries with cold climates or who do not have an abundant coastal area, such as Argentina, the United States, Uruguay, Germany, Italy and France.

The volume of foreign tourism in Brazil surpassed seven million people in 2012, but a comparison with other locations in the globe is made by making an assessment: Brazil is not using all its touristic capacity. Brazil corresponds to approximately 1.5% of the destinations, and far from the United States' international tours which represents approximately 10.5% of worldwide destinations.

Over the past 10 years, Brazil has stabilized as a regional power with a strong agriculture, which became self-sufficient in oil with the discovery of reserves in the coast, with the payment of debts to the IMF and the development on diplomacy (SALEK, 2010).

The country is exerting an influence on the cooperation area, for developing countries, due to its market, the political and economic field. With this, Brazil is increasingly attracting international looks; the result of this development, the country became the seat of the most important sporting mega-events.

When one thinks of the recognition by tourists and fans of the sport that the host countries have received before, during and after the event, and the media attention given to aspects inherent to countries such as culture, politics and level of development alone, propagates the fact that hosting an event of this magnitude generates a positive impact on the local economy, with potential regional and global implications (PETERSEN-WAGNER, 2013).

There is also the fact that hosting events of this magnitude also generates a euphoric environment, with potential positive socio-cultural impacts, such as creating a sense of community and national identity (PETERSEN-WAGNER, 2013).

With international mega-events, Brazil could expand both the natural tourism, as well as promote the development of economic and business tourism, and may improve the national infrastructure.

Aquarela Plan describes the image of a very attractive Brazil, exploring the natural beauty, the joy of the people and their cultural diversity, and promotes tourism in the country through political speeches and marketing plans (MINISTRY OF TOURISM, Brazil, 2010).

It basically has three parts, an analysis of 2004-2006, when they were preparing to receive the mega-events., 2007 - 2009, the period of the Pan American (Rio de Janeiro, 2007), and the latter part of 2010-2020. In this last period major mega-events will be occurring, World Military Games (Rio de Janeiro, 2011), Rock in Rio (Rio de Janeiro, 2011, 2013 and 2015), Rio +20 (Rio de Janeiro, 2012), World Youth Day (Rio de Janeiro, 2013), Confederations Cup (Brazil, 2013), World Cup (Brazil, 2014) and the Olympic Games (Rio de Janeiro, 2016).

There is a possibility that the country brand is strengthened which is a strategic asset that can be used by all nations seeking economic growth. Several countries, particularly in Latin America and Africa, with few exceptions, have negative images from consumers, leading scholars and international opinion builders due to characteristics such as drug trafficking, pollution, crime, political and economic instability. But these problems were solved by some nations over the years through the construction and strategic brand management of country programs, which are used to improve the perception of the country compared to other states and attract international investment. This management is vital to the growth of a nation and to add value to their products factor, since it increases the strength and credibility in the international arena (HSM MANAGEMENT, 2004).

To highlight this scenario as competitive and innovative, it is suggested that countries should make efforts to strategically manage their image enhancing and strengthening their points of emphasis and aiming to correct its flaws (KOTLER; GERTNER, 2004). In the Brazilian perspective, as there is a massive investment for tourism of natural resources, the authors recommend allocating more investments to develop the economy and tourism to attract foreign investments and industries, according to this theory. For this to occur, it is recommended to obtain complete success. There is a relationship of mutual cooperation between the government, the business sector and the media (MELO; BRENNAND, 2004).

## SPORT AND CULTURE

This part is devoted to analyzing the relationship between sport and the country's culture, its influence on the country and to make an ideological revision.

Instruments employed in cultural intervention, such as language arts, and other myths, let individuals or groups achieve a vision of reality. They are cultural instruments, collective mechanisms used by everyone (SODRÉ, 2001).

The greatness that football currently has, can typically be deployed between both internal and external mediation tools. Internally, football has been trying to remove children and youths from urban violence and places for them to focus on the sport. Externally, it has been covering the global representation of Brazil in the field of sports and enabling the strengthening of the international politics of the country.

The Brazilian reality can be seen in the opposite way. The Institutionalist Perspective, in which to insert the political and economic macro-processes, continuing the logic of political economy, the country analysis is plotted, seeking to overcome problems, since the cultural perspective is emphasizing the customary elements of reality. The author calls this perspective "the tradition of home", familiar, habitual, while the first is the "street" form. In the world of "home" people are worthy and in harmony and there, in the street world, individuals are struggling for life.

Brazilian football can portray this view, since its reality encompasses both perspectives: within the home, there is football in its purest form, compromised only with sport itself, facing the pleasure and worth for its pure and simple representation. Within the street, you will find the art of football, played on the stage of globalized media, serving as a showcase of stylized Brazilian culture.

In Brazil, from north to south, from east to west, "football is an important Brazilian cultural heritage." And we do not see this aspect only by the amount of stadiums and football museum collections around the country. It is proven, especially: searching for the technical mastery of the ball that encourages the daily lives of children early on in the show, developed in the field in 90 minutes of play, the matches held on weekends as a pick-up game, in the football schools today scattered across almost the entire country. These are elements of heritage manifested by the body, which can be associated with rituals before a match, such as singing the national anthem with hand on the heart. All these elements are part of country's identity. (BASTOS, 2013)

Those identities are produced by specific regulatory frameworks, institutional structures and value structures together. These identities determine how people should behave in society. (RAMALHO, 2006)

Bringing this thought to football in Brazil: it is observed that we live in a culture permeated by new identities, and prominently among them, football, especially in recent times. It is an identity element of Brazilian culture to the world, much as the carnival, but with a much more dynamic representatives. It is the scope that reaches all social classes. It is the continuity of the process, uninterrupted.

More than any other sport, Brazil is experiencing this reality, and there is no way they did not disclose the strategies of their foreign policies. You could say that what the footballing activity involves, in its functioning, approaches a subject of domestic interest, since it comes to alleviate social problems, with effects even in the economic stabilization of the country.

The structure of sport to work states that even though similar, they are as different as the "mechanization of human movement." This mechanization refers to aspects such as technological language, income, method, bureaucratization and rationalization processes that limit spontaneity, which are scarcely found in the sport. The ideology would in fact to strengthen the sport aspects such as the yield strength of society, creating a sort of "unity" between ideal body and spirit (VAZ, 2013).

The ideology that permeates the sport is currently no explicit diffusion of political thoughts, as occurred in Mussolini's Italy, but the underlying ideas. For example, Brazil wants to strengthen its capacity to intervene in the world, and seek to occupy a permanent seat in the Security Council. For this the government has been making continuous efforts since their early days in office. In addition, there is the capitalist empire, acting on all behaviors and taking the sport one of their means.

Football has become a hub for which many have interest: the owners of clubs, sports companies with their products, advertising companies, the media and the interest of the players themselves. But regardless, football exerts the same attraction for fans. Its popularity due to the simple way of playing and the possibility of access of people of any age is perhaps its greatest asset.

The global appeal of football is based on national attractive football. This aspect may be related to what Hall and Ramalho da Rocha said about identity: it is involved in the processes of representation and works in conjunction with the institutional structures and values.

Moreover, the interposition between the two attractions can mean that countries like Brazil, where the passion for football is fed, do not respond by further expansion of football, but for its biggest influence and cultural penetration. And that is what instigates the completion of the World Cup, from the point of view of sport. From another point of view, as Hobsbawm:

> The Cup itself probably does not have any political background in particular, but, like the Olympics, is almost certain to be vulnerable to pressures and diplomatic or otherwise of the most powerful countries promises. (HOBSBAWM, 2006)

As a manifestation of capitalism, football is seen as a selling product: the clubs were transformed into joint stock companies, and the sport began to be produced as a commodity. With this, players who were stars before, much admired, but were not rich, became idols, with million dollar contracts, as well as news media.

Thus, it is understood that a World Cup no longer represents a showcase in which specific products are exposed.

In turn, the windows no longer pose to marketing each country, which consists of three aspects: identity, personality and communication. Within the Football World Cup, the author explains:

> Identity can be simplified as the sum of history and the present. It communicates associated information and values that allow to define whether we are talking about a country that was once or a country that has been and is now. Personality is the sum of what it done and how it is done, and that also leads to information on economic, technological, social realities, among others. Above all, the Brazilian way of living life, watching the games and making tourists value the difference that Brazilian people are today, feature foremost in customer satisfaction surveys after the trip to Brazil. Communication is what we will communicate and how these elements will be reported in relation to Brazil, the World Cup and cities. (CHIAS, 2010, p. 2).

From the capitalist perspective, in Brazil, football would not question the true cultural identity of the country, because football is there as one of its elements. Brazil has football as a tradition. It lives as an enthralling sport. But at the same time, Brazil had no way to escape the world's capitalist economy without putting a margin to progress and obviously to keep surviving. The country then also stands as one of the greatest football spectacles.

The memory of football encourages revisiting memorable flights of players, or rather of the stars of the art moving the football and old radio and television narrations are transmitted on Internet sites and blogs, appear on television programs while reaffirming the space that football occupies in the daily life of Brazilians. Rebuilding the moves, the dribbles and ball passes reiterates and reinforces its identity aspect as cultural heritage of the nation, the specificity of being Brazilian. (BASTOS, 2010)

## IMPACTS AND LEGACY OF MEGA-EVENT

This part is dedicated to talking about the types of impacts and consequently bequests that may come to the host country, as well as where these factors begin and end.

The impacts of a Sporting Mega-event may be tangible or intangible. Tangible impacts mention those possible impacts of measurement, for example, the variation in employment rates, Gross Domestic Product ( GDP ) and tourism flow, which may be direct, indirect or both.

The direct impacts are those directly linked to the achievement of the Mega-event, and those indirect are linked to the developments of Mega-events, and its calculation can be done by means of a multiplier.

Intangible impacts otherwise, are those whose individual aspect makes the task of measuring them very complex, for example, increasing the happiness of the population, improving the image of a city or country before the world, regional pride etc. In addition there are some approaches that allow a certain type of review of such impacts (MAENING; ALMERS, 2008).

The ex-ante studies can reach considerable positive effects without needing a shock with reality, since the previous results are availed by the government and other groups interested in making the mega-event.

Since the claim until the period between the acquisition of the right to host the event and its realization, the government and other interest groups, seeking evidence through ex-ante studies, the benefits that may cause Mega-events across the population; such as increasing the number of jobs, growth of business opportunities, increased tourism, GDP growth, among others; test to explain not only the costs but also the enormous changes that occur in the host cities. As Owen (2005) says:

> Mega-events such as the Olympic Games require large sums of public money to be spent on venues and infrastructure improvements. In order to justify the use of public funds, economic impact studies are often commissioned with invariably large inflows of money that will have a long term positive effect by such means as job creations and visitor spending. (OWEN, 2005, p.1).

The projections given by studies commissioned by or with an interest in the event are the best possible. But there are serious grounds for questioning the credibility of these forecasts (TUROLLA, 2009).

Besides the distrust caused by political interests covered in these studies, the experiences of previous events have confirmed that the ex-ante estimates are almost always overestimated. Studies done after the completion of mega-sporting events have found that nothing comes close to the figures disclosed by prior governments or companies directly involved in the implementation of the event. According to a study published by Golden Goal Sports Venture:

> In fact, most studies commissioned by the candidate cities have economic impacts so positive that end up providing the basis to justify public investments.

The problem is that past events analysis does not confirm initial forecasts, and the host cities end up with a legacy of debts, idle infrastructure and expensive maintenance, which end up putting in doubt the feasibility of hosting the games. (GOLDEN GOAL, 2010, p.2).

Any type of ex-ante analysis covers many propositions and makes salvation about the state of the economy and the answer to the headquarters of the mega-event (DWYER ET AL., 2005). Therefore, ex-post studies are now being managed with the objective of determining whether the predictions of the ex-ante studies were right. What proves most of them is the absence of evidence showing the relationship between sporting mega-events and positive economic impacts (OWEN, 2005).

Comparing the results of the economic variables after the completion of the mega-event with the same variables specified in ex-ante studies is theoretically easy. The greatest difficulty in making the calculation of economic impacts after the event is the challenge of distinguishing economic changes related to normal development of the city or region with the event versus the economic changes that would happen if there was no event. Nevertheless, there is an approach that attempts to overcome this difficulty (BAADE; MATHESON 2002).

There are, however, other types of impacts caused by sports mega-events of a more private nature and measurement is even more difficult than the tangible economic impacts. These are intangible impacts.

Those who trust in the ability of a mega sports event to generate positive long-term effects in the host region argue that the intangible effects are much more important than the tangible ones. As they say Pellegrino and Hancock (2010):

> In many cases, a detailed economic impact analysis is just one component of the decision based more on visionary benefits such as improved public image, increased stature in the global marketplace, community pride, and long-term economic development. There is nothing wrong on basing the decision on these kinds of broad and intangible objectives. In fact, while a detailed economic impact analysis is necessary for due diligence, from a host's perspective achieving the long-term objectives and vision for change are ultimately far more important than short term profits and losses. (PELLEGRINO; HANCOCK, 2010, p.3)

Critics of the benefits promised by the realization of sporting mega-events, however, consider the fact that the intangible effects not being measurable is somewhat worrying. According Matheson (2006):

In addition, if the lion's share of the benefits of an event is intangible, this is a significant cause for concern since this type of benefit is most likely to be based upon assumption and guess work. While sports boosters often suggest that the exposure a city receives during a mega-event is invaluable to the area, in the words of University of Chicago economist Allen Sanderson, "Anytime anybody uses the word „invaluable," they are usually too lazy to measure it or they don't want to know the answer.(MATHESON, 2006, p.8)

However, these events cause changes in psychological character to the regions. Studies suggest that the level of happiness of a region should increase when it hosts a sporting mega-event (SZYMANSKI; KUPER, 2009). Other studies indicate that a higher level of happiness in a region translates into higher productivity (COATES, HUMPHREYS, 1999). Events such as the FIFA World Cup is always remembered by the possibilities for own marketing and image building, which produces protracted effects for the nation in relation to its competitive environment (MAENING; ALLMERS, 2008).

One way to get the image effects promoted by holding a mega sports event is the Anholt Nation Brands Index. States are assigned on a quarterly global survey evaluating their cultural, commercial, political and human aspects, investment potential and tourist appeal.

The results are combined to produce a full ranking. The NBI, created in 2005, depicts an improvement in the position of Germany after the completion of the World Cup in 2006. Areas such as the operational part, security, hospitality and domestic marketing, influence the image shown through the event (MAENING; PORSCHE, 2008).

The Montreal Olympics (1976) were the beginning of studies on the economic impacts of mega-events. Sports, since the mega-event, generated debts that were paid decades later, after years of its completion, the Barcelona Olympics (1992) is the beginning of literature on the legacies of sports mega-events.

Barcelona emerged a new city, transformed by games whose legacy continues today. You can set that mega-events are being observed as Sporting chance to change the cities through the design of a positive long-term legacy.

The authors who address the legacies of sports mega-events do not disregard the immediate economic impact, but lessen its importance, due to its short term nature and low modification. Based on this perspective, a sporting mega-event may focus on deficits and not cause the expected economic impacts and, yet, be positive for a country, since it achieves its objectives in the long term (PELLEGRINO; HANCOCK, 2008).

There is an immense variety of sports that can provide legacy, unfortunately, they do not have a satisfactory and comprehensive definition of legacy, and there is no satisfactory definition for what is claimed (VILLANO, TERRA, 2008).

There is some similarity between what is considered legacy and what the intangible impacts of conducting sporting mega-events are, which increasingly contribute to the disorder regarding the terminology.

Inserted in this variety of possible bequests, it is valid to categorize them into tangible and intangible. Therefore the entire infrastructure of the mega-event can be considered as a tangible legacy, because it is likely to take economic cost-benefit. It has the cultural impact of the mega - event, and can be considered intangible heritage, as its effects reflect in various ways, sometimes to validate changes , sometimes, causing  the host city to be seen as a failed project (MAZO et al. 2008).

With these difficulties , it is likely that the best setting for legacy has been provided by Preuss (2006) which defines legacy generically, planned or unplanned, positive or negative, tangible or intangible, such as structures that remain before, during and after sporting events and fully or partially captivate civil society .

Additional to the problem of definition, there is difficulty in measuring. Literature shows that the legacy of mega-events is multidisciplinary, dynamic and defined by local and global factors (MAZO et al. 2008). Nevertheless, bequests vary between host cities, events and historical moments, so it is scarce to analyze the legacy of mega-events from previous experiences (benchmarks). The exclusively economic analysis loses legitimacy in the sense that there is no economic study that has calculated the effects of the legacy of sports mega-events.

## BRAZIL AS HEADQUARTERS OF WORLD CUP 2014

The FIFA World Cup is an event of sporting competition, with awards. The event has been planned in advanced. The organization and coordination involves a large number of people, aiming to convene a large number of people in the same physical space at any given time, facing a common idea (MARTIN, 2003).

As for size, the event of the World Cup is classified as macro-event, which involves the activities around it, since the location is itinerant to be based in various places of the world, and the category is selected and directed to the same public time, respectively. It involves the crowd watching the games in the stadiums and viewers who watch it on television . In summary, it is an open event. (MARTIN, 2003)

In view of this opening and being defined as "the biggest media event of the planet" the 2014 World Cup in Brazil has the following projection: over 40 billion people will watch the broadcasts; every spectator present at a stadium represents more than 10,000 viewers watching for screens and television (BERNASCONI, 2009).

This projection allows us to understand the scope of all the movements that will be made by Brazil during the World Cup, while being able to size the importance of the planning phase. This is one of the most strategic stages of the event, because it is the one that outlines what the country wants to achieve with the event, in addition to programming directly related to football games.

The opportunity to host the Football World Cup in 2014 opened a range of expectations for Brazil, beyond the changes and transformations required by FIFA (some already mentioned).

This range includes areas immediately related to the event and the activities related thereto, which operate as a chain. As an example, there is tourism.

Mota (2006) says that an event like the World Cup moves the entire economy of the host country, especially tourism. For example, she cites the outcome of the 2006 World Cup in Germany, which was attended by over 1 million fans in games.

Among the tourists visiting the country during the games, there are those who are also attracted by the historical and cultural aspects of the place, meaning an offshoot of tourism, for which size cannot be predicted. Thus, the domestic economy will be fueled substantially.

Bernasconi (2009) states that a World Cup "should be understood as an exceptional instrument of international marketing for the host nation" which discloses its attractions and the various elements of their culture, significantly inserting itself on the global tourist map and worldwide economy.

This author points to the Cup as a great opportunity to carry out internal works in several areas, although the best result is going to be the positive legacy to be established in 2005. Among the aspects contributing to this legacy are:

The urban renewal of major metropolitan areas of the country;

Improvement and expansion of local, regional and national infrastructure;

Creating a set of multipurpose stadiums and arenas in major Brazilian cities;

Train inhabitants for incoming tourism and services in general quota, considering that the event has huge visibility and will perhaps represent the "biggest media event of the planet."

Santovito (2010) refers not only to the tourist movement during the World Cup event, but also in its effects upon the return of tourists to their country of origin. This is a "spread a positive image of the place, which can generate the arrival of other tourists" tourism event (the World Cup is a big event) that promotes tourism and leisure.

According to this author, in the economic sense, the capture and promotion of events are held to the activities that give social and economic returns to the cities that host the games and the country. Internally among the benefits brought by tourism events are:

Help the balance between supply and demand, reducing the problems of seasonality around the holiday seasons;

Creates flows of people, adding value to offer;

Serves as a tool for communication and marketing;

Stimulates tourist events to stay longer in the city , spending more than the leisure tourist;

It gives visibility and value the culture as well as its economic and social assets, inserted into programming as a backdrop destinations;

Promotes the role of tourism which consists of receiving and issuing locations;

Generates business and motivates public policies;

Creates opportunities for jobs and investment , improving income distribution and uptake of currency;

Provides international prestige of the host country and the cities in which the games are played through a spontaneous generated media event.

As stated, the countries, when applying to host an event such as the FIFA World Cup, FIFA do not judge just by sporting spirit, as it was then. Today it is a football spectacle, which is globalized and mainly reckoned with capitalist criteria, as a business, goals are drawn in advance, so that their results serve as reinforcement to their ideology.

From the political point of view there are also set goals and developed plans that interact subliminally in the strategic planning of the event. In other words, there are several fronts that incorporate an event of this magnitude, all seeking to reach their targets.

Focusing on the political aspect, the prestige that Brazil can get hosting the World Cup 2014, it is first important to remember the almost unique social representations of the country abroad, until quite a few years ago.

> Social representations are ways to interpret, understand, categorize, feel and read the world. They are produced in social interaction processes of communication, work, culture, finally in everyday life, making them expressions of a given society, of a particular social group, in a specific historical moment, as well as forms of social mediation since, through them that subjects will relate and act. (MOSCOVICI, 1978, p. 66).

Pictures of sun, beach, carnival, the beautiful women and football, denoting pleasure, beyond the images of slums and hunger indexes, records of great poverty, associated with very negative images of violence and child prostitution for example, long served as a statement of what Brazil had to offer the world.

Meeting these images, broadcast in various media, primarily in direct contacts between tourists and visitors coming unproductive foreign policies, such as the adopted during the military dictatorship authoritarian and exclusionary.

After that period, the Sarney Government's, protectionist policies that influenced the whole foreign policy were being replaced, observing a trend introduced by globalization. Governments of Fernando Collor / Itamar Franco started an adaptation of the country to the international system. In terms of Fernando Henrique Cardoso, the focus was to replace the reactive schedule dominated by the logic of autonomy through distance for a proactive international agenda, determined by the logic of autonomy through integration (VIGEVANI et al, 2003)

The Lula government's foreign policy, among others, has developed an essentially critical stance in relation to globalization and trade liberalization, reaffirming the search market access to developed countries.

More than that, the Brazilian government, through its realistic, and pragmatic, universalist foreign policy comes to correct the course of the previous policies based on the principles of autonomy and development insertion of the country in the international system in a less vulnerable way to Brazil, as stated previously. (SARAIVA, 2005)

As part of its foreign policy, Brazil has intervened more effectively in peacekeeping missions of the United Nations in bilateral operations (Haiti , Timor-Leste , among others) and in missions resulting from cooperation with Portuguese-speaking Countries (CPLP) in operations multilateral.

The Brazilian government has been investing heavily in Brazil's image in the international ground, including already being considered a prominent member of the World Forum in Davos and participating of the meetings of the G20, with India in the struggle for liberalization of the World Trade Organization (WTO).

With these areas of action in the course of its activist foreign policy, Football World Cup 2014 meets the interests of the government as to whether to enter with autonomy among developed countries.

> For Brazil, the 2014 World Cup is the opportunity to take a leap to modernization and display not only its organizational capabilities, as well as its economic strength to attract investment and the many attractions that can transform the country into one of the most important tourist destinations the world from the near future (SOUZA, 2009, p. 2).

The internal pressure from big business is big, after all, the worldwide exposure for the 2014 World Cup is a possibility of consolidation of many domestic products, brands, and this is a worldwide presence, since the event brings together representatives from across the globe.

The event of the 2014 World Cup will be a point of concentration of various interests of Brazil in relation to foreign investment in the country and vice versa , the formalization of agreements and routing troubleshooting, among others . In this "gap", a multitude of products will be exposed, articulated, but the great weight to Brazil's foreign policy is what Brazil wins in the international political scene from there.

In the Brazilian diplomatic agenda itself, there is shared access to the markets of developed countries; maintenance mechanisms that favor developing countries to implement policies that permit the production of commercial balances and not deepen the dependence on foreign capital. (ALMEIDA, 2010)

## CONCLUSION

This last part is devoted to final conclusions of this work. Additionally an analysis of the challenges and opportunities that Brazil may have to face and even a precise set of policy recommendations and good practices will be suggested.

## *OPPORTUNITIES*

Even before the World Cup begun, it was already generating businesses and jobs, as many companies will be hired to organize and prepare the infrastructure for the event. During the competition, the tourist flow is unparalleled according to some consultants. The increase would be equivalent to 14% of movement throughout the country. An increase of 600,000 tourists in the months of June and July 2014 is estimated

This huge potential revenue generator needs to be harnessed, not only before and during the competition, but after its completion as well, in order to leverage future business. Brazil will now have better tourist infrastructure with new businesses and jobs created due to this event.

During the World Cup it is expected that the segments of website development and support for software implementation, consulting, training companies and providers of small business services, serving major companies in the infrastructure sector, will have reduced demand for their services during the event, since whatever they produce will have to be ready by the beginning. Therefore, for these segments, the business prospect should begin as soon as possible and concentrate all their efforts in this period.

The remaining segments listed above intensify their services instead, due to the increase of tourist flow. The strategies planned before the event should become actions. Tourism companies should seek a joint performance with mutual indications of their services. In particular, they reinforce strategies to increase the average length of stay of tourists, tour packages and trips to other local or regional attractions.

After the World Cup, the greatest legacy the event will leave the resulting effort that companies will own, which is aiming to reach a level of excellence expected by the public. As a result, those who invest in improving the quality of their services will have achieved a new level of competitiveness to work permanently in the market after the end of the event. This means that the 2014 World Cup will be an incentive and a means to invest in improving the management of companies, due to the significant increase in sales during the event. Therefore, the Cup should be seen not as a tight time but as an opportunity to promote the company's development in the long term. Another legacy that the competition will leave will depend heavily on tourist perception of some factors:

Public and private services (transport, telecommunications, internet, etc.) Infrastructure;

Quality of service;

Degree of enchantment with the attractions of nature and local culture;

Effectiveness of promotional and communication for the future tourist return strategies.

In particular, companies should develop promotional offers to encourage tourists to return, thinking about special discounts for returning, followed by third party offer attractions that are not done for all groups, among others. In other words, it's time to enjoy the personal contact to make future sales. If the perception of value is positive, there will be a sustainable growth of tourism in the country, because the tourists will recommend visiting Brazil to others depending on their satisfaction. Moreover, in 2016 the Olympics are marked and that, despite being held in Rio de Janeiro, they can attract business opportunities to other regions.

## CHALLENGES

Contrary to the opportunities there are some challenges to overcome. The Government and private sector should work together to overcome major obstacles that present themselves. Below is the analysis of the main challenges and difficulties on the table 1:

Table 1: Challenges and Difficulties.

| Challenges | Difficulties |
|---|---|
| Timely Completion of the stadiums | Lack of manpower in construction. |
| Preventing the collapse of airports | Poor infrastructure and few alternatives and low capacity to serve passengers. |
| Attendance of foreign visitors in the host cities | Difficulty of service in a foreign language, poor quality services and service. |
| Urban transportation | Poor public transport, no good alternatives to displacement of large audiences, difficulty access to stadiums. |
| Provide efficient communication services | Bad Infrastructure and communication services. |
| Provide skilled labor | Low investment in staff training. |
| Public and private security | Any public safety, as private, are of low quality. The risks are huge for tourists. |

**Source:** Authors own elaboration.

## RECOMMENDATIONS OF PUBLIC POLICIES AND GOOD PRACTICES

First of all, it is important to highlight that the practice of having a section on academic work devoted to recommendations for public policy and good practices refers to the tradition of some American research centers and institutions, such as the Peterson Institute for International Economics and particular, the School of Foreign Service (SFS) at Georgetown University. This tradition recognizes that such policy prescriptions have their natural limitations. Initially, they are not absolute and admittedly do not constitute doctrines of any kind. Rather, only normative prescriptions, with the sole intention of being based on conclusions, inferences and evidence of scholarly work on the methodological rigor. More than guide the formulation and implementation of public policies, they suggest providing new inputs for critical debate about them (BUENO, 2012).

The following recommendations for public policies were grouped into three different subsections. The first contains recommendations for the municipal and state levels; the second is directed to the Federal Government; and the third special interest groups (civil society and private sector).

## CITIES AND STATES

In addition to the 12 host cities, 184 were defined as other tourist destinations during the event and realized a significant increase in visitors.

This guide recommends three essential elements:

Integration between municipalities and states;

Use of public space for the development of a culture of peace;

Preventing crime and policing.

Partnering with States not only allows obtaining financial resources, but also that the security actions of municipalities are integrated with the strategies that will be developed by the police and the federal government.

The aim is to enable positive experiences in organizing major events such as the Carnival and Parintins Party, and projects that prioritize safety, to be replicated in other municipalities. Actions that increase safety and improve the living conditions of the population in these cities, connecting public safety in the development and social integration.

Sports activity is still recommended as a strategy to engage the youth, seizing the moment to put public policies on sport in place as a way not only to broaden public participation in the event, but also promote better health, well-being, quality of life and mainly the prevention of violence through peaceful occupation of public spaces in the city.

## FEDERAL GOVERNMENT

We need the federal government to invest primarily in five key areas: airports, security, access roads, transport in cities and hotel chains.

Today, a major problem in Brazil is in the structure of its airports. Few of those are prepared to receive large volumes of passengers as it is expected for the period of the World Cup. It can be said that only the Galeão Airport in Rio de Janeiro and Guarulhos Airport in Sao Paulo have this condition.

Insecurity takes over our country. But it is clear that it is not only Brazil who suffers from it; there is insecurity everywhere in the world. The difference is how the authorities deal with this problem.

Brazil needs to revise most of their public safety planning. Some actions, such as the eviction of Rio hills by local police help improve the country's image before the tourists arrive. However, it is likely that most such attitudes should be taken and in all the cities that will be World Cup hosts.

Preparing security for the period of the World Cup, and taking that experience to apply it day-to-day after the event, will earn Brazil many points with the international public opinion, and thus expect a significant increase in tourism due to natural beauty and entertainment options we already have. We just need to provide the necessary security for our visitors.

Ground transportation is very common during the World Cup, and is also widely used by tourists visiting the country. There is a necessity to invest more on the road conditions and to provide security for those who choose the roads to attend World Cup matches. After this great change, all tourists who enjoy our roads will enjoy the ride in a safer more practical way.

Cities should invest in alternatives that make public transportation efficient and more objective, avoiding trouble and making it easier for tourists. It is crucial that we have buses circulating on a larger scale, to join all points of the city and also have fair prices on airfares.

But the most important thing about this is that cities have become aware that the investment should not be restricted only to the period of the World Cup. We need to show tourists that this level of organization will be kept after the event, because when that same tourist who comes to cheer for his country in the World Cup, opts for Brazil for vacation, they will be looking for all the infrastructure they found here before.

Incentives for hotels to offer differentiated services and superior quality than the one served today should come from the government. Brazil has many good hotels and is ready to receive tourists, but not all tourists have the same conditions for staying in a big hotel. Several tourists keep their savings to make a special trip in their lives, and possibly the accommodations are not among the biggest investments they are willing to make.

Good and cheap hotels may be critical to attract more tourists to Brazil, and also stimulate local tourism. Therefore, investment in this area, and then its maintenance, will bring many positive results for tourism in Brazil.

## PRIVATE AND CIVIL SOCIETY INITIATIVE

We all should have greater involvement in state politics. The initiative seeks to ensure greater private participation in infrastructure investments, thereby using the instrument through the Public-Private Partnerships (PPPs) in the viability of investments.

We try to seek greater efficiency in the implementation of the Union budget, ensuring the achievement of planned investments, so we propose a technical and economic priority in the selection process works, so as to try to reduce bureaucracy in procurement processes.

Together we provide courses with environmental licenses to entrepreneurs whose projects were approved uninitiated, analyzing legislation to ensure the principle of legal defense in administrative procedures in order to reduce excess stoppages of works; finally, balancing the action of the control organs with the need to hold the areas of Executive purposes.

# REFERENCES

ALMEIDA, Paulo de. **A política externa do novo governo do presidente Luís Inácio Lula da Silva: retrospecto histórico e avaliação programática.** Revista Espaço Acadêmico, ano 2, n° 19, 2002.

ANHOLT, Simon. **The Importance of National Reputation.** Foreign and Commonwealth Office, King Charles St, London, 2008. <http://www.simonanholt.com/Publications/publications-other-articles.aspx>.

BAADE; MATHESON. **Bidding for the Olympics: Fool's Gold?.** 2002 <http://citeseerx.ist.psu.edu/viewdoc/download?doi=10.1.1.399.2989&rep=rep1&type=pdf>

BASTOS, Sênia. **O futebol como patrimônio cultural do Brasil.**

< www copa2014turismo.gov.br >.

BERNASCONI, José Roberto. **Copa do Brasil 2014.** 2009.

<www www.sinaenco.com.br/noticias_detalhe.asp?id=49>

BUENO, Ironildes. **Paradiplomacia Econômica:** Trajetórias e Tendências da Atuação Internacional dos Governos Estaduais do Brasil e dos Estados Unidos. 1ª Edição. Brasília: Verdana, 2012

CHIAS, Josep. **Brasil 2014: uma visão a partir do marketing e do turismo** <www.copa2014turismo.gov.br2010>.

COATES, D.; HUMPHREYS, B. **The growth effects of sport franchises, stadia and arenas.** Journal of Policy Analysis and Management, v. 18, n. 4, USA, 1999.

DWYER, L.; FORSYTH, P; SPURR, R.. **Estimating the impacts of special events on an economy.** Journal of Travel Research. 2005. 43: 351-359.

GOLDEN GOAL. **Calculando o impacto econômico de mega-eventos esportivos.** Golden Goal, Rio de Janeiro, 2010. <http://www.goldengoal.com.br/br/downloads/retorno_jogos_olimpicos.pdf >.

HELD, David; MCGREW, Anthony, **The Global Transformation Reader,** Cambridge, Polity Press, 2000.

HOBSBAWN, Eric. **Interview. Agência Carta Maior**, 2006. <www.recid.org.br>

KECK, M., SIKKINK K.. 1998. **Activists Beyond Borders: Advocacy Networks in International Politics**. Ithaca: Cornell University Press

KELLER, K. **"Building customer-based brand equity"** *Journal of Marketing Management*, July/August, 2001.

KOTLER, P.; GERTNER, D. **O marketing estratégico de lugares**. HSM Management. São Paulo, 44th edition. may/june 2004. p. 62

MAENING, W; ALMERS. **South Africa 2010: Economic scope and limits**. Hamburg Contemporary Economic Discussions, n. 21, Hamburg, 2008.

MAENNIG, W. PORSCHE, M. **The Feel-Good Effect at Mega Sport Events: Recommendations for Public and Private Administration Informed by the Experience of the Fifa World Cup 2006**. Hamburg Contemporary Economic Discussions, n. 18,

Hamburg, 2008.

MARTIN, Vanessa. **Manual prático de eventos**. São Paulo: Atlas, volume 1, 2003.

MATHESON, V. **Mega-Events: The effect of the world's biggest sporting events on local, regional, and national economies**. College of the Holy Cross, Department of Economics, Faculty Research Series, Paper n. 06-10, 2006

MAZO et al. **Em Busca de uma Definição de Legado na Perspectiva de Mega-eventos Olímpicos**. In: Legados de mega-eventos esportivos. Brasília: Ministério do Esporte, 2008.

MELO, F., BRENNAND, J. **Empresas socialmente sustentáveis**. Rio de Janeiro: Qualtimark, 2004.

MINISTRY OF TOURISM, Brasil. Brasília, 2012. <http://www.dadosefatos.turismo. gov.br/dadosefatos/estatisticas_indicadores/principais_emissores_turistas/>.

MOSCOVICI, Serge. **A representação social da psicanálise**. Rio de Janeiro: Zahar, 2° edição, 1978.

OWEN, J. **Estimating the cost and benefit of hosting olympic games: what** can beijing expect from its 2008 games? Department of economics. Indiana State University, 2005.

PELLEGRINO, G; HANCOCK, H. **A lasting legacy: How major sporting events can**

**drive positive for host communities and economies**. <http://www.deloitte.com/ assets/DcomGlobal/Local%20Assets/Documents/Public%20Se

ctor/dtt_ps_lastinglegacy_160209.pdf>

PETERSEN-WAGNER, Renan. **Por que sediar um megaevento esportivo?**. <http://www.copa2014.turismo.gov.br/copa/copa_cabeca/detalhe/artigo_renan_ petersen.html>.

RAMALHO, Antônio. **O Brasil e os regimes internacionais**. In: ALTEMANI, Henrique; LESSA, Antonio C. (Org.) Relações internacionais do Brasil. Temas e agendas. 2$^{nd}$ vol. São Paulo: Saraiva, 2006, p. 75.

SALEK, Silvia. **Brazil: No longer 'country of the future'**. BBC News, march 6$^{th}$, 2012. <http://www.bbc.co.uk/news/business-17270649>.

SARAIVA, José Flávio Sombra. **Dois anos da política externa de Lula.** 2005.

SODRÉ, Muniz. **Reinventando a cultura: a comunicação e seus produtos**. 4$^{th}$ edition. Petrópolis: Vozes, 2001.

SOUZA, Marcelo de. **Vitrine ou vidraça? O que o Brasil espera da Copa?** 2009. <www.copa2014.org.br/noticias/Noticia.aspx?>

SZYMANSKI, S.; KUPER, S. **Soccernomics: why England loses, why Germany and**

**Brazil win, and why the U.S., Japan, Turkey and even Iraq are destined to become the**

**kings of the world's most popular sport**. New York: Nation Books, 2009.

TUROLLA, F. **A economia da Copa. Conjuntura da Infraestrutura**. Associação brasileira da infraestrutura e indústrias de base, São Paulo, 2009.

VAZ, Alexandre Fernandez. **Teoria crítica do esporte: origens, polêmicas, atualidade. Esporte e Sociedade** Revista Digital. ano 3, n.7, nov. 2007/fev. 2008 < http://www.lazer. eefd.ufrj.br/espsoc/html/es102.h>

VIGEVANI, Tullo; OLIVEIRA, Marcelo F. de; CINTRA, Rodrigo. **Política externa no período FHC: a busca de autonomia pela integração.** Tempo Soc. v.15, n.2, São Paulo Nov. 2003

VILLANO, TERRA. **Definindo a Temática de Legados de Megaevento Esportivos.** 2008. http://www.listasconfef.org.br/arquivos/legados/Livro.Legados. de.Megaeventos.pdf

# FOREIGN POLICY AND SECURITY: DEVELOPMENT AND IMPACTS OF THE "BRAZILIAN DEFENSE POLICY" DURING LULA DA SILVA'S ADMINISTRATION (2003-2010)

Lorena Bitencourt Madureira[6]
Fábio Albergaria de Queiroz[7]

## INTRODUCTION

The foreign policy of a country is, in general, influenced by domestic and international variables, as pointed out by Robert Putnam (1988). Moreover, it is worth noting that foreign policy-makers are often guided by their own perceptions and values about the world and the role of their country in this anarchical complex system. Consequently, when some of these actors are replaced, more specifically the chief of the executive branch, insofar as the context of national or international scenario changes, it allows the identification of some underlying vicissitudes in foreign policy orientation.

In this context, the defense and security agenda of any country, by its nature, stands as an important vector of foreign policy. In sum, and obviously taking into consideration that the following premise is a simplification that does not depict all the features of such a complex field, what we commonly see in such area is how a determined country acts to protect itself from perceived threats. Concomitantly, these perceptions contribute to shape the related defense policy orientation. But, what happens after a Head of State's replacement? A rupture or the continuity of the agenda initiated by its predecessor?

In this regard, this chapter aims to analyze Luiz Inácio Lula da Silva (2003-2010) administration's proposal for the national defense area, how it was implemented and its implications for Brazil's foreign policy. Thus, to accomplish the proposed tasks, firstly, it is necessary to understand the foremost features of Lula's predecessor, Fernando Henrique Cardoso (FHC).

---

6 Graduate student in Law and Intelligence at Catholic University of Brasília; Re searcher at NESEDI/UCB (Center of Studies in Security, Strategy, Defense and Intelligence from the Catholic University of Brasília)".
7 The aforementioned author conducted this work during a Postdoctoral Fellow at the Institute of International Relations of the University of Brasília (IREL/UnB) with financial support from CAPES (Brazilian Coordination for the Improvement of Higher Level Personnel).

In his administration, Fernando Henrique Cardoso (1995-2002) fostered important advances on Brazil's national defense policy. In 1996, the National Defense Policy (PDN) was created: an initiative that sought to define the country's strategic priorities on defense and security. One of the most outstanding legacies of Cardoso's administration in the area of defense is the current structure that settled civil control over the armed forces with the creation of the Ministry of Defense in 1999.

In turn, Lula, yet a presidential candidate, demonstrated concerns about the national defense subject. According to Oliveira (2005), along the presidential race, Lula shaped his speech to be accepted by the military audience. As president, Lula promoted substantial advances on that field. The second National Defense Policy was formulated in 2005 as an effort to upgrade the conceptual framework presented in its previous version. He also established the so-called National Defense Strategy (END) in 2008, a more emphatic and affirmative normative tool.

In short, Lula's administration changed the emphasis given to some points in Brazilian foreign policy and the treatment given to the national defense area, which gained greater prominence in the previous administration. Although military expenditure had increased gradually since Cardoso's administration, in Lula's term, negotiations and initiatives to strengthen the Brazilian military sector broadened discussions on national defense.

## FOREIGN POLICY, DEFENSE AND SECURITY IN FHC'S ADMINISTRATION (19952002)

As pointed out by Vizentini (2005), one of the priority lines of FHC's foreign policy was the concentration of efforts to raise Brazil's international influence and position by highlighting, for instance, its aspiration for a permanent seat in the United Nation's Security Council (UNSC).

By analyzing the issue, Cervo and Bueno (2011) argue that this desire was launched in 1994, but was put aside in the first year of Cardoso's administration, although in his discourses FHC had frequently defended the Security Council's reformulation in order to make it more legitimate, inclusive and representative as a mechanism of global governance.

In general, the Brazilian foreign policy during Cardoso's administration was characterized by the so-called pursuit of autonomy through participation, a conceptual description that, in accordance to Vigevani and Cepaluni (2007), may be defined as the emphasis given on adhering to international regimes without losing its management capacity on foreign policy. According to the authors, FHC sought to internalize many changes based on "liberal premises", an always remembered feature of his administration, materialized in actions like the deepening of a privatization program in areas such as steel milling, telecommunications and mining resulting in the sale to the private sector of government-owned enterprises such as *Telebras* and *Companhia Vale do Rio Doce*.

## The Defense Policy on FHC's administration

On Cardoso's administration the debate about its defense policy was increased. Alsina Jr. (2003) defined the line adopted by FHC in the defense sector as a low profile one. At the domestic level, the absence of classical perceptions of external threats, the general lack of knowledge about the instrumentality of military power and the disinterest of some important political actors on military issues are elements that contributed to such scenario.

In spite of the aforementioned low appreciation, according to Oliveira (2002) before Cardoso's administration, only Geisel (1974-1979) effectively took care of the military apparatus. In an analysis of the civil-military relations, Martins Filho (2000) highlights that FHC's administration sought not to displease the military even in a context of economic crisis. In fact, during this period military budget boosted, as shown in the following table elaborated with data provided by the Stockholm International Peace Research Institute (SIPRI).

### Table 1: Fernando Henrique Cardoso's military expenditures (1994-2002)

| Variable | Fiscal Year | 1994[1] | 1995 | 1996 | 1997 | 1998 | 1999 | 2000 | 2001 | 2002 |
|---|---|---|---|---|---|---|---|---|---|---|
| Balance in millions of Brazilian Reals | Jan-Dec | [7,040] | 13,140 | 14,145 | 15,021 | 16,662 | 17,898 | 20,753 | 25,682 | 28,224 |
| Percentage of GDP | Jan-Dec | [2] | 1.9 | 1.7 | 1.6 | 1.7 | 1.7 | 1.8 | 2 | 1.9 |

Source: SIPRI (2013). Available on: http://milexdata.sipri.org/result.php4

Also according to Martins Filho (2000), Cardoso's administration was characterized by institutional innovations. In this regard, the establishment of the National Defense Policy (PDN) in 1996 and the creation of the Ministry of Defense (MD), in 1999, were initiatives intended to create mechanisms for coordinating efforts between diplomats and military externally. The creation of the Government Council's Chamber of Foreign Affairs and National Defense (Creden), through Decree No. 1,895 of May 6th, 1996, was an important institutional advancement in this regard.

It was intended to formulate policies, establish guidelines and approve and monitor programs and actions to be implemented in matters relating to: international cooperation in security and defense issues; border integration; indigenous people; human rights; peacekeeping operations; drug trafficking; immigration; intelligence activity; security for critical infrastructure; information security; and cyber security.

President Cardoso was also concerned with the lack of coordination between the three branches of the armed forces - the Army, the Navy and the Air Force - notably in the early days of his administration, and it was clearly noticed in the creation of the MD, as highlighted by Alsina Jr. (2003).

## National Defense Policy (PDN/1996)

The first National Defense Policy, formulated in 1996, is a key instrument to understand the relationship between Cardoso's administration's foreign and defense policies. The document expresses the national defense strategy based on the international integration model desired by the country at the time. According to Soares and Silva (2012), the 1996 PDN was the first document of its kind in the country's history and it innovated by establishing guidelines to joint external actions among military and diplomats in the context of security issues. Oliveira and Soares (2000) argue that despite of being received with little credibility in Brazil, it was well received abroad. According to Oliveira (2013), the PDN indeed set a first definition of what the national objectives in the area of defense would be, although vague and imprecise in some aspects.

More critically, Miyamoto (2004) asserts, for instance, that the PDN was far from actually being called a guide for the Brazilian defense policy. According to the author, the goals expressed in the PDN did not define what the country's perception on defense and security was, to the point of clarifying and justifying the intended actions behind the document´s planning. So, it was nothing more than a confused and imprecise letter of intent.

Regarding the international scenario, the PDN mentions some of the so-called "post-cold war threats", and also highlights the core features of the regional context. In general, South America was presented as a peaceful area despite the presence of some sources of instability. It is worth saying that the South Atlantic was included as one of the priority environments for the Brazilian interests. The perception of the aforementioned potential threats is what makes room for the inclusion of subjects such as drug trafficking and the action of the organized crime on the defense agenda. The PDN section devoted to the analysis of such aspects (Item 2.1) declares that:

> At the regional level, there are remaining areas of instability that can frustrate Brazilian interests. The action of armed groups that operate in neighboring countries, the limits of the Brazilian Amazon, and international organized crime are some of the points capable of generating apprehension.

In spite of revealing, so far, the concern about the Amazonian region, it does not appear prominently in the document. The region is explicitly mentioned in only two instances of the PDN according to Teixeira Júnior and Nobre (2012). The document also highlights the following statement: "politics are centered in an active diplomacy in the direction of peace and a deterrent strategy of defensive character" (BRASIL, 1996). From this assertion, it can be inferred that diplomacy was seen as the country's main resource of defense and any action should only be carried out in front of a real situation of menace (Oliveira, 2013).

More specifically, the PDN establishes twenty different guidelines. South America is the subject presented in the first guideline, which also determines that Brazil should actively contribute to world and regional peace. Although the Amazon explicitly appears only twice, at least three other guidelines in the document indirectly indicate how to deal with such issue, in guidelines about the system monitoring, control or management of border areas the enhancement of the military presence in it is one of these guidelines.

Considering what was said, Alsina Jr. (2003) develops the central claim that the PDN was confusing and difficult to understand if presumed as a security or defense policy. Moreover, the author argues that the creation of the MD and the formulation of the PDN were not able to enhance a closer and deeper relationship between foreign and defense policies. However, during Cardoso's administration, efforts were undertaken to renew the PDN under the responsibility of Geraldo Quintão, his Minister of Defense (2000-2002), but the project was only completed at the end of President Lula's first term.

## FOREIGN POLICY, DEFENSE AND SECURITY IN LULA DA SILVA'S ADMINISTRATION (2003-2010)

Despite its efforts to modify the emphasis formerly given to some points of the Brazilian foreign policy, Lula's administration, in many aspects, could be seen as a continuity of FHC's. According to Vigevani and Cepaluni (2007) the strategy brought about by Lula could be properly defined as the search for "autonomy through diversification", an empirical construction based on the following assumptions: (1) search for a greater international equilibrium by mitigating all kinds of unilateral practices; (2) strengthening of bilateral and multilateral relations in order to increase the country' influence on international political and economic negotiations; (3) thickening of diplomatic relations in order to take advantage of a greater economic, financial, technological and cultural exchange; and (4) avoidance of agreements that may compromise the country's long-term development.

In other words, Almeida (2004) points out that these basic premises of Lula's administration gave strength to the popular idea of "changing the world" through the inclusion of social issues in international debates and forums, whenever possible. And regardless some of his emphatic assertiveness about the failures of the existing normative tools in providing the ascension of developing countries into a more inclusive world, Lula frequently seemed to have no objection concerning the Brazilian integration into the globalized world, since Brazil's sovereignty and interests were kept and respected. By acting this way, Soares and Silva (2012) asserted that Lula increased the degree of Brazilian foreign policy autonomy and understood that security and defense are important variables in this search for a more participative international insertion. As told by Soares (2011), the goals of the Lula administration's foreign policy, some in continuity with the previous administration, strengthened the area of defense. So, considering this assumption, let's see how these improvements came to be.

### The National Defense Policy (PDN/2005)

The new 2005's PDN version, according to Almeida (2010b), retained the essence of the previous one but with slight structural changes. In short, it tried to adapt the content of the first document to a changing and challenging national and international realities besides of being notably more precise on the outlined objectives. As emphasized in the original text, the 2005 PDN:

> It is the document of highest level of defense planning and aims to establish

objectives and guidelines for the preparation and application of national capacity-building, with the involvement of the military and civilian sectors, in every sphere of national power (BRASIL, 2005).

By considering both domestic and international environments of analysis, this new normative structure brought some reflections about Brazil's role in terms of the international security agenda setting, and also demonstrated concerns about the establishment of the concepts of State Security and Defense in order to avoid the risk of conceptual stretching[8].

In spite of the increasing debate about national defense in Brazil, according to Oliveira (2005) the country was still in the opposite direction in relation to the regional trend of adopting a version of the White Book of Defense. Notwithstanding all the different perceptions of its real meaning and importance, the PDN was clearly helpful in establishing some core concepts under the Brazilian point of view. Thus, according to the National Defense Policy:

> I-Security is the condition that allows the country to preserve the sovereignty and territorial integrity, the attainment of its national interests, free of pressures and threats of any kind, and to guarantee citizens the exercise of constitutional rights and duties;

> II- National Defense is the set of measures and actions of the State, with an emphasis on military expression, for the defense of territory, sovereignty and national interests against threats mainly external, potential or manifest (BRASIL, 2005. Item 1.4).

It was also noted that the document adopted an extended concept of security, which indicated that international security should not be understood merely on the perspective of the traditional political and military threats. More than that, the security concept should be broader in order to allow the inclusion of threats stemming from other sectors such as the environmental, societal and economic ones (Oliveira, Viana e Silva, 2011).

In general, the 2005 PDN, according to Okado (2012), was important because it allowed breaking the apathy related to the lack of thinking regarding Brazil's national

---

8 Conceptual stretching means the uncritical application of concepts to new issues and problems which may have inadvertently led to the expansion of these concepts to include new cases, rather than to rethinking if these cases really fit in the given definition.

defense and conditions created for the formulation of a new strategic plan that took place in 2008.

Therefore, the efforts in order to restructure the strategic field in the country did not end with the PDN renovation. Lula has committed to the development of the White Book of Defense, but failed to comply during his eight-year term. The innovation brought by his administration regarding the structuring of the Brazilian strategy, both the form and the arrangements, was the National Defense Strategy in 2008 (ALMEIDA, 2010b).

a) The international scenario and its reflections on PDN

Regarding the international environment, the 2005 PDN emphasizes the asymmetry of power among its actors and, as said, the danger posed by the so-called new threats to the security of states. Furthermore, the section highlights some foreign policy priorities such as the improvement of multilateralism and the securitization[9] of environmental issues and transnational threats. Thus, the document asserts that:

> The prevalence of multilateralism and the strengthening of the principles established by international law and sovereignty, non-intervention and equality between States, are promoters of a more stable world, aimed at the development and welfare of mankind.

> The environmental issue stands as one of the concerns of humanity. Countries in possession of great biodiversity, huge reserves of natural resources and huge areas to be incorporated into the productive system can become object of international interest.

> (...) Currently, non-State actors, new threats and the contrast between nationalism and transnationalism pervade the international relations and security arrangements of States. The transnational offences varied in nature and international terrorism are threats to peace, security and democratic order (BRASIL, 2005. Items 2.3, 2.4 e 2.6).

---

9 Securitization is the process in which an actor facing a threatening situation tries to put the object to be protected (referent object) in a locus of decision immune to the ordinary rules of the political scenario. As a result, they may use all the necessary means to solve the problem, including force.

b) The regional scenario

The 2005 PDN makes it clear that Brazil belongs to South America and, thus, the South Atlantic is strategically important for its security, but not equal to or greater than the subcontinent. This point represents a difference in relation to the previous document that dispenses similar treatment to both South America and the

South Atlantic. Another point worth noting in the document is the way the peaceful condition of South America is described by affirming that:

South America, far from the world's main focuses of tension and free of nuclear weapons, is considered a relatively peaceful region. Additionally, processes of democratic consolidation and regional integration tend to increase regional reliability and the negotiated solution of conflicts (BRASIL, 2005. Item 3.4).

Another issue that we point out about the regional scenario is an indication of the importance of strengthening a closer relationship and cooperation among the Amazonian countries. In this regard, it is more emphatic than the previous version, as follows.

c) The Amazon

The Amazon appears as a paramount issue in which the main threat is the action of non-state actors as well as pointed out in the 1996 PDN version. Furthermore, the 2005 PDN introduces a more expansive view on the Atlantic slope of the Amazon (Blue Amazon), that figures, along with the "Green Amazon" as a "priority area for national defense" (BRASIL, 2005. Item 6.12).

According the PDN, in order to counter the threats to the Amazon, actions focused on strengthening the military presence, effective state action and expansion of cooperation with neighboring countries, aiming at the defense of natural resources and environment must be performed.

Thus, the guidelines regarding the Amazon establish:

Increase military presence in the strategic areas of the South Atlantic and the Brazilian Amazon;

Implement actions to develop and integrate the Amazon region, with the support of society, aiming, in particular, the development and vivification of the border region; (BRASIL, 2005. Item 7)

Teixeira and Nobre (2012) analyze that the 2005 PDN is in accordance to the Brazilian geopolitical tradition by arguing that the presence of armed forces in the region is essential to both national defense and security. They also argue that the Amazon's integration from Brazil's defense perspective begins to gain more prominence.

So, the proposition of concrete actions gains more space. Despite its advances, the authors say that the relation to the guidelines the PDN is generic. That's because, sometimes, it confuses the attributions and responsibilities of the Ministry of Defense and the Ministry of Foreign Affairs.

## The National Defense Strategy (END/2008)

The National Defense Strategy was launched on December 18, 2008 through Decree No. 6,703 and presented a unique format listing the proposals for the area of national defense, in matters of shape, size and content. By proposing a brief comparison between the last PDN and the END, Oliveira (2009) indicates that the former should be a reference to the last one, but rather than recognize its roots the END does not even mention the National Defense Policy, as if it had been formulated as an unprecedented document in the field. Indeed, the two plans are full of common themes, both are purposeful in their projection into the future, but their styles are different.

To Saint-Pierre (2010), the development of the END was the first time that Brazil has made public its global and regional view, exposing the perception of the challenges and threats and disposition of forces to curb them. The same author argues that the END appeared to provide the need of a White Book of Defense[10]. This is because many of its South American neighbors had their own White Books of Defense, which revealed the Brazilian deficit regarding this matter.

In the words of the former Brazilian Minister of Defense, Nelson Jobim (2008), since the end of the military administration (1964-85), the civil power avoided addressing the defense issue. There was a common perception that it was up to the

---

10   The White Book of Defense is a public document, in book form, which exposes the government's view about defense. This document is presented at national and international community. The Brazilian White Book of Defense was launched in 2012.

military sector to take control of the defense policy. In the academic environment, the consequence was the lack of interest by most of the researchers about defense issues. The relationship between civilians and the military brought traces of retraction in that period.

In order to correct such distortions, according to Jobim (2008), President Lula initiated the preparation of the plan that would later be the END. Accordingly, Jungmann (2010) points out that the END first expressed Brazil's need to point itself the best way to walk in, underlined by the international system changes. On the other hand, it reveals that the country, conscious of its goals and interests, placed itself for the first time in its history, in relation to its strategic future.

According to Oliveira (2009), the END uses the expression "national security" in a democratic aspect to include issues such as intelligence systems, terrorism and counterterrorism, security infrastructure, chemical and nuclear security, cyber security, tropical diseases, joint international rescue operations, etc. Equally important, the document proposes the political, economic and strategic regional integration without compromising the national nature of Defense. The analysis of the END fundamental elements will be divided into two parts: a) Document's overview; and b) Guidelines.

## a) Document's overview

In general, the first part of this document presents the central arguments about national defense. Brazil's peaceful tradition is emphasized as a way to confirm this sense present along the Brazilian history.

> Brazil is a peaceful country, by tradition and conviction. It lives in peace with its neighbors. It runs its international fairs, among other things, adopting the constitutional principles of non-intervention, defense of peace and peaceful resolution of conflicts. This pacifist trait is part of the national identity, and a value that should be preserved by the Brazilian people (BRASIL, 2008b, p.08).

The document proposes to involve civil society in the debate about defense issues and present the principal defense actions to them. Furthermore, three structural topics were pointed out in the document:

> The first structuring axis deals with how the Armed Forces should be organized and guided to better perform their constitutional mandate and their assignments in situations of both peace and war (…).

The second restructuring axis refers to the reorganization of the defense industry, in order to ensure that the equipment needs of the Armed Forces are met and be based on technologies that are domestically mastered.

The third structuring axis discusses the composition of the Armed Forces' troops and, consequently, about the future of the Mandatory Military Service (BRASIL, 2008*b*, p. 10).

Based on these topics, the document focused on the relevant explanation of the armed forces functions and their chances of application. The protection of air, sea and land areas, the risks that converge on each of them and the work of armed forces gains special attention in the propositions of the document. The second larger END's section corresponds to the Implementation Measures. It aims to complete the first part of the document, with the purpose of contextualizing its goals, and establish its application and transitional measures that would lead Brazil to the role outlined by the Strategy.

As long as the propositions to the national defense area in the second section were made, generally, the performance possibilities of the armed forces are conceptualized and the vulnerabilities of national defense listed. Moreover, the section contains the explanation about each action regarding to: structure of the Armed Forces; Science, Technology and Innovation promotion; consolidation of the defense Industry; Education, Mobilization, Logistics, Command, Control and Training propositions of actions.

It is also up to the second part of the END to identify the documents to be established as a result and complement to the Strategy. The END pursued to set up a strategy that establishes standards of behavior for the armed forces and generates concrete results regarding the structure of the Brazilian strategic thinking. Thus, it is inferred that the strategy did not predict an end of its formulations, but long-term actions that would give rise to new debates related to the area and continue the efforts to establish the profile to be traced by Brazil based on its defense.

The END structure revealed the concern of Lula's administration to raise new topics for discussion on national defense and enhance the society knowledge about the armed forces strategies of action, facing the value added by the END to the conceptualization of their formulations.

Saint-Pierre (2010) also concludes that all its strategic aspects the END presented concerns about the Brazilian interests regarding international and sub-regional contexts. Taking into account the sub-regional framework, the END encourages integration of South America based on the understanding that regional military cooperation, as well as the integration of the defense industrial base, is essential to reduce the potential of conflict in the region. The document also proposes the preparation of the armed forces to a greater involvement in UN peacekeeping missions.

The National Defense Strategy was not welcomed unanimously by the military and researchers in the area. For Almeida (2009), even if it were an implementable strategy, it would not have the effects that the drafters intended to. In a subsequent study, Almeida (2010a) recognizes the imprecision of the proposals concluding that the document did not constitute a strategy, but the simulation of what should be one and it is not a defense one because it does not clearly define what the real threats or challenges for Brazil are.

The U.S., through its embassy in Brasilia, has also criticized the END insofar as the text presents derogatory content regarding the Brazilian concern for the defense of the Amazonian region according to the following extract:

> One of the most notable elements of the strategy is the focus on the defense of the Amazonian region. Although the document maintain that this region faces constants security challenges as a function of uncontrolled borders and the potential instability in neighboring countries, he also dives into the traditional Brazilian paranoia concerning to the activities of non-governmental organizations and other shadowy foreign forces that are popularly seen as potential to the sovereignty of Brazil (FOLHA ONLINE, 2010a).

## b) Guidelines

The first guideline suggests, as means of defense strategy, the use of "Dissuasion". It proposes, as strategy, "to dissuade the concentration of hostile forces in the terrestrial borders, in the limits of the Brazilian jurisdictional waters, and prevent them from using the national air space" (BRAZIL, 2008b, p.04). According to it, in order to dissuade someone, you need to be prepared to fight. For Oliveira (2009), this concept as expressed in Guideline 16, creates the central block of the END, because it is the base for the next ones. According to the author, it was not about dissuasion, but on how to exert it.

Guideline 16 is of paramount importance since it contains END's core principle, according to Oliveira (2009). Its determination is for "Structuring the strategic potential around capabilities". Also according to the aforementioned author, its relevance is noted for three reasons: primarily because Brazil has interests to defend through its military power that even when you have no defined and declared enemies, there are threats against your security. Secondly because "organization around capabilities" rehearses an unusual level of coordination between the armed forces. Finally because it will contribute to the development of a national military identity, once before belonging to the Air Force, Navy or Army, officers are all from the armed forces.

Regarding the restructuring of the armed forces, at least three guidelines specifically provide this information. The doctrinal, operational and territorial change should be guided by the principles of monitoring, control and presence and mobility of the Armed Forces, as expressed in the Guidelines 2 and 5. The reorganization of the Armed Forces is based upon the unification of military operations and the creation of new military command structures, as defined by the 7th Guideline of the END.

In the terrestrial borders and in Brazilian jurisdictional waters, the Army, the Navy and the Air Force units perform, above all, vigilance tasks (BRASIL, 2008b, p. 14). Guidelines 8, 9 and 10 of the Strategy launch points on the territorial distribution of the Brazilian military contingents, they warn about the importance of transferring troops to the border areas highlighting the Amazonian region. Guideline 11 proposes the improvement of the armed forces logistics capabilities, especially in the Amazonian region regarding transportation, command and control. Guideline 21 addresses the potential for military mobility and also asserts that the ability to dissuade depends on the ability to mobilize and to renovate material and human resources.

Due to this, it was possible to achieve what was expressed in Guideline 15, which proposes an optimizing policy for the use of human resources and in Guideline 23 which raises the claim of maintaining the compulsory military service, launching basis for the personnel composition and proposing that young people exempted by recruitment service must instead perform social service.

In relation to the military capabilities and skills, the END indicates the obligation to be prepared with flexibility and integration between the forces possible attack, as arranged in the Guidelines 12, 13 and 14. The END also addresses the use of military force to ensure law and order, under the Federal Constitution, as pointed out in Guideline 17 for national defense.

# IMPLEMENTATION OF LULA'S ADMINISTRATION PROPOSAL TO THE NATIONAL DEFENSE

## Domestic scenario

Once Lula's desires regarding the structure of national defense and security are understood, it is necessary to explore some actions that affirm his line of reasoning. Lula's administration inherited the armed forces with lack of material and an uncertainty about its missions, according Winand and Saint-Pierre (2003). However, Oliveira (2004) points out that the main military definitions that approximate foreign policy and national defense derive from the FHC's administration.

Lula da Silva had the mission to establish clear roles for regarding the Ministry of Defense. Oliveira, Brittes and Munhoz (2012) analyzed the MD's role in Brazilian foreign policy and concluded that Lula's administration and its ministries maintained the lack of legitimacy inherited from the previous government.

Lula, in a Message to Congress in 2003, emphasized the importance of the Amazonian Protection System (SIPAM) and of The Amazon Surveillance System (SIVAM), initiated in 2002 on Cardoso's administration. According to Lula da Silva:

> The Amazonian Protection System is being implemented and directed to promote the sustainable development of the Amazon, through knowledge and information from a large database, contributing to meet the general guidelines arising from the Integrated National Policy for the Legal Amazon and the airspace surveillance in accordance with the National Defense Policy.

> (...)the Amazon Surveillance System now has large land-based radars and aircraft fitted with equipment for aerial surveillance and remote sensing, as well as attack aircraft based at different points of the region (BRASIL, 2003).

The institutionalization of SIPAM and SIVAM was highlighted during Lula's administration. Moreover, the administration succeeded in important efforts in Calha Norte Program (PCN).

> Created in 1985, the Calha Norte Program is really important to ensure the presence of the State in the Amazon, strengthening the sovereignty and territorial integrity in the region, through measures and actions to address the most serious needs of the area, in particular the socio-economic character that plague underserved populations, with the goal of setting a man on the earth (BRASIL, 2003).

The project revealed continuity from the previous administration with increased emphasis. Under Lula's term, PCN expanded its area of operation to 10,938 km of border, which represents 25% of the national territory. Both PCN and SIVAM aim to defend, protect and guarantee the territorial integrity as well as combating illegal actions and stimulating sustainable development (NASCIMENTO, 2005).

In 2004, the Army was granted new powers with Complementary Law number 117. It manifested the concern about the frontiers. The law stipulated the Army to exercise police functions along the borders. The assignment of new functions to the land force confirmed the need to protect and to occupy the Amazon (OKADO, 2012).

In harmony with the concerns in defense the whole national territory, Lula launched Decree No. 6,592, on October 2nd, 2008, about national mobilization. The Decree regulates the National Mobilization System (SINAMOB) and defines foreign aggression as: "(...) harmful acts or threats to national sovereignty, territorial integrity, the Brazilian people or national institutions, although it does not mean invasion of the national territory" (BRASIL, 2008c). The innovation in its definition is the intended legitimacy to act outside own borders when threatened.

Replying END's proposal, Lula's created the Higher State Armed Forces (EMCFA), when he sanctioned on August 25th, 2010 the Complementary Law number 136. The creation of EMCFA proved a point of continuity of efforts that begun during FHC's administration, confirming a unified view in the armed forces. Furthermore, Soares (2011) points out that the possibilities of articulation between the armed forces and the police power of the Navy and Air Force in the border regions increased, which was an attribute of the Army only. According to Soares and Silva (2012), the Law has two central merits: first, the increase of political control over the armed forces, and the incorporation of the National Congress into the defense debate.

As Soares and Silva (2012) conclude, Lula also increased the political control and the institutional alignment of the Armed Forces, but failed to increase the Brazilian military power in order to make it an effective tool to protect the national interests. In consequence, Lula struggled to institutionalize the use of the military as an instrument of foreign policy.

The table below shows the military expenditures of Lula's administration. The first line shows the balance in millions of Brazilian Reals through the eight years administration and the second line presents this value as of GDP percentage.

## Table 2: Lula's military expenditure

| Variable | Fiscal Year | 2003 | 2004 | 2005 | 2006 | 2007 | 2008 | 2009 | 2010 |
|---|---|---|---|---|---|---|---|---|---|
| Balance in millions of Brazilian Reals | Jan-Dec | 25,829 | 28,508 | 33,080 | 35,686 | 39,887 | 44,841 | 51,283 | 59,819 |
| Percentage of GDP | Jan-Dec | 1.5 | 1.5 | 1.5 | 1.5 | 1.5 | 1.5 | 1.6 | 1.6 |

Source: SIPRI (2013). Available on: http://milexdata.sipri.org/result.php4

### International and regional scenario

In regards to the international cooperation on defense and security, Lula's administration made a coherent movement with the option of prioritizing relations in South America. Lula's administration increased the autonomy degree of Brazilian foreign policy and understood that security and defense as important variables for the Brazil's international insertion. Moreover, Lula brought to the field the goal of keeping South America as a Brazilian area of influence, as demonstrated by the creation of the Council of South American Defense (CDS) and the mission in Haiti (SOARES AND SILVA, 2012).

Lula's administration has promoted the creation of Union of South American Nations (UNASUL) and, within this institution, the creation of a Council of South American Defense, confirming its concern about the sub-regional scenario (SAINT-PIERRE, 2010). At the UNASUL creation ceremony, Lula highlighted the importance of the regional context and the intention of creating the Council:

> I am convinced that now is the time to deepen our South American identity, also in the field of Defense. Our armed forces are committed to peacebuilding. The presence of many of our countries in MINUSTAH, the UN force that ensures security in Haiti is an example of that determination. We must articulate a vision of Defense in the region founded on common values and principles, such as respect for sovereignty and self-determination, territorial integrity of States and non-intervention in internal affairs.

So, I put my Secretary of Defense in charge of carrying out consultations with all the countries of South America on the establishment of a South American Defense Council. I think we should discuss this decision here. With this same spirit I propose holding in Brazil, in the second half of this year, a meeting that would detail the functioning and objectives of the Council (AMESUR, 2008).

The CDS goals were to articulate a common position among South Americans regarding peace operations and humanitarian crises, to promote the exchange of experiences, to hold military exercises simulating humanitarian crises, to encourage and strengthen defense industry in the region, to foster mutual trust among members and contribute to cooperation against natural disasters, however, being a military alliance was not the purpose. The Council has demonstrated the maturity of countries in the region by taking responsibility in the resolution of problems and regional political crises, without interference from outside countries, mainly the United States (SOUZA NETO, 2011).

Colonel Carlos Eduardo Barbosa da Costa (2012) expressed that the CDS was the first concrete step since the Rio Treaty (1947) to construct an identity in the region about their security problems. Costa (2012) contends that the Council represents an option to reduce the mistrust among the countries of the region and it provides a positive point to the defense industry development with common base.

Silva (2010) points out that the invitation to the Mission of the United Nations Stabilization in Haiti (MINUSTAH) was a result of a conscious and continuous foreign policy of the Brazilian administration. Diniz (2006) concludes that the Brazilian international role built over time, gave it the responsibility to lead the peacekeeping operations in Haiti in 2004, MINUSTAH. According to the author, the Brazilian participation in MINUSTAH was linked with Brazilian interests, for example, the claim to a permanent seat on the UN Security Council.

Based on this perception, Costa (2012) argues that "the increasing involvement in peacekeeping missions, as in the case of Haiti, shows our determination to exercise soft power and gradually change the relation of how states 'play' on the international board". In this regard, Lula expressed in the 2004 UN General Assembly, the idea of new paradigms for international relations, which we can be understood as the idea of reorganizing the political game in the international scenario.

> We need to develop strategies that combine solidarity and firmness, but with strict respect for international law. That's how we serve Brazil and other countries of Latin America to the convening of the UNITED NATIONS to contribute to the stabilization of Haiti. Whoever defends new paradigms in international relations, could not omit on a concrete situation (CORRÊA, 2007).

Souza Neto (2011) highlights that the participation in the MINUSTAH emphasizes the Brazilian diplomacy during Lula's eight years administration: the incorporation of the armed forces to foreign policy and Brazil's project for the region. According to the author, the mission in Haiti revealed a regional leadership, coupled with the military capacity, and "a way to express the desire to be part of global decisions".

An important element of conformity between the security agenda and foreign policy is the search for a permanent seat in the UNSC. Lula applied a different perspective compared to the previous administration on this issue. In his inaugural speech the president proposed: "We will defend one reformed Security Council, representative of contemporary realities with developed and developing countries from various regions of the world among its permanent members" (BRASIL, 2008a).

Lula's administration was guided by the realization that the UNSC should be more representative of the contemporary world.

> Reflecting a power configuration almost 65 years ago, the current composition of the Council is not the most functional for the effective routing solutions to the problems of international peace and security. A reform that expands the Council in permanent and non-permanent categories, with the entry of larger number of developing countries in both, and also foresaw the reformulation of its methods of work, would meet the imperatives of giving the largest organ representativeness and transparency, so as to enhance the legitimacy and effectiveness of its decisions (MRE, 2011).

In 2004, Brazil was allied to countries that would form the G-4 (Germany, India and Japan) to present a proposal to extend the UNSC. The countries have set up a plan to guide the actions of the four in the reform process (MRE 2011). Almeida (2004) argues that since the beginning of Lula's administration high priority was assigned to the achievement of a permanent seat in the Security Council. In his speech at the UN General Assembly in 2004, Lula established the arguments:

> Only the Security Council can confer legitimacy to actions in the field of international peace and security. But their composition must adapt to the reality of current days, and not to perpetuate the post-world war or the cold war. Any reform that is limited to a new guise for the current structure, without increasing the number of permanent members is insufficient (CORRÊA, 2007).

The Brazilian application for a permanent seat in the UNSC was considered a point of honor of the foreign and security policy during Lula's administration, although not expressed in the END (ALMEIDA, 2009). The reformer speech by Lula and the alliance with the G-4 were constant during the mentioned period.

Accordingly to Samuel Alves Soares (2011), Lula adopted a declared leadership. This refers to the Brazilian efforts to occupy a prominent place in the international scenario. As well as the option for diversification of partnerships, the author reports this according to diversify in order to lead, the defense agenda of this administration.

## CONCLUSION

The analysis of Brazil's defense policy agenda during Lula's administration led to the implementation of a new proposal for the defense area resulting in efforts to restructure the strategic plan and to redefine priorities, through diplomacy, expanding the Brazilian search for cooperation on security and defense fields. In fact, Cardoso and Lula observed the security issue through different aspects. Lula's administration presented changes of emphasis and methods regarding foreign and defense policies in Cardoso's administration.

Lula's administration represented, therefore, a set of other priorities and prominent themes rather than a discontinuity of the previous agenda. At the institutional level, Lula's efforts represented continuity with the previous administration. The documents established during his eight year term presented its innovative points and also the strengthening of the discourse initiated by FHC.

In the domestic scene, Lula's administration has confirmed the concern of Cardoso's administration to establish a unified vision for the armed forces. Lula continued the renovation of Brazilian strategic thinking. It proved the increase and emphasis given to the available themes in this debate.

Lula's defense agenda revealed the interaction between domestic and international spheres. The 2005 PDN increased the emphasis on the regional context and demonstrated the change of view on in the international scenario. The END followed the same direction based on regional context and demonstrated concern about the international scenario.

The Amazon was highlighted on the documents elaborated in the course of Lula's administration and South America became a priority in the Brazilian defense policy. The END stressed on the need to relocate armed forces as an instrument of foreign policy, as well as preference for regional cooperation in the defense area.

Concerning to the actions in regional and international scenarios, Lula's administration has shown compliance with the prospect of Cardoso's administration related to South America, it was evidenced in the CDS foundation. Furthermore, it represented continuity in Brazilian participation throughout peacekeeping operations.

Moreover, Lula related to Brazil's participation in peacekeeping operations through the search for a permanent seat in the UNSC. At this point, there was a disruption in relation to the previous administration. Lula's administration upstretched the search for international support and demonstrated throughout its actions the priority in the UNSC reformulation.

# REFERENCES

ALMEIDA, Carlos Wellington de. Política de defesa no Brasil: considerações do ponto de vista das políticas públicas. **Opinião Pública**, Campinas, v. 16, n. 1, jun. 2010a, p. 220-250.

ALMEIDA, Paulo Roberto de. **A Arte de NÃO Fazer a Guerra:** novos comentários à Estratégia Nacional de Defesa. Meridiano 47 vol. 11, n. 119, jun. 2010b p. 21-31.

_____. Estratégia Nacional de Defesa: comentários dissidentes. **Mundorama**, 14/03/2009. Disponível em <http://mundorama.net/2009/03/14/estrategia-nacional-de-defesa-comentarios-dissidentes-por-paulo-roberto-de-almeida/> Acessado em 13/05/2013

_____. Uma política externa engajada: a diplomacia do governo Lula. **Rev. bras. polít. int.**, Jun. 2004, vol.47, n.1, p.162-184.

ALSINA JÚNIOR, João Paulo Soares. **A síntese imperfeita:** articulação entre política externa e política de defesa na era Cardoso. Revista brasileira de política internacional, Brasília, v. 46, n. 2, dez. 2003.

AMERSUR. **UNASUR-Discurso del Presidente Lula da Silva** Jun. 2008. Disponível em: <http://www.amersur.org.ar/Integ/UNASUR0806.htm> Acessado em: 29/10/2013.

BRASIL. **Decreto no 5.484, de 30 de junho de 2005**. Aprova a política de defesa nacional, e dá outras providências. Brasília, 30 jun. 2005.

_____. Ministério das Relações Exteriores. **Discursos selecionados do Presidente Luiz Inácio Lula da Silva**. Brasília, DF: Fundação Alexandre de Gusmão, 2008a

_____. **Estratégia Nacional de Defesa**, Decreto nº 6.703, de 18 de dezembro de 2008b

_____. **Decreto Nº 6.592, De 2 De Outubro De 2008c.** Regulamenta o disposto na Lei no 11.631, de 27 de dezembro de 2007, que dispõe sobre a Mobilização Nacional e cria o Sistema Nacional de Mobilização- SINAMOB. 64

_____. **Mensagem ao Congresso Nacional, 2003**. Brasília: Presidência da República, Secretaria-Geral da Presidência da República, 2003.

_____. **Política de Defesa Nacional**, 1996.

CERVO, Amado Luiz; BUENO, Clodoaldo. **História da política exterior do Brasil.** 4. ed., rev. ampl. Brasília, DF: Universidade de Brasília, 2011

CORRÊA, Luiz Felipe de Seixas (org.). O Brasil nas Nações Unidas, 1946-2006. Brasília: Funag, 2007.

COSTA, Carlos Eduardo Barbosa da. Tendências mundiais e seus reflexos para a defesa brasileira. **Revista Brasileira de Inteligência**. Brasília: Abin, n.7, jul. 2012.

DINIZ, Eugenio. **O Brasil e as operações de paz**. In: OLIVEIRA, Henrique Altemani de; LESSA, Antônio Carlos (org.). Relações Internacionais do Brasil: temas e agendas. São Paulo: Saraiva, 2006, vol. II, p. 303-337.

FOLHA ONLINE. **EUA fazem duras críticas à Estratégia Nacional de Defesa.** 01/12/2010a. Disponível em: <http://www1.folha.uol.com.br/poder/839335-eua-fazem-duras-criticas-a-estrategia-nacional-de-defesa-leia-telegrama-em-portugues.shtml> Acessado em: 18/05/2013

JOBIM, Nelson. A Defesa na agenda nacional: o Plano Estratégico de Defesa. **Interesse nacional,** ano I, n. 2, p. 09-16, julho/setembro 2008.

JUNGMANN, Raul. Estratégia Nacional de Defesa (END) *In:* **Segurança Internacional:** Perspectivas Brasileiras. JOBIM, Nelson A.,ETCHEGOYEN, Sergio W,

ALSINA, João Paulo (Orgs). Rio de Janeiro: Editora FGV,2010

MARTINS FILHO, O governo Fernando Henrique e as Forças Armadas: um passo pra frente dois Passo Atrás. **Revista Olhar.** Ano 02, N. 4, Dez. 2000

MINISTÉRIO DE RELAÇÕES EXTERIORES. Reforma da Governança Mundial:

Reforma e Ampliação do Conselho de Segurança das Nações Unidas. **Balanço de Política Externa 2003/2010.** 2011

MIYAMOTO, Shiguenoli. O Brasil no cenário Regional de Segurança *In:* **O Brasil no cenário internacional de defesa e segurança.** J.R. de Almeida Pinto, A.J. Ramalho da Rocha, R. Doring Pinho da Silva (orgs) Brasília, Ministério da Defesa, Secretaria de Estudos e de Cooperação, 2004.

NASCIMENTO,Durbens Martins. A Política de Defesa Nacional para a Amazônia e suas consequências ao Programa Calha Norte. *In:* **Revista Humanitas.** Mar- 2005.

OKADO, Giovanni Hideki Chinaglia. **Política externa e política de defesa:** uma epifania pendente. Dissertação (Mestrado). Universidade de Brasília, 2012.

OLIVEIRA, Andréa Benetii Carvalho de. **AMÉRICA DO SUL NA POLÍTICA DE DEFESA NACIONAL: estudo comparativo das políticas de 1996 e 2005.** Encontro Nacional da Associação Brasileira de Estudos de Defesa de 2013.

OLIVEIRA, Andréa Benetii Carvalho de.; VIANA E SILVA, Caroline Cordeiro. **Política de Defesa Nacional, Estratégia Nacional de Defesa e Doutrina Militar de Defesa:** América do Sul e Segurança Regional. 2011

OLIVEIRA, Eliézer Rizzo de. A defesa nacional no governo Lula. **Atlas Comparativo de la Defensa en América Latina.** Buenos Aires: Resdal, 2005.

_____. A Estratégia Nacional de Defesa e a reorganização e transformação das Forças Armadas. **Interesse nacional**, ano 2, n. 5, p. 71-83, abril/junho de 2009.

_____. Ministério da Defesa: A Implementação da autoridade. **Research and Education in Defense and Security Studies** August 7–10, 2002, Brasilia, Brazil.

_____.A visão brasileira de segurança hemisférica. **Seminário Defensa Europa – América Latina**. Santiago, Chile, 30.01.2004

OLIVEIRA, Eliézer Rizzo; SOARES, Samuel Alves. Forças Armadas, direção política e formato institucional. *In:* CASTRO, Celso; D'ARAUJO, Maria Cecilia (Orgs). **Democracia e Forças Armadas no Cone Sul.** FGV, Rio de Janeiro. 2000

OLIVEIRA, Guilherme Ziebell de.; BRITES, Pedro Vinícius Pereira.; MUNHOZ, Athos. O Papel do Ministério da Defesa na Política Externa Brasileira para a

América do Sul. **Seminário Brasileiro de Estudos Estratégicos Internacionais Sebreei**. 20 a 22 de junho de 2012 Porto Alegre/RS, Brasil

PUTNAM, Robert D. Diplomacy and Domestic Politics: The Logic of the Two-Level

Games *In*: **International Organization.** Boston, v. 42, n. 3, p. 427-460, Summer.1988.

SAINT-PIERRE, Héctor Luís. A Defesa na Política Externa: dos fundamentos a uma análise do caso brasileiro. **Análise de Conjuntura**, n.8, ago. 2010

SILVA, Marcos Valle Machado da. Política Externa, Segurança e Defesa nos Governos Lula e Cardoso. **Revista Debates** (UFRGS), v. 4, p. 159-177, 2010. 67

SIPRI. **Military Expenditure Database 2013.** Disponível em: <http://milexdata. sipri.org/result.php4> Acessado em 18/05/2013

SOARES, Samuel Alves. A defesa na política externa da Era Lula: de uma defesa elusiva a uma liderança proclamada. *In:* FREIXO, Adriano de (COORD.) **A política externa brasileira na era Lula.** Rio de Janeiro, RJ: Apicuri, 2011.

SOARES E SILVA, Fernando José Sant'Ana. O poder militar brasileiro como instrumento de política externa In: **Defesa nacional para o século XXI**: política internacional, estratégia e tecnologia militar / Edison Benedito da Silva Filho, Rodrigo Fracalossi de Moraes (orgs). – Rio de Janeiro: Ipea, 2012.

SOUZA NETO, Danilo Marcondes. A política externa brasileira nos oito anos do governo Lula: legados e lições para a inserção do Brasil no mundo. In: PAULA, M (org.). **Nunca antes na história desse país...?** Um balanço das políticas do governo Lula. Rio de Janeiro: Fundação Heinrich Böll, 2011.

TEIXEIRA JR, Augusto Wagner. NOBRE, Fábio Rodrigo Ferreira.Mudanças no significado estratégico da Amazônia nas políticas e na Estratégia Nacional de Defesa. **Revista de Geopolítica.** Natal - RN, v. 3, nº 2, p. 113 – 123, jul./dez. 2012.

VIGEVANI, Tullo; CEPALUNI, Gabriel. A política externa de Lula da Silva: a estratégia da autonomia pela diversificação. **Contexto Internacional**, Rio de Janeiro, vol. 29, n. 2, p. 273-335, julho/dezembro 2007

VIZENTINI, Paulo Fagundes. **Relações Internacionais do Brasil** – de Vargas a Lula. 2. ed. São Paulo: Perseu Abramo, 2005.

WINAND, Érica Cristina Alexandre. SAINT-PIERRE, Héctor Luís. A questão da defesa e as Forças Armadas Brasileiras nos primeiros meses do governo Lula. **Ponencia preparada para el VI Seminario sobre Investigación y Educación en Estudios de Seguridad y Defensa** (REDES 2003), CHDS, Santiago de Chile, 27 al 30 de octubre de 2003.

# THE INTERNATIONALIZATION OF THE BRAZILIAN FASHION INDUSTRY UNDER THE PERSPECTIVE OF KNOWLEDGE

Rayanne de Souza Soares
Rodrigo Pires de Campos

## INTRODUCTION

The International Market and the fashion business have been two recurring themes in the contemporary scenario and have been responsible for improving the economy of many countries.

Brazil is no different. With a textile industry that generates nearly $33 billion annually, according to the Brazilian Association of Textile and Garment, ABIT (2010), which corresponds to 3% of Brazil's GDP, the fashion segment contributes to the recovery of the Brazilian economy.

Data collected by ABIT in 2010 and updated in 2011, identified the country as the fifth largest textile producer in the world and the fourth largest garment industrial park. These numbers are achieved with the work of 1.7 million employees, representing 16.4% of formal employment in the country.

The sector also presented other prominent numbers in 2010, as investments which amounted to $2 billion, being the second sector that generates the most jobs in the country.

Following the continuous increase in globalization and aiming to expand their brands and reach new markets, Brazilian companies have moved towards the internationalization of its products.

According to ABEST, in 2003 the organization exported $3 million in sales. In 2006 there was a jump to $12 million and in 2012 ABEST acquired the value of more than $18.3 million, exporting to 66 countries.

During several decades such as the 1910s', 1920 s' and 1930 s', Brazil's textile industry suffered due to strong European influences. Cuts and fabrics were dictated in Europe and came to Brazil without any kind of adequacy to Brazilian climate and cultural background.

In the 1940s' during the Second World War a blockade took place on the import of fabrics, and Brazil was forced to invest in the textile and garment sectors. It was in this context that Alcaeus Pena emerged with his most famous creation "A baiana", the first genuinely Brazilian costume used by Carmen Miranda which became a great hit inside and outside the country, consequently releasing a fashion style and also promoting the Latin American culture.

Ever since, until the time when the first Brazilian fashion schools were created in 1980, there have been several changes in the identity of Brazilian fashion. In the 1950s' there was a rise of haute couture that did not last long, for soon came the decentralization of fashion and a constant movement of young people who were going through a military dictatorship and used fashion as a mean of freedom of speech.

Fashion, during the period of the dictatorship, was less luxurious. Since couture was in decline in Brazil, and what was seen in the streets were "many different styles and materials such as synthetic and rustic fabrics, geometric and floral prints, romantic fashion and long and short unisex skirts, glitter and punk, jeans and sportswear. "(Afiune, 2008)

Coinciding with the time of the creation of fashion schools, in the 80s' the fashion industry in Brazil began to obtain fame not only nationally but also internationally The fashion industry before this period was just a sector looking for inspiration outside the country (mostly in Europe and the United States) and was not able to build its own characteristics.

Currently we notice that the situation differs from distant times and the opening of the market in the 90s' allowed greater Brazilian participation in activities abroad. In order to maintain this participation and primarily so they could stand up to competing products, it was necessary to develop a product that possessed some distinction from others and that had the face of Brazil.

In 2002, Sebrae conducted a survey called "Brazilian Face" that sought to identify the strongest and most evident national characteristics that can and should be valued in building a positive image of the nation.

According to Sebrae (2002), some of the most important features of Brazilian identity are: nature, material culture, social culture through economic demonstrations, social differentiation and forms of grouping, education, social relationships, time management culture, rites, social control, and the ideal culture of communication, awareness of nature, men and values, among others.

In identifying what Brazil is, the concept of "Brazilianness" comes to light. According to Freyre (2009), Brazilianness is a characteristic and specific way of being of the Brazilian people, the result of its history and social and cultural miscegenation. In the field of fashion, Freyre (2009) argues that Brazilianness is in the tropical ecology and in the miscegenation through shapes, colors and appearances.

The concept of Brazilianness used in fashion finds support in Avelar (2009), in which Brazilianness can add original features to the product, with the use of fabrics, shapes, colors, volume and the overlapping of these elements. Avelar's notes (2009) are consistent with those of Neira (2008, p. 1), who considers that the nationalist ideal is translated into clothing by colors, volumes and shapes that are part of the "visual grammar of fashion."

Accordingly, Silveira et al. (2009) adds to the debate by holding that the creation of the Brazil brand should be based on the appreciation of national culture and the rational use of materials related to ecological and innovative design.

Brazilian fashion is composed of different aspects that make up a unique mixed style, of the culture of the five Brazilian regions. This style is named Brazilianness. (ABEST, 2012).

After highlighting important features about Brazilian fashion products, it is necessary to identify what leads its producers into becoming interested in the expansion of their business and the desire of taking their products abroad.

On that purpose, this paper will seek to discuss these issues regarding the importance of studying the internationalization of Brazilian fashion and furthermore developing research on the knowledge perspective of entrepreneurs in the sector when looking for an international insertion.

According to Cunha (2011), the contributions of knowledge management are presented as a viable way so that the companies can overcome the existing barriers and reinforce its presence in the international market: Identifying the knowledge factors of the internationalization, whether marketing, cultural, entrepreneurial or networking knowledge is critical to achieving more sustainable and less risky internationalization. Developing a strategy for national insertion is therefore essential for a company that wants to internationalize.

# THE IMPORTANCE OF STUDYING ENTERPRISE INTERNATIONALIZATION AND BRAZIL IN THE INTERNATIONAL MARKET

To begin, it is necessary to present the meaning of internationalization of companies, since the work revolves mainly around this concept. In sequence, the reasons to internationalize, the relevant strategies and Brazilian image over international trade will be presented.

Internationalization, which can be defined as an increasing and continuous process of company involvement with operations in other countries outside of its home base, is an old and widely studied phenomenon (BRAZIL et al, 1996). It cannot be considered a phenomenon of our days, if we note that trade between nations is lost in time. However, the size, growth and features that internationalization reached in recent decades is what makes this phenomenon relevant, giving it new life and a renewed interest (DIAS, 2007).

An internationalized company is a phenomenon that can be characterized based on several dimensions. For example, Welch and Luostarinen (1988) and Chetty (1999) emphasized some aspects: method of overseas operations ("how"), markets served ("where"), sales objects ("what") and organizational structure, financial and personnel. The main issues concerning the internationalization process of firms circle around five basic questions: why, what, when, where and how companies internationalize.

Literature concerning internationalization is extensive and several papers on the subject have already been exposed for learning. Below are some authors who conceptualized the topic:

• For Melin (1992), internationalization is the largest dimension of the ongoing strategy process in most companies. It determines the current development and changes in scope, business ideas, guiding actions, principles organizations, nature of managerial work, domination of values and rules convergence;

• According to Carlson (1975), the internationalization process resembles walking cautiously in unfamiliar terrain. Overseas operations involve cross national borders, which creates additional uncertainty. The lack of knowledge of local business conditions, customers, bureaucratic procedures, fluctuation in exchange rates, tariff and non-tariff barriers and getting information together, contribute to increasing uncertainty;

In a world full of changes, with the progressive liberalization of world trade, international expansion has been the business response to the general increase of competition and threats to their survival.

Below, crucial points will be analyzed: Why, when, where and how to internationalize.

## Why internationalize?

There are many reasons why firms internationalize. Stephem Hymer, (1978 , p.100 cited LIMA , 2010), who was one of the first authors to write about international business, had already observed that one of the incentives would be competition with national companies, which means to excel, expand product and obtain higher profits, for which it is necessary to seek alternatives such as moving production elsewhere. Moreover, companies are urged to go international to cope with foreign companies that are very strong competition in the consumer market. The competitiveness contributes to the capital and companies to internationalize, since market forces begin to act globally. The author also states that sometimes the internationalization of a company can provide more advantages and benefits as what it had in its place of creation, nationally. It is very important that the company uses the strategy of internationalization to grow in sectors where international competition is intense, so "the question becomes investing abroad or to end up being bought out by powerful investors " (Almeida, 2007).

Cintra and Mourão (2005) also note that reasons to internationalize are: overcoming tariff and/or nontariff barriers, the "culture" of the company, the need to develop the technology, diplomacy and economic stimuli to internationalization by the government. The importance of internationalization can be understood from Keedi's claims (2007, p. 19), which highlight that foreign trade "[...] is also driven by relationships between countries, which need to exchange goods due to the most various reasons, and may not be related to the abundance or lack of resources, working capital, among others."

That is why the internationalization of an organization can be held so that the countries involved achieve their goals, with reciprocal benefits (Keedi, 2007). Czinkota et al. (1999 apud DIAS, 2007) indicated that the main motivations for internationalization as a set of eleven factors that assemble in proactive motivations (including the advantages in terms of profits, technology, unique products, exclusive information, the commitment of management, tax benefits and economies of scale) and reactive motivations (which include competitive pressures, excess production capacity, saturation of the domestic market and proximity to customers and landing ports).

Brito and Lorga (1999) present a proposal that at first glance seems similar (in terms of nomenclature) to Czinkota, but in reality it is not, since it is more comprehensive and complementary. Therefore, it is suggested that there are three types of motivations: proactive, reactive and mixed (motivations that result from a combination of proactive and reactive). At a level of proactive motivations, the growth strategies of the company are highlighted (in which facing the difficulty of growing in the domestic market, given increasing competition, restrictive policies of business expansion and the lack of sophistication from consumers, among others, the company chooses to internationalize), as well as the advantages of the opportunities created with a new market (usually these opportunities are detected by business partners of the company in a particular market or are the result of poor performance by the partner, which leads to a reformulation of the company's strategy. The legislative changes are also considered in the market, leading to the strengthening of its attractiveness). Reactive motivations include internationalization by entrainment (result of the need of the company to follow the movement of its client to a new market) and the imperatives of the business itself (there are businesses that are by nature international, for example airlines; on the other hand there are activities that do not have regular demand or require a higher dimension than the national market). Mixed motivations consider the geographical proximity and cultural and linguistic affinities, risk reduction (through geographical diversification), cost reduction and benefits from scale economies (the search for cheaper production factors and markets with less stringent laws in environmental and tariff terms, the proximity of sources of raw materials, as well as scale economies in production), the use of the image of the country (which may potentiate the internationalization of domestic enterprises given their negative or positive international image) and government support (the country of origin and/or destination).

The view of Teixeira and Diz (2005) resembles the previous one, showing six factors: access to cheaper and "better" resources, the highest return on investment, increased market share, escape from importation or importation quotas, the response to customers and competitors and access to competencies.

Simões (1997) summarizes the motivations of internationalization as follows:

1) Endogenous: need for growth of the company; use of spare capacity; achievement of scale economies; exploration of competencies, technologies; risk diversification.

2) Characteristics of the markets: domestic market limitations; perception of dynamism of the foreign markets.

3) Relational: response to competitors; monitoring clients; approaches by foreign companies.

4) Access to resources abroad: lower production costs abroad; access to technological knowledge.

5) Government Incentives: government assistance (country of origin or host).

**When to internationalize?**

To be introduced in the international market, the company needs to prepare itself by constructing detailed and elaborated strategic planning. Planning begins with a thorough study of the country in which they intend to invest, so that the exporting process is successful. Consequently these exports will become frequent as they bring development and growth for the organization, both domestically, and in foreign markets (SILVA, 2008).

Several questions need to be analyzed in the internationalization process. One must decide how to initiate sales; what can be explored and what the company has as per capacity of exporting; if the product has market acceptance, and what these markets are (MINERVINI, 2001).

When deciding to export, the company needs to assess the strengths and weaknesses rationally and coherently. But still there may be decisions that need to be taken through intuition. The company also needs to plan the process carefully to achieve the expected results; act responsibly in order to inspire confidence to prospective buyers; and preparation to reach different decisions from the planned ones when the unexpected happens (CIGNACCO, 2009).

**Where to internationalize?**

Choosing the market to export to is very important since it will determine the success or failure of the internationalization of a company. At this moment, one takes into account the advantages and disadvantages of working in that particular place, geographic constraints, the advantages of the location and also the psychic distance, "which is the sum of certain factors such as the differences of language, education, legal and business practices, culture, industrial development, among others "(JOHANSON and VAHLNE, 1990).

## Means of internationalization

As for the entry modes, there are several proposals by different authors. Cateora and Graham (1996) suggest the following classification: export/import; licensing; joint venture; consortium; partially owned subsidiary; 100% owned subsidiary.

Root (1982) summarizes some differences between the export entry strategy and the local production strategy, from which we can emphasize: the long-term involvement, the systematic selection of target markets and entry ways, the greater allocation of resources, the adaptation of products taking into account local preferences (and not only technical/legal mandatory requirements) and the effort of controlling the distribution channels inherent to the more demanding local deployment strategies.

The same guidelines used by the previous authors, Viana and Hortinha (2005 apud DIAS, 2007) suggest the analysis of the entry modes considering ways of access for export, with production in the domestic market (direct export, indirect export) and ways of access with overseas production (production contract, licensing, franchising, technology transfer, service contracts, management contracts, consortium, strategic alliances, joint ventures and full ownership by direct investment).

Some examples of entry modes into foreign markets are presented below:

## Export

Exporting is the most used mode by companies in their international expansion processes (Salomon and Shaver, 2005). Simões (1997) defines export as a mode of operation in which the products are sold in a different country from the one they were manufactured in. Some advantages: low financial commitment, a decreased risk (comparing to other strategies) and ease (also relative) of operational procedures. It enables the achievement of scale economies when production activities are concentrated in the limit, in one place.

According to Nicola Minervini (1997), the exporting needs vary from each company and there are various motivations for exporting: the need to operate in a market volume that ensures an industrial dimension of the company; casual requests from exporters; difficulties with domestic sales; better utilization of the seasons; possibility of more profitable prices; best production schedule; extension of product's life cycle; risk diversification, improvement of the image with suppliers, customers and banks; balance against the entry of competitors in the domestic market; for a development strategy of the company.

According to Abrantes (1999), the internationalization strategies are no longer just the traditional export to a distant, partially unknown client, or the opening of a branch abroad for the use of the comparative advantages of the host country, but are propagated over many forms as the intrafirm trade, characteristic of multinational companies, cross-investment between companies from different countries, and especially different types of industrial and commercial cooperation agreements involving companies of varying sizes, financial firms, governments, supranational institutions, etc.

For José Júnior (2005), exporting brings development for the country and better relationship with the partner countries. On that matter, Ludovico (2008, p.22) also notes that "On the one hand, you get a margin of safety with commercial clients of various economic levels and on the other immunizes us against seasonal crises in the domestic market."

## Licensing

Licensing is an agreement whereby a company transfers to another the right to use certain knowledge (know-how) and/or exploit industrial property rights (trademarks, patents, designs or models) for a payment, usually expressed through royalties. (SIMÕES, 1997)

Cateora and Graham (1996) consider that this is a low risk agreement, proposing a more concise definition: a contract that transfers the rights and methods of production to a company of a third country in exchange of royalties. Slater (1997) argues that this contract may include technical assistance, engineering services or staff training. Therefore that type of contract is commonly used by companies with strong brands or high technological know-how that lack the necessary resources for internationalization (e.g. financial and human).

## Franchising

Another way of entering the global market is Franchising, very similar to licensing. In this process there is an agreement between the franchisor and the franchisee in which the first grants the right to use the trademark and business product/service through the payment of royalties by the second. So that the foreign markets are able to take better advantage of the expansion opportunities they adopt the master franchise. "With this system the franchisor gives a local entrepreneur the right to sell franchises within a territory, which can be a region within the country or group of countries" (KOTABE, HELSEN, 2000).

Companies are able to capitalize a winning business formula by expanding overseas with a minimal investment. It must be clear that the franchise encourages the franchisee to grow (LIMA, 2010). Simões (1997) believes that franchising is a privileged mode of internationalization, which enables rapid international expansion with reduced costs, being a system that feeds its own growth process.

## Joint Venture

Joint venture is a legal concept originated from the practice that may be understood as a business collaboration agreement. It corresponds to a form or method of cooperation between independent companies, denominated in other countries as a partnership between companies, joint venture or association of undertakings. The essential feature of the joint venture agreement is the realization of a common project, project whose duration can be short or long, but with a fixed deadline. It is the conclusion of a contract between two or more companies, which are associated, creating or not a new company to undertake a productive or service economic activity for-profit. (MIRANDA and MALUF, 2009).

## Consortium

A consortium consists of the combination of several companies generating a new organization. Although sometimes it can be confused with a joint venture, the consortium is generally a term reserved for activities of a commercial nature (WELCH and PACICIFICO, 1990).

## Subcontracting

Subcontracting is an order by a company (called principal) of products or parts of products - or mere operations on them - to another subcontractor based on pre-established specifications. In order to ensure that the products or operations meet the pre-established requirements, it is common that there is a transfer (in addition to technical specifications) of technological know-how and even machinery and equipment, this being formalized through autonomous contracts of technical assistance or licensing. (BRITO, 1993)

After presenting the key elements of internationalization, the role of Brazil in international trade will be discussed and analyzed in general terms.

### Brazil in International Trade

The history of trade and growth in Brazil has certain boundaries, which is a pattern and complexity of our own economic structure and evolution. It contrasts well with economic development and the persistent business expansion in Europe and Asia. Brazil met, since the post-War, considerable alternation between periods of greater or lesser growth, not necessarily with an expanding economy concomitant with the international trade.

These periods were interspersed with crises (currency and financial) and macroeconomic imbalances. It was the country of miracle to stagnation, before trade liberalization in the nineties. Since then, it has sought to consolidate economic stability and support sustained growth (SARQUIS, 2011).

Brazil, before the 1990s, had their protected industries in the domestic market and this led to the stagnation of the economy in the country. The opening of the economy in this same decade brought with it many problems. When this happened, many business owners were not prepared to face competition arising from the insertion of foreign products and even international companies in the Brazilian market had the same issue (SINA, 20).

All these changes have led national entrepreneurs to seek to upgrade and constantly grow their business to stand up to competition and remain in the market (Nose JR, 2005). However, there is still a part of Brazilian exporting companies that lack international consciousness. They are unaware of the benefits of exporting, and usually only know the disadvantages of entering the international market (LUDOVICO, 2008).

What can be seen is that Brazil has been increasingly devoted to reaching international customers, trying to overstep its boundaries. Directions to international trading are not easy to follow and they require a lot of work. However, the benefits of entering the international market can be huge and positively affect the national economy when performed successfully.

## FASHION INDUSTRY IN BRAZIL AND ITS INTERNATIONALIZING

The fashion market in Brazil is moving an average of $29 million per year in their main fashion weeks. In 2010, 30,000 formal businesses that operate in the clothing sector invested more than $180 million. Brazilian production is highly fragmented, since approximately 16% of production comes from large companies, with the remaining in the hands of medium and small confections, which employ an average of 71% of work force (POOL BRASILEIRADA TEXTILE AND CLOTHING. 2010; FERRARI 2011; PINTO 2011 apud PINTO AND SOUZA, 2011).

Brazilian textile complex is composed of approximately 4,391 textile industries and 18,000 registered confectionaries. The large number of informal enterprises in the garment sector, according to unofficial estimates, surpasses in quantity those of the incorporated enterprises.

The garment sector in Brazil is currently the second largest employer of people, disputing the first place with construction (BURGARDT, 2007). This represents about 1,500,000 formal workers, considering the economically active population. Much of what is produced, however, is consumed domestically. Nevertheless, Brazil already has overseas customers and some of them were won by Brazilian fashion, which is materializing our lifestyle which is our way of life, customs and Brazilian culture into the products, something that seems to have demand abroad. Moreover, in addition to printing these values, companies are looking for channels to promote and distribute their products (PINTO E SOUZA PINTO, 2011). According to Burgardt (2007), the identity of fashion clothing becomes relevant; however having an identity is not the only difference that conquers the foreign market, but the value that it represents to the consumer. Therefore, investment in this communication gap is crucial to stimulate demand.

Although the garment sector employs a substantive workforce, its participation in the economy has declined over the competition of foreign products in the Brazilian economy - popular Chinese and Indian products have a workforce with much lower costs and represents international brands, whose quality and design attract the more affluent classes. One way to circumvent competition via cost is to invest in quality and design, in order to increase its share in the growth of Brazil's gross domestic product via increased exports, which requires creativity and competitiveness. These items can be achieved through business strategy, focused mainly on the direct relationship between innovation and firm performance. (CAMERA, AND SALVADOR PIZAIA, 2007)

The improvement in the quality and design, as well as the development of unique products that conquer demanding and high purchasing power consumers around the world, has been a growth strategy adopted by some companies. Therefore, they have innovated and created alternative markets without limitations of growth imposed by economic constraints and a smaller or less affluent market. It is noteworthy that the strategy has been favorable for products and national fashion business, with coordination between the links in the textile chain that involve the improvement of the quality of the fibers and yarns, design, manufacturing, technology, fashion and packaging design appeal of the products.

According to RECH (2001), Brazil is investing more in competitiveness of design to differentiate products and gain a wider share in the international arena. In the international ranking of the largest textile exporters, Brazil occupies the 21st place. Brazilian exports have been less dynamic than those of other segments of the economy and are strongly found in North America and the European Community, which together absorb about 67% of Brazilian exports, focusing on thread products, cotton fabrics and garments (Feghali; DWYER, 2004).

According to the Institute of Industrial Studies and Marketing - IEMI, much of this production comes from textile companies with more than 500 employees on its staff. Organizations in this listing represent more than 50% of output and employment and account for a growing share of exports. These companies are located predominantly in the Southeast. But in recent years, large productions units have been transferred for the Northeast Region, mainly due to tax incentives, the availability and lower cost of skilled workforce in the region. In the confection segment, there is a large concentration of businesses in the state of São Paulo, followed by Rio de Janeiro, Minas Gerais and Santa Catarina.

The process of internationalization of Brazilian companies seems to develop, irreversibly, as companies of all sizes move towards the international arena, in search of new markets, gaining strategic positions, diversifying risk, or in some cases, only to satisfy the desire to internationalize its entrepreneurs (Mansur 2011).

Studies in the domestic apparel industry point that much of the production of clothing is made by small businesses. According to the Brazilian Association of Clothing, around 94% of the production of garments is done by micro, small and medium enterprises (BRAZILIAN ASSOCIATION OF CLOTHING, 2010).

The definition of small and medium enterprises (SMEs) is adopted as those that do not occupy a dominant position or a monopoly on the market and is run by its owners, who take the business risk. SMEs are not yet linked to big companies or financial groups (Gonçalves; Koprowski, 1995).

Technological development and the Brazilian investment in the apparel sector have made Brazil a country able to compete internationally in the fashion and styling segment. However, one must understand that factors such as improving and specializing the workforce is going to facilitate the Brazilian fashion industry to stay in tune with the technical standards required by the market and to gain competitiveness against its international competitors, balancing expenses and profit, price and quality. (Feghali, Dwyer, 2004).

Brazilian brands such as Forum, Csklen, Cia. Marítima, Maria Bonita, Poko Pano, Triton, Ellus, Iódice, Cavalera and Vide Bula are recognized abroad for their quality and luxury products. Designers like Alexandre Herchcovitch, Tufi Duek, Cecília Prado, Glória Coelho, Lino Villaventura, Reinaldo Lourenço and Carlos Mieli are consecrated and internationally admired (CAMERA, AND SALVADOR PIZAIA, 2007).

These brands and Brazilian designers have come to adjust their products to the international market through achievements of marketing abroad, which is essential to spread and consolidate the Brazil Brand (or Nation Branding, according to Simon Anholt).

For Anholt (2008), the combination of the words "nation" and "brand" has a lot of resonance. Considering that the national reputation is a crucial issue for governments, he coined in 1996 the concept of national brand, claiming that the reputation of the countries was similar to images of products and brand companies, since it could influence the opinions and behaviors of foreign markets, multilateral organizations, tourists, students, businessmen, international media and other "audiences".

Anholt (2008) says that the concept of Nation Branding was first coined in 1998. In the beginning it related to the way countries decide as for the rest of the world. According to Potter (2009), the concept evolved into the marketing and implementation of corporate, public and private sector ideas to sell an improved version of a foreign country image through place, city, country, or nation brand. To mark a nation means designing a unique national identity (POTTER, 2009 p. 6). The brand is best described as the idea of a customer about a product; the "brand state" includes the ideas of the world on a particular country (HAM, 2001).

The quest for continuous improvement makes the brand grow increasingly. Therefore growing helps convincing that the internal culture is vibrant and engaging.

In a short period of time, Brazil went from anonymity in the fashion world to stand as a pitcher and exporter of professionals and style. Awareness and the work produced the momentum of the country in the global fashion market. This caused the country to go through an economic boom that exceeded the broad limits of the fashion world. As Brazil gets trendy, tons of Brazilian pieces sold abroad with different labels made in

Brazil have their prices multiplied by two to twenty times, depending on the product (Feghali; DWYER, 2004).

To conquer the international space, it's no use being only a successful brand. Sometimes you have to adapt to the market you want to export to. A piece of clothing that is successful in Brazil will not always have the same impact in another country for various reasons such as weather, customs, cultures, religions, etc. An example of this adaptation is the Cecilia Prado brand, which focuses on the production of longer dresses for the Middle East market. (CAMERA, AND SALVADOR PIZAIA, 2007).

**What the Brazilian government has done to collaborate with the expansion of the Brazilian fashion industry abroad?**

Government assistance relating to the shares of Apex-Brazil primarily provides funds for the development projects of the Agency (BRAZIL, 2003). For the apparel industry, there are two specific sectorial projects: Project + B (Integrated Sector Project for Internationalization of Brazilian Fashion), which was established in 2003, in partnership with the Brazilian Association of Fashion Designers - ABEST – and aims to increase exports of branded products to markets such as China, the United States and France, as in the design of ABEST are countries that represent the Asian market, the United States and Europe, where there are partnerships with local commercial agents - who are responsible for negotiating the Brazilian products with distributors such as networking department and other retail stores -; and TEXBRASIL Program (Strategic Program of the Brazilian Textile Chain), created in 2000, in partnership with the Brazilian Association of Textile and Clothing Industry - ABIT – which aims to prepare companies in the textile and apparel industry interested in marketing their products in other countries, for markets such as Argentina, Australia, China, Colombia, United Arab Emirates, United States, France, Peru, Dominican Republic and the United Kingdom - countries with which Brazil has signed bilateral trade agreements related to this area, or participating in negotiation integration and economic complementation (APEX, 2013; TEXBRASIL 2013). Project + B promotes the export of Brazilian clothing products to partners abroad, through the unification of actions for the internationalization of each company, and also provides opportunities for the participation of these companies in international fairs. The TEXBRASIL program also promotes the export and internationalization of clothing companies, preparing them for this purpose. It also helps the participation in international fairs and presentation to buyers and journalists from international fashion. The difference between the two is that companies not associated with ABIT can join TEXBRASIL, while only companies associated with ABIT and ABEST can participate in the Project + B (APEX, 2013; TEXBRASIL 2013).

# STRATEGIES AND KNOWLEDGE REQUIRED FOR THE NATIONAL PRODUCT INTERNATIONALIZATION

The garment industry has faced difficulties and obstacles with the exchange rate policy, high interest rates, huge taxes, logistics problems and unfair Chinese competition are factors that hinder industry growth. However, the quality of design, technology, factories, professionalism, responsibility to environment and social concerns adopted by Brazilian companies have cornered more space in national and international markets. (CAMERA, AND SALVADOR PIZAIA, 2007).

Still, according to the authors, the process of internationalization of companies focuses on the establishment of the basic assumptions of international strategy, industrial innovation, and business strategies of foreign direct investment. The internationalization strategy of the company has to be crafted initially by sales agents and distributors, and then establish a physical presence in the country in which you want to incur. This slow introduction overseas market is due to the high cost of installation on foreign country. There are expenses concerning market research, preparation of the distribution network, product storage, transportation logistics and fulfillment of technical requirements or specific market demands. Failure of an internationalized company represents a significant loss of foreign investment. (Garcia, 2005).

Being present on the international market requires planning and implementation of a set of actions that, in turn, are part of the company's strategic planning. This planning requires organization, the company's mission definition in the target market, determining the objectives and goals to be achieved, assessment of opportunities and difficulties, analysis of the behavior of these new consumers, identifying and evaluating competitors, positioning the company in the new market, identification of trading partners and sales offices (showrooms, representatives) and their requirements, advisory press and dissemination costs (advertisements, press days and events). Furthermore it is essential not to lose sight of the participation in major fashion events (fashion weeks, trade fairs, among others), the format of the work to be adopted – through own distribution or through partners - the option of opening stores and franchises and setting of the control mechanisms for monitoring these plans. (MANETTI, 2006).

The search of the international market for a Brazilian company cannot simply be motivated by a question of expediency or even exchange of favors because Brazil is fashionable. After all, who can ensure that these factors will last long?

According to Lopez and Gama (2007), it is known that many products have failed in foreign markets because they did not meet the taste and local standards. The cultural distance, spending habits or promotional practices are barriers to overcome. However, one resource is left for the exporter: to adapt the product to the target market.

In markets that are very different from ours, some products may have decreased or even rejected potential sales. These differences may be climatic, social, cultural, or can be related to the availability of local raw materials, the existence of alternative products, lower level of income, the availability of hard currency to make purchasing, government import barriers, among others.

When a product is a sales success in the local market, a strategy for achieving success in exporting is the choice of similar markets abroad. Thus, only minor changes will be needed in the product or maybe none. To meet the expectations of the market, the company puts its product under the same conditions of competition and makes its product more attractive than its competitors (LOPEZ AND GAMMA, 2007).

Web knowledge involves social networking and business that facilitate the internationalization of enterprise networks. The knowledge of the network refers here to the network itself (as the locus of knowledge). Cultural knowledge of a foreign market refers to the knowledge of values, customs and ways of thinking that market.

The business knowledge refers to knowledge of the existence of opportunities and how to explore them.

Opportunity recognition is critical to the survival and growth of the firm. Shane (2004) defines entrepreneurial opportunity as "a situation in which a person can create a new means-ends framework for recombining resources that the entrepreneur believes will yield a profit." Some proposals have been presented to explain the factors that lead to the identification of opportunities. Kirzner (1973) refers to the identification of opportunities as the attention of the entrepreneur, while Shane (2004) proposes two factors behind the recognition of opportunities: absorptive capacity (prior knowledge) and cognitive processes (intelligence). For Baron (2004), opportunity recognition are results of a cognitive process, such as identifying something new with a potential value (Mejri and Umemoto, 2010).

## CONCLUSION

We note that in the current Brazilian scenario the number of companies that specialize and seek a differential for Brazilian products to stand out among foreign products has increased, since competitiveness has been growing and is nowadays crucial for products to have something that differentiates them among others as a rule for survival in the market.

This research sought to discuss the internationalization of companies working in the fashion industry in Brazil, its importance for the country's economy, its features and basic knowledge to run fewer risks in joining a distinguished setting of their national environment.

The concept of internationalization was defined. Internationalization involves taking a product beyond its borders. It means developing a strategic plan so that a particular company can operate in a market that is not its home.

It is observed that this phenomenon is not new since trade between countries is lost in time. The ways of performing this process have been improved and are more recurrent and common today. Taking a national product overseas has become something natural for anyone who has a great business view and knowledge to do such an accomplishment.

The initial section aimed to present the reasons that lead companies to internationalize what the determining factors for choosing the future markets are, and when and how to perform this procedure.

It became clear during the analysis of internationalization that, by venturing into the overseas market, the company can achieve more advantages and benefits than in their place of creation due to the increased competition, the lack of sophistication of consumers, among others. Therefore, it is necessary to have a good company growth strategy, a detailed study of the country in which they intend to invest and good use of the opportunities created in a new market. Among the motivations that lead a company to expand are: monitoring the movement of the client to a new market, geographical, cultural and linguistic proximities, and willingness to grow.

Moreover, it is clear that when deciding to internationalize the company the pros and cons need to be analyzed and evaluated with care since good planning is essential to get the desired results.

The second part brought the main focus of the Brazilian fashion industry and its internationalization. This section was initially assigned to show the numbers in this segment, whether economic or social, the country and the characteristics of companies that operate in this sector.

It is evident that Brazilian product competition with international markets is extremely high. Countries that feature the latest technology, operating in the luxury market for a longer time or countries that excel at low cost tend to stand out and are more attractive in the eyes of customers. However, Brazil has not been intimidated, and has continued its endeavor to remain and expand its share in the international markets. Therefore, stamping a Brazilian brand to the products has been key. Bringing consumers a product that is differentiated and at the same time does not remove the features of the Brazilian people has been crucial, since it becomes attractive for many. However, it is worth remembering that sometimes it is necessary to adapt the product to the market that you want to target, either in terms of climate or culture, among others.

This persistence has allowed the Brazilian producer to work with products that meet the most diverse clients, which has contributed to the distinct brand names to gain space outside the country, since it has invested in quality and design, as well as only developing products that conquer demanding consumers.

We noticed that in a short period of time, Brazil came out of the anonymity and was released as an exporter of fashion professionals and style.

The third and final section deals with the international insertion strategies and knowledge that a particular company should have to obtain in order to achieve international success.

Internationalization cannot be purely and simply motivated by the desire to become internationally known. There should be a thorough study, which will help the business achieve its goals. Setting goals and making a detailed planning is of paramount importance. Thus, the following should be evaluated: the target market, the behavior of new consumers, the opportunities and difficulties, culture, business partners, marketing practices, among others.

Among the primordial types of knowledge necessary to internationalize a company are market and cultural knowledge and business networking. Recalling Cunha (2011), the contributions of knowledge management are presented as a viable way, so that companies can overcome existing barriers and strengthen its presence in the international market path, besides it being fundamental to achieve a more sustainable internationalization and take fewer risks.

At the end of this article, we can highlight that Brazil has increasingly devoted itself to conquer external customers and trying to go beyond their limits. Arriving in an overseas market is not a task we consider easy and it requires hard work, but it sure will be worth it, since the benefits of entering the international market can be huge and positively affect the national economy when successful.

# REFERENCES

ABIT – Associação Brasileira de Indústria Têxtil e de Confecção. Disponível em<*www. abit.org.br/*|>.

ABEST – Associação Brasileira de Estilistas. Disponível em <*www.abest.com.br/*|> .

ABRANTES, A. A internacionalização empresarial numa economia mundializada. *Milllenium, 15.* 1999.

AFIUNE, C. D. **História da moda Brasileira**. Centro Universitário Feevale – ICET – Desing de Moda e Tecnologia. Novo Hamburgo, 24/06/2008. Disponível em <http:// www.slideshare.net/carolafiune/portiflio-histria-da-modabrasileira#btnNext>.

TEXBRASIL.Serviços. 2013. Disponívelem :<http://www.texbrasil.com.br/ texbrasil/Servico.aspx?tipo=24&pag=1&nav=0&tela=Servico> .

ALMEIDA, André (Org.). **Internacionalização de empresasbrasileiras:**perspectivas e riscos. Rio de Janeiro: Elsevier: Campus, 2007.

ANHOLT, Simon. **The Importance of National Reputation**.Foreign and Commonwealth Office, King Charles St, London, 2008.Disponível em: <http://www. simonanholt.com/Publications/publications-other-articles.aspx>.

ASSOCIAÇÃO BRASILEIRA DO VESTUÁRIO. Relatório anual 2010. Disponível em: <http://www.abravest.org.br>.

AVELAR, S. *Moda, globalização e novas tecnologias.* São Paulo: Estação das Letras de Cores, 2009.

BRASIL, H. V.; LEONEL. J. N.; ARRUDA, C.; GOULART, L. **Pesquisa de campo sobre internacionalização das empresas brasileiras**. In:BRASIL;ARRUDA (ends.). Internacionalização de empresas brasileiras. Rio de Janeiro,Qualitynark, 1996.

BRITO, Carlos Melo. **Estratégias de internacionalização e cooperação empresarial**. Faculdade de Economia do Porto. Workingpaper n° 38, 1993.

BRITO, C. e LORGA, S. *Marketing Internacional,* Sociedade Portuguesa de Inovação, Porto – 1999.

BURGARDT, Lilian. **O sucesso da moda brasileira**. Disponível em: <http://www. universia.com.br/materia/materia.jsp?materia=13222>.

CÂMARA, M.; SALVADOR, M.; PIZAIA, M. **Internacionalização de empresas brasileiras do Setor Têxtil**. Disponível em <http://aplicativos.fipe.org.br/enaber/pdf/52.pdf>.

CARNEIRO, Jorge; DIB, Luis Antônio. **Avaliação comparativa do escopo descritivo e explanatório dos principais modelos de internacionalização de empresas.**INTERNEXT – Revista Eletrônica de Negócios Internacionais da ESPM, São Paulo, v. 2, n. 1, p. 1-25, jan./jun. 2007.

CARLSON, S.**How foreign is foreign trade?** Acta Universitatis, StudiaOeconomiaeNegotiorum II, Bulletin 15, Uppsala, Suécia, 1975.

CATEORA, P.R. and GRAHAM, J.L. (1996), *International Marketing*, McGraw–Hill, New York.

CIGNACCO, Bruno Roque. . **Fundamentos de comércio internacional para pequenas e médias empresas**. São Paulo: Saraiva, 2009. 309 p.

CINTRA, R.; MOURÃO, B. **Perspectivas e estratégias na internacionalização de empresas brasileiras.** Focus RI Assessoria e Consultoria em Relações Internacionais. São Paulo, 2005. Disponível em: <http://www.focusri.com.br/artig7.htm>.

CHETTY, S. **Dimensionsofinternationalizationofmanufacturingfirms in theapparelIndustry.**EuropeanJournalof Marketing, v. 33, n. 1/2, p. 121-42, 1999.

CLETO, Marcelo Gechele. **Proposta de estruturação da transferência de tecnologia intra-firma para produção no exterior em empresa brasileira:** o caso da Metal Leve S.A. Florianópolis: UFSC, 1996. (Tese de Doutorado) – Universidade Federal de Santa Catarina.

CUNHA, Camilla Sara Gonçalves. **O processo de internacionalização de micro e pequenas empresas sob a ótica do conhecimento**. (Dissertação de Mestrado). Universidade Católica de Brasília, 2011.

CZINKOTA, M., Ronkainen, I.,Moffett, M. (1999), *International Business*, The Dryden Press, 5th Edition, Orlando.

DIAS, Manuela Cristina. **A internacionalização e os fatores de competitividade: o caso Adira**. Porto, 2007. Dissertação (Mestrado em Economia). Faculdade de Economia, Universidade do Porto.

FEGHALI, Marta Kasznar; DWYER, Daniela. **As Engrenagens da Moda**. Rio de Janeiro: Ed. Senac Rio, 2004.

FERRARI, Beatriz. **Moda brasileira quer brilhar além das passarelas**. Disponível em: <http://veja.abril.com.br/noticia/economia/moda-brasileira-luta-para-brilhar-alem-daspassarelas>.

FREYRE, G. *Modos de Homem & Modas de Mulher*. 2ª ed. São Paulo: Global, 2009.

GARCIA, Renato. **Internacionalizaçãocomercial e produtivanaindústria de cosméticos:**desafioscompetitivos para empresasbrasileiras. Disponívelem: <http://www.scielo.br/scielo.php?pid=s010365132005000200003&script=sci_arttext>.

GONÇALVES, Antonio; KOPROWSKI, Sido. O. Pequena empresa no Brasil. São Paulo: EDUSP 1995.

HAM, Peter van.**The Rise of the Brand State**. Foreign Affairs set./out. 2001. Disponível em: <http://www.foreignaffairs.com/articles/57229/peter-van-ham/the-rise-of-the-brand-state>.

HILAL, Adriana, HEMAIS, Carlos A. **O Processo De Internacionalização Na Ótica Da Escola Nórdica:** Evidências Empíricas Em Empresas Brasileiras . RAC – Revista de Administração Contemporânea.v. 7, n.1, jan., fev. e mar. 2003.

_____. **O Processo De Internacionalização segundo a Escola Nórdica**. In: In: ROCHA, Ângela. A Internacionalização das Empresas Brasileiras: Estudos de Gestão Internacional. 1.ed. Rio de Janeiro: EditoraMauad, 2002.

HYMER, Stephen. **Empresasmultinacionais: Ainternacionalização do capital.** [Rio de Janeiro]: Graal, [1978]. 118 p.

KEEDI, Samir. . **ABC do comércio exterior:** abrindo as primeiras páginas. 3. ed São Paulo: Aduaneiras, 2007. 174 p.

KOTABE, Masaaki; HELSEN, Kristiaan. **Administração de marketing global.** São Paulo: Atlas, 2000. 709 p.

LIMA, Thais Tolentino de.**Internacionalização de empresasbrasileiras:**Estudo de caso Arezzo. Centro Universitário de Belo Horizonte – UniBH, 2010

LOPEZ, José Manoel Cortiñas; GAMA, Marilza. **Comércio exterior competitivo**. 2. ed. São Paulo: Aduaneiras, 2005. 466 p.

LUDOVICO, Nelson. **Exportação:** você está preparado?: Vamos eliminar a interrogação!. São Paulo: STS, 2008. 168p.

MANETTI, A. Oportunidade no mercado internacional para empresas brasileiras dentro do segmento da moda.*In*: Anais do 2º. Colóquio Nacional de Moda, Salvador, BA, de 03-06 out/2006.

MANSUR Elisa de Rooij. **Internacionalização da moda:**Estudo de caso da Osklen. PUC – Rio, 2011.

MEJRI,K.;UMEMOTO,K.**Smallandmedium-sizeenterpriseinternationalization:** Towards the knowledge-based model. Journal of International Enterepreneurship.p. 156-167, 2010.

MELIN, Leif. **Internationalization As A Strategy Process**. Strategic Management Journal, 13, p. 99-118, 1992.

MINERVINI, Nicola. **O exportador.** 3.ed São Paulo: Makron Books, 2001. 394 p.

_____. **O exportador:** ferramentas para atuar com sucesso nos mercados internacionais. 4. ed. São Paulo: Prentice-Hall, 2005. CD-ROM

MIRANDA, Maria Bernadete e MALUF, Clovis Antônio. **O contrato de** joint venture **como instrumento jurídico de internacionalização de empresas.**

NEIRA, Luz Garcia. A invenção da moda brasileira.Caligrama – Revista de estudos e pesquisas em linguagem e mídia. Vol. 4, no 1, Jan/Abr. 2008.

NOSÉ JUNIOR, Amadeu. **Marketing internacional:** uma estratégia empresarial. São Paulo: Thomson, 2005. 323 p.

PINTO, Marcelo M. B. **Frombasictofashion in theapparelindustry:** a studyaboutupgrading in valuechains. 2011. 229 f. Tese (Doutorado) – Universidade do Vale do Rio dos Sinos, São Leopoldo, 2011.

PINTO, Marcelo Machado Barbosa e SOUZA, YedaSwirski de.**A internacionalização de empresas que produzem valor intangível:** uma investigação sobre uma empresa brasileira de moda praia. REDIGE v. 2, n. 3, dez. 2011.

PORTO, Thiago Farias. Softpower and nation branding: the international projection of Brazil's image (2001-2012). Trabalho de Conclusão de Cursoapresentado à UniversidadeCatólica de Brasília, 2012.

POTTER, Evan Harold. **Branding Canada: Projecting Canada's Soft Power through Public Diplomacy.**Canadá: McGill-Queen's Press - MQUP Canada, 2009.

RECH, Sandra Regina. **QualidadenaCriação e Desenvolvimento do Produto de ModanasMalhariasRetilíneas.**Em    http://teses.eps.ufsc.br/defesa/pdf/4279.pdf, Florianópolis, 2001.

RODRIK, Dani. **Estratégias de desenvolvimento para o novo século.** In: ARBIX, G. et alii. (Org.). Brasil, México, África do Sul, Índia e China. Diálogo entre os que chegaram depois. São Paulo: Edusp/Unesp, 2002.

ROOT, F.R. (1982), **"WhyEveryCompanyNeeds a Strategy for Global Competition?"**, *Management Review*, 71 (5), p. 34

SALOMON, R.and SHAVER, J. M. (2005), **"ExportandDomestic Sales: TheirInterrelationshipandDeterminants"**, *Strategic Management Journal*, 26, pp. 855–871.

SARQUIS, José BuainainSarquis. **Comércio Internacional e Crescimento Econômico no Brasil**, FUNAG – Brasília, 2011.

SAUVANT, K. **O investimento direto estrangeiro dos BRIC** (Brasil, Rússia, Índia e China) no exterior. In: ALMEIDA, A. **Internacionalização de Empresas Brasileiras**. Rio de Janeiro: Elsevier. 2007. p.37-77.

SINA, Amalia. **Marketing global:** soluções estratégicas para o mercado brasileiro. São Paulo: Saraiva, 2008. 361p.

SILVA, José Ultemarda.**Gestão das relações econômicas internacionais e comércio exterior.** São Paulo: Cengagelearning, 2008. 200p.

SEBRAE – Serviço Brasileiro de Apoio às Micro e Pequenas Empresas. Disponível em <*www.sebrae.com.br/*□ >.

SILVA, José Ultemarda.**Gestão das relações econômicas internacionais e comércio exterior.** São Paulo: Cengagelearning, 2008. 200p.

SILVEIRA, C. G.; PINHEIRO, O. J.; GOYA, C. R. *CaupéJóias* – Projeto de Pesquisa em Design de Joalheria: *da Brasilidade à Sustentabilidade. In*: V CIPED, Bauru, SP, 10-12 de out/2009.

SIMÕES, V. C. (1997), A Internacionalização das Empresas Industriais Portuguesas: Características e Perspectivas, Conselho Económico e Social, Fev. 1997.

TEIXEIRA, S. e DIZ, H. (2005), **Estratégias de Internacionalização**, Publisher Team, Lisboa.

TEXBRASIL.Serviços. 2013. Disponívelem : <http://www.texbrasil.com.br/texbrasil/Servico.aspx?tipo=24&pag=1&nav=0&tela=Servico>.

VICENTE, Décio Pereira. **Criação e desenvolvimento de produtos em empresas brasileiras de moda internacionalizadas.** (Dissertação de Mestrado) – Universidade de São Paulo, Ribeirão Preto, 2009.

WELCH, L.; LUOSTARINEN, R. **Internationalization: evolutionof a concept.** Journalof General Management, v. 14, n.2, p. 34-55, 1988.

WELCH, L. e PACIFICO, A. (1990), **Management Contracts**: A Role in Internationalization, International Marketing Review, Vol. 7, No. 4, pp. 64-74

# DEVELOPMENT OF AMERICAS DURING THE POLITICAL EMANCIPATION

George Henrique de Moura Cunha
Adrilane Batista de Oliveira
Luiz Alberto Macedo Carvalho

## INTRODUCTION

The institutional hypothesis states that some societies are organized to support the rule of law. This hypothesis also argues that the institutions are a set of rules and regulations that determine the incentives and constraints of a society. As mechanisms of social regulation, institutions may be economic or political, as in the case of companies and electoral systems. They can also be formal and codified as a written constitution or *common law*[11] . (ROBINSON *apud in* FUKUYAMA, 2008)

Among the institutional key elements could be highlighted: Respect for landowner rights laws, restrictions over the actions of elites and equality of opportunities in order to ensure a fair play, private investments and boost the economy. The historical evidence found in the Americas renders the most viable institutional hypothesis to explain the discrepancies between the United States and Latin America. While the Portuguese and Spanish American institutions have limited the regional development, the opposite happened on the thirteen colonies. The English colonization has always encouraged innovation, technological development, enhancing local institutions (democracy), the use of emerging technology from the industrial revolution. The model of organization and functioning of current institutions, despite the profound changes after independence, has its origins in the colonial period. The continuity of these institutions was maintained due to power distribution and political balance strategies. Examples of maintenance of institutional structures: Control of El Salvador by 14 families, the inalterability of colonial bloodlines between owners and elites in Costa Rica, the oligarchy of landowners in the Northeast of Brazil, the Creel dynasty in Mexico and the domain of Liberal Conservative parties for 150 years in Colombia. Even after the formal democratization and changes in political institutions, these elites remained in political power and continued to determine the economic institutions. (ROBINSON *apud in* FUKUYAMA, 2008)

---

11 Common Law

The role of institutions established by the metropolises in the development of the colonies is the subject of discussion in current debates about the differences in the economic trajectories of the United States and Latin America. The main question is whether the underdevelopment of the colonies is due only to the institutions or the historical accidents of every nation are elements that must also be included in this analysis.

Assigning the current problems of the Americas to malformation of institutions during the colonial period is anachronistic and is a weak argument. Other historical events also had an impact on socio institutional formation in the region, such as slavery and other forms of forced labor, the formation of local executive power and its performance. These events have had crucial importance in supporting Latin American balance. (ROBINSON *apud in* FUKUYAMA, 2008)

For example, the American Constitution, despite suffering amendments over time to abolish slavery, allow the vote of women and raising taxes, has been in force for over two hundred years. But this notion of constitutional stability does not cooperate with the comparative development.

The aim of this study is to describe the role of institutions in economic formation of the main countries of the Americas during the political period of independence between the eighteenth and nineteenth centuries.

## THE ROLE OF INSTITUTIONS ON THE INDEPENDENCE PROCESS

The great colonial expansion of the fifteenth century led to the creation of many different colonies by Europeans, some successful and others not. The institutions established in the American colonies were controlled by small Europeans groups that were aimed at own benefit. The European colonization model had overexploitation on the its basic foundation, with economies based on the export of primary goods, use of slave labor and high taxation of the local population. Institutions that would ensure equality, human rights, justice and other social demands would hinder the explorer plan for the region and therefore have not been installed.

In regions where the implementation of the operating model was impossible, institutions were introduced to guarantee the landowners rights, as in the case of the thirteen colonies. Different from Iberian colonies, the settlers who established on north of the continent stemmed from societies fragmented by rivalries and wars in Europe. At the beginning of colonization, both North and Latin America, were at the same stage of development. However in America, Spanish population density was higher and some of its companies as Aztec, Inca and Maya, had their own way of social organization, established institutions, advanced agricultural methods, studies in areas of mathematics, astronomy and advanced engineering.

In the nineteenth century, the operating mode of *corregimientos* added to problems in the metropolises (Spanish succession war, French revolution, continental blockade, one of the Portuguese royal families to Brazil in 1808, among others) made the Spanish crown ever more distant from the colony increasing abandonment and encouraging many *creoles* to seek political independence.

The independence processes in the Americas are therefore not fruit of a political initiative or ideologies generated in the colony, but weaknesses and misfortunes from Iberian metropolises within the context of European rivalries and wars. When Spain proved unable to govern their overseas possessions, key figures from the New World explored the void and took power and did not find strong resistance. A constitutional crisis devastated all the colonies in Latin America. The independence were introduced without much commotion, causing surprise to embryonic entities whose purpose was to promote the exchange of Lords. This kind of anarchical negativism provided the *caudilhismo macho* [12](LANDES, 2003).

Latin American institutions were characterized by a lack of direction, unity and nationality. While a mobilization by civil society was insignificant. While a mobilization by civil society was insignificant, governance in general, was assumed by landowners. These landowners were responsible for the police power, provided security, jobs and labor.

In this period, one of the biggest contrasts was the constitutional process that occurred on the occasion of the independence of the United States and Revolt in Mexico. In 1810, the Hidalgo Revolt, led by Father Miguel Hidalgo, was responsible for shaping the political demands made by the Mexican elite. When Guanajuato was plundered, the rebels stood to indiscriminately kill all white people. It was another class war, or even ethnic, than an independence movement, whose goal was to unite the elite. The possibility of popular participation through political independence was something that was contrary to the interests of political elites. Therefore, Mexican elites viewed the Constitution of Cadiz, which allowed popular participation, with extreme skepticism, and never recognized its legitimacy.

---

12 The *Caudilhismo* was a kind of political regime characterized by grouping a community around a political leader. The *Caudilho* was the highest figure of this regime. A person had full powers, a "father of the nation ', responsible for basic services (health, education, security); was responsible for making improvements, to build what was needed using this privilege to subtract as much as he could of the population.

In 1815, after the return of Fernando VII to the throne, the Constitution of Cadiz was annulled. When they tried to regain control of its colonies in America, the Spanish Crown faced no major problems in Mexico. However, in 1820, Hispanic troops were gathered in Cadiz to restore Spanish authority, mutinied against King Fernando VII. The national army joined the movement and King Ferdinand VII found himself compelled to restore the Constitution of Cadiz and again convene the constituent assembly, which was more liberal proposing, including the abolition of slavery. The constituent assembly also attacked the special privileges such as the right of the military to be tried in its own criminal courts. Faced by this document, the Mexican elites decided to continue supporting the independence movement.

Augustin de Iturbide, leader of the independence movement, published in 1821 the Iguala Plan which presented a vision of an independent Mexico. The plan included a constitutional monarchy and removed the provisions of the Cadiz Constitution pleasing local elites.

The independence project received prompt support and immediately Iturbide organized the Mexican secession. Benefiting of its position in the movement and the weakness of political institutions Iturbide became emperor and quickly, a dictator. In October 1822, he dissolved the Congress sanctioned by the Constitution and replaced by a board of his choice. Although Iturbide has not resisted in power, this kind of events would be repeated several times in Mexico on the nineteenth century.

In the same period, England reassessed its policy for the continent. In an attempt to increase its influence in Latin America, British troops invaded Buenos Aires in 1806. The *Porteña* population showed no willingness to make the switch from Spanish domain by the British and expelled the British soldiers. The English onslaught motivated the *creoles* to fight the invaders, consolidating resistance to new invasions. Being an important maritime trading center, Buenos Aires was exposed to external, intellectual and economic influences. The agro pastoral base of its economy also aroused both the landed interests as the commercial speculators who were aware of the benefits of freer trade. (BETHELL, 2001)

The settlers waited for the right moment to achieve independence. And this happened in 1808, when Napoleon deposed the Spanish royal house and his brother Joseph Bonaparte was elevated to the Hispanic throne. England received special privileges because, "he had saved Brazil" for the Portuguese crown. These privileges were incorporated into treaties negotiated by Lord Strangford in 1810, which established preferential tariffs for British goods and special legal rights to British merchants. At the same time, the Portuguese pressured the British and agreed to limit the transatlantic slave trade to Brazil, with a view to their gradual abolition. Strangford, almost inevitably, also became involved with the issues of the Plata region. Before the revolution of 1810, he negotiated with the viceroy the opening of Buenos Aires to the English trade; later, when the revolutionary government declared their loyalty to Fernando VII, he was able to maintain informal relations with the government without violating the Anglo-Spanish alliance. The situation across the river is a little more complex, in Uruguay. In September 1808 a joint government was established in Montevideo, led by the Spanish governor and was intended to take Uruguay, not from the domain of Seville, but from the Viceroy of Liniers, accused of Bonapartist tendencies, which dissolved as soon as Seville Liniers replaced by a peninsular reliable, Baltasar Hidalgo de Cisneros. While it lasted, the joint of Montevideo received considerable local support, mainly because it appealed to the feelings of political and commercial rivalry with Buenos Aires.

In 1809, the attempt to create a joint in Buenos Aires was also a target for Liniers. One of his first creators was Martin de Alzaga, a wealthy peninsular merchant, who managed the *cabildo* against the British invasions and headed now an important local political faction. This faction covered the native Spanish and prominent Creoles as Mariano Moreno, a lawyer who later headed the radical wing of the revolution in Río de la Plata. Even if Alzaga has been accused of republicanism by their enemies, the only clear goal of the group was to unseat Liniers, or for personal reasons, suspicion of disloyalty, or for new political possibilities. The coup attempt was failed because Liniers had the support from the vice-regal bureaucracy and *creole* militia, which was quite satisfied with the position he had reached under the aegis of the viceroyalty. Montevideo remained loyal to the Spanish Regency until 1814, but its interior was led by Uruguayan patriots who refused to accept the government authority of Buenos Aires. Strangford tried to preserve the English neutrality between these groups and at the same time contain the Portuguese who coveted the Spanish province.

## ARGENTINA

Buenos Aires was during this period, one of the most politically active centers. The most important political event was the "May Revolution" of 1810, where Viceroy Cisneros (Liniers successor) accepted grudgingly to keep a *cabildo aberto*[13] that delegated to the *cabildo* to compose a joint. However, before the joint could work, protests emerged, organized by commanders of creole militia and others who saw in the Spanish monarchy crisis an opportunity to make changes in the colony. The rebels won and on May 25 a joint was formally established that did not include the viceroy and was chaired by Colonel Cornelio Saavedra, a merchant from Alto Peru but long established in Buenos Aires.

---

13 Open Cabildo

This period of revolutions and changes did not mean legal or institutional innovations. The opening of the port to trade, continued as the Viceroy Cisneros had previously established on a provisional basis, having been proposed by the joint no innovation. Equality policies have been implemented and gave mestizos the same rights as other members of society. The rhetoric of egalitarianism enthused and encouraged the population to combat privileges of royals and peninsular Spaniards, who began to suffer discrimination in public employment and in the calculation of their contributions. The audience judges were exiled for suggesting that the board should recognize the Regency Council of Spain, which was replaced by a new Supreme Court.

In 1810, an even more harsh treatment was directed to those involved in an attempt against the revolution. This occurred in Cordoba, where the judiciary has positioned contrary to the requirements from Buenos Aires joint. Among the rebels of Cordoba was the hero of Buenos Aires defense against British troops, Santiago Liniers, who had moved to other cities after he left the post of viceroy in 1809. Despite its importance, Liniers was executed with other leaders of the movement.

A good reference of this revolutionary movement was Mariano Moreno, in charge of the joint official newspaper, the *Gaceta de Buenos Aires*. Moreno used its pages to prepare public opinion to accept broader changes in the future. His articles had a slightly defense of republican government and political independence. In the interior of Argentina, the revolutionary government achieved a political support of local oligarchies, or at least part of them.

> The conflict between political factions did not end with the death of Moreno. The government's joint was fully dissolved in 1811 and was replaced by the First Triumvirate and later by the Second Triumvirate and in 1814 by a Supreme Director. In 1812, aiming to please the English, the slave trade was banned and European immigration was stimulated, causing direct impacts on local trade. The lack of adopting a position in favor of independence, by some sectors of society, including Moreno's followers who founded the Patriotic Society in order to continue the revolutionary process. At the same time the *Loja Lautaro* was founded, an organized secret society in semi Masonic guidelines. Among the founders was José de San Martin, national hero, who was a career officer in the Spanish army. His participation in Lautaro Lodge and in the broader political scenario of the revolution marked the emergence of a new political force: the regular army, whose officers, were mostly from the beginning of the revolution, recruited from the population and were therefore not career soldiers like himself; however were at least serving to balance a largely saavedrista urban advocacy. The union of the political heirs of Moreno, San Martin and other army commanders associated with the Lautaro Lodge, weakened the saavedrista group, which controlled the First Triumvirate, and it was dissolved in October 1812. The Second Triumvirate was an instrument of the Lautaro Lodge and the Constituent General Assembly and became a National Congress in 1813.

As suggested by his title, the Assembly should adopt a constitution for the vice-kingdom, which would be called United Provinces del Rio de la Plata. In practice, this never happened, it did not even reach a declaration of independence, although a symbolic affirmation of national sovereignty was made through acts such as the adoption of its own flag, currency of issue and the creation of a national anthem. A package of reforms was also proclaimed, including a law of free birth, extinction of slavery, the abolition of legal torture and nobility titles, a prohibition on linking real estate and many other measures. These reforms had an anti-clericalist character. The abolition of a weakened and widely discredited Inquisition did not generate much controversy, but the law prohibiting all persons under thirty years to take vows was a serious coup in religious orders and had exactly that purpose. The Legislative Assembly program caused minimal impact on the basic structure of society because the titles of nobility and related assets did not exist or were without strict importance. The effect of the principle of free birth was lower on the institution of slavery than the recruitment of slaves for military service with the promise of freedom if they survived.

## BRAZIL

Not unlike Spain, Portugal was economically isolated in the late eighteenth century, with limited natural resources and modest military and naval power. Brazilian re-exports - mostly sugar and cotton in the eighteenth century - were essential to the equilibrium of Portuguese trade balance. Its main trading partner was England, which provided Portugal - and indirectly Brazil -manufactured products (mainly textiles) in exchange for wine, olive oil - and Brazilian cotton. By treaties dating back to the late fourteenth century, England was also the guarantor of the independence of Portugal and territorial integrity of the Portuguese empire.

Napoleon pressed the Portuguese crown to take part in the Continental System and to break their ties with England, its traditional ally and trading partner. Portugal was in a quandary when the British government affirmed that while he could not protect Portugal, he was determined not to let Brazil stay under the French rule. After much hesitation of the Portuguese royal family, they finally accepted the British offer of a naval escort to Brazil.

Conflicts of interest, economic and political, real and potential, with the metropolis grew. At the same time, at the same time not only the relative economic backwardness from Portugal regarding its most important colony was recognized, but its political and military weakness as well. In the militia, the army in cases of external attack or slave revolt was formed by farmers officers and soldiers who were free men, with the exception of most important cities, where the organization of militia was based on color and occupation.

The rising discontent increased with the permanence of the Portuguese family in Brazil. The Brazilians had much closer ties with the metropolis than others *creoles* in Latin American colonies. The most persistent criticism to Portuguese absolutism and political system imposed to Brazil came from Hipólito José da Costa, who, from June 1808 to 1822, published in London an influential liberal newspaper, the *Correio Brasiliense.* (BETHEL, 2001)

In March 1817, some farmers and slave owners pressed by low profits from exports of cotton and sugar and high prices of the captives, joined to priests, judges, the residents (small farmers tenants and squatters) and artisans in a military revolt that culminated in the proclamation of the Republic of Pernambuco. The constitution of the republic included religious tolerance and the "equal rights", but defended property and slavery. The revolt spread quickly through the states of Alagoas, Paraíba and Rio Grande do Norte, but then lost the empire. England refused to encourage the revolt, since the desire of the English was, after securing the opening of the ports, to maintain the stability and unity of Brazil. Two British merchant ships transformed the blocked Recife by the sea with an army sent from Bahia, loyal to the command of governor Arcos, from Rio de Janeiro, and in May 20, 1817, the rebels surrendered. The 1817 Revolution, which lasted two and a half months, revealed the existence of nationalist and liberal ideas, including the military. Major cities and military units began to be covered with Portuguese troop's repression, sending signals.

Meanwhile in Portugal a liberal-nationalist revolt exploded in the city of Porto with participation of the military and the population. The economic situation was critical. With severe budget problems, Portugal had difficulties to make the payment of civil and military staff.

In 1820, the Liberals formed a provisional joint to govern Portugal and demanded the immediate return of the king to Lisbon. They were quickly to impose the Extraordinary General Courts and Constituents, responsible for writing and approving a new constitution. By the guidelines of November, the courts would be elected for Portugal, choosing one representative for every thirty thousand free citizens. It was expected to be installed in Brazilian captaincies, provisional governing together loyal to the Revolution of Porto, who should supervise the elections to the Courts. The main objective was to restore Brazil to the condition of previous Portuguese colony to 1808.

The struggle against absolutism in Brazil began with the military. In January 1821, the Portuguese troops stationed in Belém rebelled and formed a liberal governing board for the region of Pará, which joined later the states of Maranhão and Piauí. This joint was declared as immediately ready to promote elections for the Courts of Lisbon.

On 10 February, in state of Bahia, with a similar military conspiracy, led by soldiers with liberal tendencies against absolutist officers, ousted the governor Conde de Palma and installed a provisional joint aiming at a liberal constitution for the United Kingdom of Portugal and Brazil. Its members were most Portuguese, but received support from many prominent Brazilians. In Rio de Janeiro, popular demonstrations in favor of the constitutional revolution and a meeting of Portuguese soldiers in the *Largo Rossio*, on February, they forced the king to reformulate the ministry and forced him to approve a liberal constitution for Portugal and Brazil. The king decreed also in line with the instructions of the Provisional Junta of Lisbon, the creation of governing joints in the provinces where there were none and the preparation of indirect elections for the Courts.

Under pressure and with no alternative, Don João VI returned to Lisbon on March 7, 1821 leaving his son, Don Pedro, as Prince Regent, leaving no other alternatives than to defend Brazilian interests in the Courts. After elected, the elite got together in January 1821 and tried to return Brazil to its older colonial status. The Portuguese bourgeoisie tried to establish its hegemony over Brazil and deny to England direct access to its ports, totally ignored the wear suffered by the colonial pact as a result of political, economic and demographic development in Brazil. In addition, the political, ideological and economic changes in Europe and America became very unlikely that among all the European great powers and Portugal was the only one able to keep its colonies in the Americas (BETHELL, 2001 p 214).

In face of the constitutional movements in the states of Pará, Bahia and Rio de Janeiro, and especially with the return of Dom João VI, the courts were avoiding Rio de Janeiro and began to deal directly with the different provincial governments of Brazil. In face of the constitutional movements in the states of Pará, Bahia and Rio de Janeiro, and especially with the return of Dom João VI, the courts was avoiding the Rio de Janeiro and began to deal directly with the different provincial governments of Brazil. In addition, in August, a new contingent of soldiers were sent to Brazil. The Courts have shown their intention to continue ruling Brazil when on September 29, it ordered that all government institutions located in Rio de Janeiro were dismantled and transferred to Lisbon. Finally, on October 18, the Prince Regent was ordered to return to Portugal. When elected Brazilian deputies, who came to the Cortes during the years 1821 and 1822, were met with insults and offenses. All Brazilian intentions to seek economic and political equality with Portugal and creation of parallel agencies of government were rejected by the Court. They also had the notion of Portuguese determination to undo all changes that had taken place in relations between Brazil and Portugal since 1808. These attitudes only increased the indignation of the colony and lit the desire for independence. In October 1822, a group of seven Brazilian deputies left Lisbon illegally, went to London and then returned to Brazil. The act was repeated by the other members as a protest against the policies in Lisbon.

Jose Bonifacio was an important figure in the Brazilian political process. His ideas on social issues were remarkably progressive – it was favorable to abolition of the slave trade and even slavery, he supported the free European immigration and land reform - but, politically, he was conservative and deeply hostile to democracy. Similarly to the Argentinian case, the local elites clashed earlier in the year 1822 through its Masonic lodges (Apostolate and Big East). This conflict, which had an ideological bias or not to convene a constituent assembly involved Jose Bonifacio and Joaquim Gonçalves Ledo radicals as the priest Januário da Cunha Barbosa, Domingos Alves White Muniz Barreto, José Clemente Pereira and Martim Francisco Ribeiro de Andrada.

On February 16, 1822, Jose Bonifacio strongly opposed to the popular representation in the elected national assembly and convinced Dom Pedro that a Council of Provincial Prosecutors composed of citizens appointed was needed according to the traditional procedures. This conviction only lasted 48 hours. On June 3, Don Pedro agreed to convene a constituent assembly. It was decided in May 1822, that no decree of the Portuguese courts would be applied without the approval of the Prince Regent. In August, Don Pedro and the Brazilian Government proclaim several "independent" acts. On September 7, 1822, Dom Pedro received the last orders of Lisbon revoked their decrees, accused their ministers, demanded once again his return to Portugal and the total submission from Brazil to the Portuguese Empire.

The Brazilian movement force for separation from Portugal came from the most important provinces of the Centre-South, São Paulo, Minas Gerais and the capital, Rio de Janeiro. Pernambuco, where the Brazilian ruling class was anti Portuguese, and where there was the revolution in 1817 and the attempted establishment of the republic, which had a small garrison, was willing to transfer its loyalty to Dom Pedro, when the authority of a Brazil was recognized as independent. The other provinces of the Northeast and North, where there still was great Portuguese military presence and a large number of Portuguese communities, who remained loyal to the Lisbon courts

There were fanciful rumors that Portugal would send a punitive expedition and, in a first stage of re-conquest, to try to separate the Northeast and the North from the rest of Brazil. These regions were geographically closer to Portugal, were not integrated economically to the Center-South of Brazil and in many ways had closer historical ties with Lisbon than Rio de Janeiro. For a complete and solid independence process, an avoided civil war and recognition of the new emperor authority over Brazil, it was imperative to attract the Northeast and the North, especially Bahia, the most important of the provinces that still remained under the Portuguese control.

## UNITED STATES AND MEXICO

The only American country that could challenge the British influence in America was the United States because it became independent in time to take advantage of the Industrial Revolution. Free of involvement or commitment to Europe, linked by proximity and feelings of Pan-Americanism and with the informal instrument of an enterprising merchant fleet policy, the young federation was apparently, in 1808, well positioned to take advantage of the weakening of the imperial ties.

In the 1720s', all 13 colonies that came to be the United States took advantage of similar governance structures. In all cases, there was a governor and an assembly representing the landowners. Women and slaves were not part of democracy. Still, political rights were quite large, compared to contemporary societies elsewhere. It was these assemblies and their leaders who met in 1774, in the first Continental Congress - the United States Independence prelude. In its view, the assemblies had both the right to determine its own composition as the right to taxation - which created problems for the British colonial government. The document drafted by delegates in Philadelphia in 1787, was the result of a long process that began with the formation of the General Assembly in 1619.

The United States Constitution did not create a democracy by modern standards. Each state should determine who the voters would be. Thus, while the northern states soon have extended the right to vote to all white men, regardless of their income or property, the south would only gradually show the same prodigality. None of them recognized the rights of women or slaves, and as the whites were being released from the limitations on the property and wealth, racial restrictions were adopted which explicitly ousted blacks of any law. Slavery, of course, was considered legitimate when the US Constitution was written and held the most sordid of negotiations regarding the division of seats in the House of Representatives among the states. The allocation would take place according to the population of each state, but the southern representatives requested that the slaves were counted. The northerners objected. It was agreed that, for the purpose of distribution of seats in the House of Representatives, each slave would count as three-fifths of a free person.

The conflict between the North and the South of the United States were repressed during the constitutional process by compiling pacts how this rule of three-fifths and similar. New settings would be added to over the years, such as the Missouri Agreement, according to which a favorable state to slavery and other scenarios would always be aggregated to the Union, in order to maintain balance in the Senate between the two positions. Thanks to these subterfuges, the political institutions of the United States remained in peaceful operation until the Civil War would resolve conflicts in favor of the North.

The Civil War was bloody and destructive. Both before and after the Civil War, however, there were no economic opportunities for a wide segment of the population, especially in northern and western United States. In Mexico, the situation was different. If the United States experienced five years of political stability, between 1860 and 1865, Mexico experienced a scenario of instability in the first 50 years of its independence, which is best illustrated by the career of Antonio Lopez de Santa Ana.

Santa Ana, the son of a colonial dignitary in Veracruz, stood out as a soldier fighting for the Spanish crown in the wars of independence. In 1821, changed sides with Iturbide and never looked back. He became president of Mexico for the first time in May 1833, but remained in power for less than a month, preferring to let his mandate to Valentin Gomez Farias. Santa Ana Gomez Farias continued their alliance until mid-1835, when Santa Ana was not to resist. Returned to the presidency in 1839, 1841, 1844, 1847 and, finally, between 1853 and 1855. In total, he was president 11 times in the course of which he presided over the loss of the Alamo and Texas and the disastrous Mexican-American War, which led to the loss of what would become the New Mexico and Arizona. Between 1824 and 1867, Mexico had 22 presidents in Mexico, many of whom came to power in ways sanctioned by law.

The consequence of this unprecedented political instability should be obvious to the institutions and economic incentives. Such inconsistency resulted in deep insecurity regarding the right to property, and severe weakening of the Mexican State, which had little authority and ability to raise revenue or to ensure the provision of public services. Indeed, although Santa Ana was president of Mexico, vast portions of the country were not under his control, which allowed the annexation of Texas by the United States.

Furthermore, the driving force behind the Mexican Declaration of Independence was the desire to protect the set of economic institutions developed during the colonial period, which was made in Mexico, in the words of the great explorer and geographer of Latin America, the German Alexander von Humbolt "the country of inequality." Such institutions, which require the exploitation of indigenous peoples and the creation of monopolies, blocked economic incentives and initiatives of the great mass of the population. While the United States began to go through the Industrial Revolution in the early nineteenth century, Mexico impoverished.

A sample of the results: In 1818 there were 338 banks operating in the United States, with total assets of $160 million. In 1914, there was 27,864 banks with total assets of $27.3 billion. Potential American inventors had easier access to capital to create their businesses. This oversupply facilitated access to resources due to the fierce competition among the institutions.

Between 1820 and 1845, only 19% of Americans were patent holders, whose parents had specific training or were from landowner families. During this period, 40% of those who registered a patent only had access to primary or lower levels of education. The United States was in the nineteenth century the most democratic country in political terms and as per the rights of property and innovation. As a counterpoint, Mexico in 1910 only had 42 seats, two of which controlled 60% of the total bank assets. Unlike the United States, Mexican banks had total freedom to charge interest rates that better favored by restricting access to the rich, who used this access to exercise control over the local economy.

## CHURCH: FUNDAMENTAL INSTITUTION IN AMERICAS

The ideological and economic support received by the contenders in the independence struggles in Latin America was offered by the Church. Most of the bishops was peninsular and identified with the interests of Spain. The Crown had the right to appoint bishops, which made them dependent and subordinate to it. There was awareness that the revolution and the liberal ideology represented to the position of the Church on the continent. The clerics whose loyalty to the crown was suspected were called back to the metropolis or simply deprived of their dioceses, as in the case of the Bishop of Caracas, Narciso Coll i Prat, and prelate of Cusco, Jose Perez y Armendáriz. Moreover, in the period between the restoration of Fernando VII in 1814, and the liberal revolution in Spain in 1820, the metropolis appointed 28 of the 42 American dioceses' new bishops with unquestionable political loyalty. (BETHELL, 2001)

The lower clergy, especially the secular, consisted mainly of *creoles* and therefore, although it presented divisions, the whole of the *creole* elite, was more inclined to support the cause of a Spanish American self-government than independence. There was a division, economic and social, between the mass of the parish priests and the ecclesiastical hierarchy and the great virtual monopoly of the peninsulars regarding the highest ecclesiastical offices. In addition, the Bourbon regime attacked the main sources of income (*capellanias* and *fucro eclesiástico* granting priests immunity from the civil justice) increasing dissatisfaction of the clergy.

Some priests played an important role in the struggle for Spanish American independence, emphasizing Miguel Hidalgo y Costilla and Jose Maria Morelos in New Spain, which induced to popular devotion, especially with the indigenous folk, to proclaim the Virgin of Guadalupe as the patron saint of Spanish-American revolution. In Quito, three priests were responsible for the proclamation of independence in 1809 and, in 1814, a list drawn up by a realistic general related over a hundred priests among the patriots. In Santa Fe de Bogota, three priests were part of the 1810 joint and nine priest participated in the 1811 Congress. In 1815, more than a hundred priests, including Hidalgo and Morelos, had been executed in Mexico. Many others, secular and regular, had been excommunicated. Sixteen priests signed the Declaration of Independence of Rio de la Plata and thirteen, the Declaration of Guatemala. In Peru, 26 of the 57 Members of Congress from 1822 were priests. The papacy had maintained its traditional alliance with the Spanish Crown against the liberal revolution, especially in the papacy of Leo XII during the period of revolutions and wars in favor of Spanish American independence. With consequent defeat, the political mistake made by the institution also evidenced the internal problems within the Church.

The Catholic Church in Spanish America emerged from the extremely weakened independence struggles. The links between the crown and the church had been so narrow that the fall of the monarchy was a serious blow to the prestige of the church throughout Spanish America. The intellectual position of the Church has been shaken. The same intellectuals who rejected the absolute monarchy also challenged the revealed religion, or at least appeared to do it. In the construction of a new political system, the

heads of independence movements sought a moral legitimacy to those who did and found inspiration, not in the Catholic political thought, but in philosophy, particularly on utilitarianism[14]

The influence of Bentham[15] in Spanish America represented a clear threat to the Church, because it gave intellectual credibility to republicanism and offered an alternative philosophy of life. The Church reacted, not through an intellectual debate, for which he was unprepared, but by a request to the State to abolish the enemies of religion. It is therefore, an alliance between Church and State.

It is not clear how much the ecclesiastical structures below the level of the episcopate had been disintegrated. Some members of the clergy died; others returned to Spain. In many places, the discipline was relaxed because of the sectarian character of the war - and the loss of contact with Rome. In general, in the post-revolutionary period

---

14 Economic doctrine based on the assumption that the actions are good when they tend to promote happiness and bad when they tend to promote the opposite
15 Jeremy Bentham was a leading proponent of utilitarianism

a religious vocation apparently became less attractive. It is possible that the Church had lost 50 percent of its secular clergy, and an even greater loss than the regular. In Mexico, for example, the number of secular clergy decreased from 4229 in 1810 to 2282 in 1834. The regular clergy decreased from 3,112 in 1810 to 1,726 in 1831. In the Franciscan province of Lima, the annual average of ordered declined from 6.9 in the three decades of 1771-1800, to 5.3 (1801-1820), 2.3 (1811-1820) and no one between 1821 and 1837. In a year after the proclamation of the Republic in Bolivia, 25 of the 41 convents of the country had closed its doors - although in this case, the hostile legislation of Bolivar and Sucre has contributed to this. (BETHEL, 2001)

The economic assets of the Church were seriously weakened by the expulsion of the Jesuits in 1767, the confiscation and sale of their properties and threatened earlier by the *Consolidação* decree from December 1804, which provided for an appropriation by the state from property and capital of the Church, was damaged even greater during the wars of independence. From Mexico to Buenos Aires, realist and patriots governments, while proclaiming their devotion to the Faith, required the aid from the Church, in a series of emergency measures, money, tithe income, buildings, land, cattle and even sometimes objects of worship.

The governments of the newly independent Spanish American republics recognized Catholicism as the state religion, but at the same time often adopted the principle of religious tolerance. The Inquisition was abolished as Protestantism was introduced by newly arrived foreigners. The consequence of this divergence between liberals and church was the transformation of this issue into a political focal point throughout Spanish America, particularly in Mexico where a major civil war emerged (1850-1860).

## CONCLUSION

Through the period and historical facts discussed, there is evidence of significant and expressive influence of poor institutional formation in economic, political and social problems existing in the Latin American continent. Therefore, it is essential to highlight two key institutions for inclusion of citizens in society: Political rights and income inequality. A good argument is that political rights promote development by protecting property rights and thus inducing investment or stimulating the demand for public goods, including productive public goods. The formal restrictions for free males were phased out in the United States around 1830, and the former freed slaves legally acquired that right in 1869, but as the regulation of elections was the prerogative of the state governments and American law always required registration voluntary, the fact that restrictions were always present. Women, in turn, obtained the right to vote in 1919. In Latin America, the male vote was generally restricted at first by a requirement of home ownership or income, and subsequently by the requirement of literacy in order to specifically exclude farm workers.

# REFERENCES

ACEMOGLU, Daron. **Por que as Nações Fracassam: as origens do poder, da prosperidade e da pobreza**. Rio de Janeiro: Elsevier,2012.

BETHELL, Leslie. **História da América Latina**. Volume III. São Paulo: EdUSP, 2001

COATSWORTH, John H. **Economic and International Trajectories in Nineteenth-Century Latin America**". Cambridge: Harvard University Press, 1998.

DONGHI, Tulio Halperin. **Dois séculos de Reflexões Sul-americanas sobre a Lacuna de Desenvolvimento entre os Estados Unidos e a América Latina**. In: FUKUYAMA, Francis. Ficando Para Trás: explicando a crescente distância entre a América Latina e os Estados Unidos. Rio de Janeiro: Editora Rocco, 2008.

FUKUYAMA, Francis. **Ficando Para Trás: explicando a crescente distância entre a América Latina e os Estados Unidos**. Rio de Janeiro: Editora Rocco, 2008

HANKE, Lewis, org. **History of Latin American Civilization: Sources and Interpretations**, vol. 2: The Modern Era. Londres: Methuen & Co Ltd London, 1967.

KRAUZE, Henrique. **Olhando para Eles: Uma Perspectiva Mexicana sobre a Lacuna em Relação aos Estados Unidos**. In: FUKUYAMA, Francis. Ficando Para Trás: explicando a crescente distância entre a América Latina e os Estados Unidos. Rio de Janeiro: Editora Rocco, 2008.

LANDES, David S. **Riqueza e a Pobreza das Nações: Por Que Algumas São Tão Ricas e Outras São Tão Pobres**. São Paulo: Editora Elsevier, 2008.

ROBINSON, James. O equilíbrio Latino-americano. In: FUKUYAMA, Francis. **Ficando Para Trás: explicando a crescente distância entre a América Latina e os Estados Unidos**. Rio de Janeiro: Editora Rocco, 2008.

# INTERNATIONAL LAW OF PROTECTION IN CASE OF DISASTER RESPONSE

Marcelo Leandro Pereira Lopes[16]
Sarah Maria Veloso Freire Lopes[17]

## INTRODUCTION

Since the disappearance of Sodom-Gomorrah and the destruction in Pompeii, big disasters populate the human imagination, which first gives them a punishment justification of the divine will. Over time, the human inability to deal with major disasters gradually developed a model of solidarity among people.

With the end of World War II (1939-1945), at international level, the individual elevation occurred due to the principle of human dignity, of actor status in international law. Because of the atrocities committed by the Nazi Holocaust, human beings received in 1848 special attention of United Nations through the Declaration of Human Rights.

Thus, the expansion of human rights protection developed in post-war eventually received international nature and, to obtain effective protection, it was necessary to develop cooperation between people and new patterns, so the concept of state sovereignty had to be adopted.

Recently, due to the many catastrophes that have generated international impact, numerous States and International Organizations have intensified discussions in view of building norms that deal about the disaster response. International aid frameworks are being regulated, and suitable alternatives to facilitate and regulate foreign aid are being developed more and more.

---

16 Doctoral candidate in Constitutional Law at the University of Fortaleza - UNIFOR. Master in Law from the Catholic University of Brasilia - UCB. Specialist in Constitutional Law from UFPI.
17 Master's Degree in Law at the Catholic University of Brasilia (in progress). College Professor.

International assistance in the event of disasters of large proportions has become decisive and can mean the most effective and quick recovery of the state or even the difference between life and death of those affected. In such cases, the creation of a model law to establish a framework of regular help and reinforce a legal preparation of a State, has been instrumental in the implementation of international assistance.

Thereby, this paper aims to analyze the possibility of intervention or the obligation of intervention, through the use of force for humanitarian purposes, to send and receive international assistance in case of disasters, as well as the possibility of a country adopting a managerial normative model of application of international aid operations, without breaking international principles such as sovereignty and self-determination of the people. For such, the bibliographical and exploratory method was used through documentary analysis of national and foreign legislation (domestic laws and international treaties) and pre-existing data (secondary data collection).

At first, the principles currently governing international relations were highlighted as fundamental for the assistance and development of normative instruments of international cooperation. After that the intensification of natural disasters, the impacts and the importance of the study in Brazil were addressed. Then, it led to the analysis of the Disaster Response Program and the Brazilian foreign legislation on the subject, concluding with the right to protect and its compatibility with the principles of International Law.

Soon after, the International Law of Disaster Response of IDRL (International Disaster Response Laws, Rules and Principles) was addressed, basically its emergence, action fronts and the countries that had already adopted model laws, highlighting yet the correlation of subsistence between sovereignty and intervention for international assistance.

Finally, it was claimed that, in order to reconcile and preserve principles such as non-intervention and sovereignty, IDRL must have the character of subsidiarity, being applied only in cases in which the affected State resources are not sufficient to combat the consequences of the disaster, and that the assistance is provided only by International Organizations.

## GOVERNING PRINCIPLES OF INTERNATIONAL LAW RELATIONS

The Constitution of the Federative Republic of Brazil of 1988 - CF / 88, in its article 4th and sections expressly addresses several principles that should govern the country in its international relations, foremost among them: national independence, prevalence of human rights, non-intervention, and defense of peace and cooperation of the people for the progress of humanity.

National independence is the first principle listed in article 4 of CF/88, basis of the other governing principles of international relations that are intertwined with sovereignty itself, as Crippa (2011) adds. In this path, Reale (*apud* CRIPPA, 2011, p.19) conceptualizes sovereignty as "the power to legally organize and enforce within its territory the universality of decisions within the limits of ethnic coexistence purposes", with the intention of self-organization and imposing its decisions. However, national independence, or even sovereignty, as recognized by the aforementioned author, is no longer recognized absolutely as in the traditional pattern, and currently find limits, mainly guided by the protection of human rights.

Therefore, human rights must be strictly respected by States, establishing a relation of solidarity between them and a sense of universal fraternity.

Bechara (2011, p. 134) emphasizes that

> Both international treaties signed up by States as national constitutions reflect the new configuration of sovereignty, qualified as the necessary measure to achieve peace and a better international harmony ordering. Sovereignty is the emanation center of concrete force that ensures the plurality, peace and state policy unit, not a rigidly ordered project or a power center to which everything converges, but a compromise of possibilities.

Bechara (2011, p. 135) adds that even the change of sovereignty conception, from the recognition of the value of solidarity, by the universal normative standard of human rights, did not empty its contents or subtracted from each State the autonomy and the self-determination capacity, because when it comes to international legal assistance, the respect for sovereignty reflects the possibility of control of foreign public acts of judicial character by national bodies.

The prevalence of human rights is another among the main principles governing the State in international relations, even limiting the excessive internal action of the State itself, indicating the constitutional recognition of the values inherent to human dignity. This principle also recognizes the importance of "globality" and legitimacy of rights inherent to the human person, in the same way that it recognizes the power of the state to adopt adverse policies directed to those who disrespect it.

Thus, on the dignity of the human person and his or her elevation as a subject of International Law, explains Jubilut (2010, p. 23):

> (...) when establishing rights and duties for the individual - and the consequent process of internationalization of human rights, which meant, in practice, the establishment of responsibility by the international community to ensure their protection. Such protection takes place on two fronts: on the one hand in the international system, with the creation of a complementary system to the internal systems of States of human rights norms; and, on the other hand, by establishing analysis criteria of the internal conduct of States, both in terms of respect for human rights and in respect to its governance.

Between the concepts of sovereignty and human rights is one of the most important axiological conflicts internationally. On the subject, the aforementioned author adds:

> This conflict has two dimensions. On the one hand it involves the question of legitimacy, in that the implementation of both concepts is interconnected, since the protection of human rights requires the minimization of state sovereignty which, in turn, evolved towards being considered not only a right but also a responsibility (the State's responsibility to its citizens), thereby gaining a vertical dimension (State-citizen) that adds to its horizontal dimension (State-State). And on the other hand, it involves the question of legality, since the protection of sovereignty appears to be much more rooted in the founding norms of International Law than the protection of human rights, which can lead to inaction in the face of serious violations of human rights on the basis of legalistic approaches (JUBILUT, 2010, p. 153).

It is noteworthy that such a conflict is evident when it the use of force is necessary for humanitarian purposes, while questioning the legality and legitimacy of the first.

In this sense, the principle of non-intervention addresses the meddling of a State into another, respecting its sovereignty and will. Therefore it consists in the non-intervention in the manifestation of its own respect for the equality and independence among States, since each State has freedom to manage themselves according to their internal organization. This principle prohibits not only armed intervention, but also interventions of diplomatic and economic order, for example. The disregard to this principle, currently, almost always manifests itself with the will imposition of one State over another in an abusive manner, not guided by any previously recognized international commitment.

The principle of defending peace brings to the State the command of measuring their actions, aiming at peace and preventing conflicts. This principle is also recognized in various international commitments, such as the American Convention on Human Rights. Its great importance is synthesized in the words of Bobbio (*apud* CRIPPA 2011, p. 122): "the peace is necessary precondition for recognition and effective protection of human rights in every State and in the international system".

J. de Oliveira Filho, quoted by Bechara (2011, p. 137) says that public order is the "social state that results from the relationship established among the representatives of the Legislative, Executive and Judiciary, as rulers, and individuals, as governed, in order to achieve the interests of both". In the Constitutional framework, it reflects the set of fundamental principles of a system.

In International Law, public order originally represented the self-defense of the sovereign legal system, determining the content of fundamental principles that underlie the State protection against external aggressions. This situation reduced the public order to a list of abstract principles, but should be protected from the irrevocable provisions, such as constitutional provisions concerning the State political organization and its foundations, such as the universal normative standard of human rights (which effectively constitute the public order).

It is noteworthy that international treaties that establish the harmonization of national legislation, outweigh the concept of national public order while achieving the required equivalence or homogeneity of procedures.

The principles of international cooperation and solidarity, in addition, relate to the means that enable cooperation among people, such as the development of legal instruments between States, such as treaties and conventions, refer to a real need in view of the current patterns of globalization. In short, the need for cooperation among people arises as it is understood that the protection of individuals is not restricted to mere territorial divisions, therefore aiming humanity's utopia of progress as a whole.

It is understood that the cooperation among people for the progress of humanity foreseen in article 4, section IX, of the Brazilian Federal Constitution expresses a solidarity value, which also corresponds to one of the fundamental objectives of the Federative Republic of Brazil, present in the aforementioned Constitution, in article 3, section I.

Thereby, the listed principles, as well as others, explicitly or implicitly recognized, have served as criteria of interpretation and integration, giving coherence to the international system by entering the country in this new reality of internationalization of relations between States. It can also be noted that these principles, even though they were listed and individualized by CF/88, are regarded as one and in harmony; there is no prevalence of some over others, as they are not absolute.

# DISASTERS AND INTENSIFICATION OF NATURAL DISASTERS

Disasters can be understood as the consequence of adverse events that generate large impact on the social environment and can be differentiated, simply, by its origin or nature, human or natural (TOBIN AND MONTZ, 1997 *et al apud* MARCELINO, 2007). This time, human disasters ensue directly from the action or omission of men, as natural disasters would be enhanced by natural phenomena.

Natural disasters are phenomena that happen in any country, in some more often than others, being the more common ones: earthquakes, tsunamis, storms and volcanic eruptions. Among the many recent examples of disasters, rather due to the proportions achieved, is recurring drought in Africa and the earthquakes and tsunamis in Japan.

According to data on natural disasters in the EM-DAT (Emergency Events Database) measured between the years 1900 and 2006, it is confirmed that the vast majority occurred in developing countries, especially in the Asian (3,699 records) and American (2,416 records) continents.

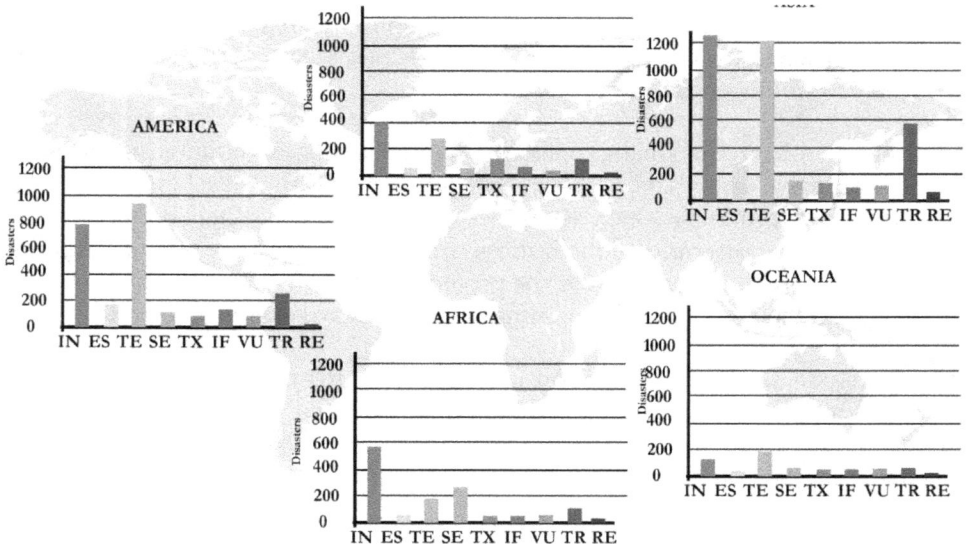

Picture 01 – Distribution by continent of natural disasters around the globe (1990-2006). Legend: IN – Floods. ES – Landslide. TE – Storm. SE – Drought. TX – Extreme Storm. IF – Forest Fire. VU – Volcanism. TR – Earthquake e RE – Wash.

It is believed that climate change in recent years may be one of the factors that has intensified, in catastrophic proportions, existing natural phenomena and, in particular, the damage caused by them.

According to data from EM-DAT (2007), in the 70s', on average, there were 90 disasters, increasing in the 90s' to over 260, with greater frequency and magnitude. It is believed that among the main factors contributing to the disaster increase are: population growth, social segregation in urban areas, accumulation of people and goods in risk areas (coastal areas), progress in registration and information technologies and global climate change (MARCELINO *et al*, 2006).

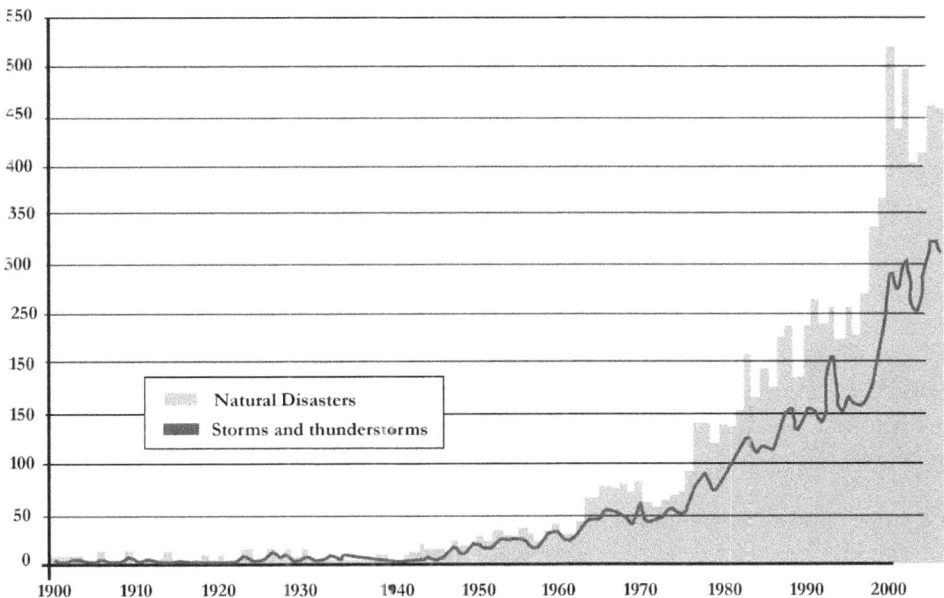

**Picture 02 – Annual frequency of natural disasters all over the globe (1900-2006)**

**Legend: Desastres Naturais – Natural disasters. Tempestades – Storms.**

**SOURCE: EM-DAT, 2007**

Among the natural phenomena intensified in Brazil, the increase in rainfall can be highlighted in southern and southeastern regions of the country, in contrast to a decrease in rates in the Northeast and North of the country, as showed by the 2007 report of the IPCC - Intergovernmental Panel on Climate Change.

According to data from EM-DAT (2007), between the years of 1900 and 2006, there was a total of 150 disasters records in Brazil. Of these, 84% were observed after the 70s', showing an intensification of disasters, with 8,183 victims and around 10 billion dollars in damage. It is noteworthy that over 60% of the events occurred in the South and Southeast.

In the last decades, despite the intensification of natural disasters records in most of the world, Brazil deals in a segmented manner and without due attention, both domestically and internationally; lacking an intensification of debates and concrete proposals of legislation and technical apparatus to respond to local and external disasters.

## DISASTERS AND GUIDELINES OF LAW DISASTER RESPONSE PROGRAMS

Depending on the country or the population, it is observed that the consequences of occurrence of disasters include: natural, those enhanced by human intervention or inability and lack of preparation of local governments in managing the incident. An example was described by Heath (2011), which occurred in 2008, when cyclone Nargis hit Myanmar and the entire low-lying coastal region of the country, reaching even its largest city, Yangon.

The storm destroyed at least 700,000 houses, much of the country's fishing fleet sank and the rice plantation of the area was compromised. However the government's inability to take care of the damage and the resistance to accept the assistance of other States and international organizations, aggravated the damage, leading to the deaths of at least 85,000 people. When humanitarian aid was finally allowed to enter the country, weeks after the disaster, its damages were already expanded.

The mentioned author also states that the French and US warships waited along the country's coast for two weeks with food, medical supplies, water purification systems, small boats and helicopters, which required to be brought to isolated rural areas.

Without permission to enter the country, the ships withdrew without delivering the aid. Initially, until the access of international aid of UN agencies and non-governmental organizations, such as the Red Cross and Save the Children, were prevented from carrying out assistance activities.

In situations like this, the issues of sovereignty and non-intervention and the need for humanitarian aid are put in confrontation, without knowing exactly the limits of action or even a possible mitigation of sovereignty in favor of the human right guard. With movements of integration and the new cooperation among people, the concept of absolute State sovereignty can be notices as disrupted, gradually sovereignty has been made more flexible and relativized, almost always in favor of human rights.

The international community has long ago recognized the need for coordination and cooperation in disaster response. Heath (2011, p. 444) points out the origins of this concern in the twentieth century:

> In 1922, the League of Nations took up a project to establish an International Relief Union (IRU), to furnish aid and coordinate relief operations in the event of disasters. 89 Twenty-four states attended the first meeting of the IRU, but the institution soon foundered under a lack of funding and growing isolationism and rearmament, both symptoms of the global depression of the 1930s. The second major attempt to formulate a convention was scrapped before the process truly began. In 1984, the Office of the United Nations Disaster Relief Coordinator (UNDRO) submitted a Draft Convention on Expediting the Delivery of Emergency Assistance to the Economic and Social Council, but, despite initial expressions of support, the Council never took action on it. More recent efforts at top-down rulemaking have all constituted non-binding guidelines and statements of principle.

Thus, with the passage of time, even without clear legal limits, there was an increase among those that promote and participate in operations in emergency cases in occurrence of disasters, help that is not always coming only from non-governmental organizations, as the Red Cross and Red Crescent, but sometimes comes directly from other States.

Along these lines, the pioneer program IDRL (International Disaster Response Laws, Rules and Principles), or currently just called Law Disaster Response Program, has been promoted since 2001 by the International Federation of Red Cross and Red Crescent Societies - IFRC, aiming to regulate help in such cases, dictating guidelines for legal preparation in disaster management. Thus, in 2007, the International

Federation has published a set of guidelines on national facilitation of relief, addressing the conditions for international aid, as well as on the granting of legal means, such as custom exemptions to internal corporate entities, privileges and immunities, when accepting international aid.

The Disaster Law program has developed the role of raising the legal issues, occurred before, during and after the occurrence of disasters, in short, protecting the international scenario of prevalence of human dignity and dissemination peace in the world. The duty to protect human rights has come to be a general command, and specifically in the case of IDRL, for the sake of help in combating and preventing disasters, whose often consequences of any occurrence of major proportions go far beyond the commitment of human rights, transcend the borders of States directly affected, resulting, for example, in reflections linked to the economy and the environment of other States, which creates another impasse, the self-protection.

As an example of the organization's activities, there is what happened in Mozambique, which is a country prone to cyclical occurrence of disasters. A policy was established based on the experience in emergency operations and existence throughout the country of a network of volunteers trained to work in several areas. The plan developed for the country sets limits and humanitarian assistance targeting guidelines.

The International Law of Disaster Response was also legally protected by the Geneva Convention since 2007, with the approval by the Member States of the International Disaster Response Law Guidelines, or simply known as the IDRL Guidelines, which have served as a parameter for models adopted in several countries, complementing and adapting to the realities of each State, since the legal management and the disasters vary widely from country to country.

In the same search molds for standardization and regulation, the International Law Commission of the United Nations (ILC) has also been trying to develop a line of action on the duty of acceptance of humanitarian aid, based on the principle of international cooperation and protection of human rights, reconciled with State sovereignty and self-determination. Therefore, it seeks to formulate and limit the duty of States to accept humanitarian aid in cases of disaster, a proposal which includes that a State should not arbitrarily refuse international help, especially when it is unable to cope alone with the damage generated or when its population is neglected or suffer for actions of their own government.

The efforts of organizations like the ones mentioned above, have emerged in an attempt to establish acceptable standards and adoption of management models before a disaster occurs. It turns out that currently there are no universal laws, although today they are most effective, and what is actually happening is the adoption of a series of bilateral and multilateral agreements, such as specific treaties, to deal with individual issues such as disaster responses in cases of nuclear accidents, however most of the principles, guidelines and declarations do not have a binding quality.

The problem here established, however, goes far beyond, since often, countries conceal their real intentions, such as economic and political interests, using the pretext of humanitarian aid to interfere in affairs of other States. To find limits and analyze case by case, where in fact help is needed, and who can, selflessly, promote real assistance along the lines of humanitarian solidarity is the main challenge for the adoption of international legislation that regulates such situation.

## BRAZILIAN LEGISLATION AND IDRL GUIDELINES - INTERNATIONAL DISASTER RESPONSE LAW GUIDELINES.

Currently, in Brazil, with the adoption of inadequate assistance and shortsighted policies by the current political guise, the internal actions of risk management and disaster responses have become priorities as the occurrence of natural disasters has become more frequent, as already mentioned above, interconnected with excess or shortage of rains, such as drought, especially in the Northeast, or even, floods and landslides, in the South, for example.

Many were the actions taken by the government to combat disasters generated by the drought, as mentioned above. Yet, recently, in 2012, a National Plan for Risk Management and Disaster Response was launched, when the National Center for Risk and Disaster Management – CENAD (*Centro Nacional de Gerenciamento de Riscos e Desastres*) was opened, aiming at the prevention of risks and natural disasters, highlighting the importance of science and technology, in early warnings and adoption of assistance measures. It is noteworthy that, as foreseen in the plan, investments for the years 2012-2014 are nearly R$18.8 billion.

Although it is not possible to measure consequences of the adoption of the plan since it has been recent and gradually implanted, it is believed that a progress and a concern demonstration aimed at an alignment with the new guise of adoption of guidelines for combat and prevention of natural disasters adopted by other countries around the world, has been created.

Yet, in April 10, 2012, the Law 12,608, which established the Protection and Civil Defence Policy – PNPDEC (*Política de Proteção e Defesa Civil*), provided on the National System of Protection and Civil Defense – SINPDEC (*Sistema Nacional de Proteção e Defesa Civil*) and the National Council for Protection and Civil Defense - CONPDEC (*Conselho Nacional de Proteção e Defesa Civil*) and authorized the establishment of an information system and disaster monitoring. Again, this law gives importance to the adoption of preventive and mitigating measures in a risk situation. It must be observed that it addresses the food distribution, mapping and monitoring of risk areas, and the application of resources.

Therefore, it can be observed that recently the country has adopted measures for the protection and prevention in occurrence of disasters, including natural ones. It is observed also that the country has the means, especially financial, to apply such measures, although it can be verified obstacles to the effective application, such as environmental, social and political limitations.

It does not always happens in other countries that, in addition to not having financial resources to deal with the occurrence of disasters, they are not open to receive foreign aid, mainly for fear of putting their sovereignty at risk, a justifiable concern, since the intervention, disguised as help, sometimes conceals other interests.

## THE RESPONSABILITY TO PROTECT AND ITS CONSEQUENCES

With the development of International Human Rights Law, the end of the Cold War and several catastrophic humanitarian crisis, there was an improvement of the debate on humanitarian intervention and an emphasis on the need to reconcile the concept of sovereignty and protection of human rights in International Law to, thereby, restore the legitimacy of non-intervention, by setting clear rules for the use of the intervention with humanitarian purpose.

The origins of the responsibility to protect, date back to a speech in 54th session of the UN General Assembly, in September 1999, when Secretary-General Kofi Annan reflected on the prospects for human security and intervention in the next century, and inquired about the way to respond to egregious and systematic violations of human rights that offend every precept of our common humanity, if humanitarian intervention is, indeed, an unacceptable assault on sovereignty.

In September 2000, the Government of Canada responded to the challenge launched by Annan, announcing the creation of the Independent International Committee on

Intervention and State Sovereignty (ICISS), opening the way for the consolidation of the concept. The report presented by the committee was entitled "responsibility to protect" and presented in December 2001, unanimously agreed by the twelve commissioners. Thus, the doctrine of "responsibility to protect" would eliminate dilemmas involving humanitarian interventions.

By using force in the protection of life and human rights, the "responsibility to protect" implies the modification of the concept of sovereignty as an absolute right for sovereignty as a responsibility, limiting the exercise of the sovereignty of the individual rather than a state sovereignty only. Thus, the primary responsibility rests with the State; if there is failure or lack of government's will to exercise such a role is when that responsibility passes to the international community.

Peres believes that

> The Responsibility to Protect solidifies on some fundamental principles. As basic principles two stand out: the State Sovereignty implies responsibility, and the primary responsibility of protection of its people lies with the State itself; where a population is suffering serious harm, as a result of internal war, insurgency, repression or State failure, and the State in question is unable or unwilling to prevent or avoid, the principle of non-intervention give away to the international responsibility to protect (2013, p. 30-31).

ICISS establishes that the "responsibility to protect" covers three different types: the responsibility to prevent (prevention focused on root causes and direct causes of internal conflict and other crises caused by man that put people at risk), the responsibility to react (includes the establishment of sanctions not involving the use of armed force and military intervention in extreme cases) and the responsibility to rebuild (includes efforts to implement justice, recovery, reconciliation, development and peace building, particularly after a military intervention).

The application of the responsibility to protect in cases of natural disasters generated restlessness in the UN, especially in relation to Cyclone Nargis, which hit Myanmar in May 2008. On the subject, it is emphasized that

> It is estimated that 138,000 people have died and 1.5 million have been displaced. The government's slowness in responding to the tragedy and their reluctance to ensure the access of humanitarian agencies without its direct control led the French chancellor at the time, founder of the NGO Doctors Without Borders, Bernard Kouchner, to propose that the UNSC invoked the Responsibility

to Protect, since the denial of humanitarian aid would be "a crime against humanity". Both western governments and ASEAN members have rejected the idea on the grounds that the Responsibility to Protect could not be applied to cases of natural disasters. In the optimistic point of view of Bellamy, fears that could arise from unilateral and misuse of Responsibility to Protect in mentioned cases would have been largely compensated by the rejection of this use by a large portion of the international community (FONSECA JR. and BELLI, 2013, p.16).

The unquestionable fact is that natural disasters consist of an undeniable reality and mechanisms to prevent and respond to these phenomena must be organized and coordinated by national and international systems.

As an example, Chile has developed a proposal for a system called "Information Exchange Mechanism on Capacities of Support for Natural Disasters" (MICADEN), which takes into account the models available in a global, regional and sub-regional level, and creates a centralized mechanism that coordinates existing resources in a dispersed manner. This proposal was approved during the X Conference of Defense Ministers of the Americas, held in October 2012 in Punta del Este, Uruguay, and the temporary presidency of the Conference of Defense Ministers of the Americas (CDMA) is now in the hands of Peru.

The approval by the UM of the Hyogo Framework for Action for 2005-2015 is noteworthy in this context, whose main objective is to strengthen the resilience of nations and communities in the face of disasters. This document was the result of the Second World Conference on Disaster Reduction, held in Hyogo, Japan, in January 2005, and became the first plan that details the type of cooperation needed from all sectors and agents to create a common management system, in order to reduce losses from disasters.

The Lieutenant General Jorge Robles Mella (2013), Chief of General Staff of the Air Force of Chile, points out that

> At the regional level, the Organization of American States (OAS) coordinates international cooperation for disaster cases through the Inter-American Committee for Natural Disaster Reduction.

> Among OAS main documents there is the Declaration of San Salvador on Citizen Security in the Americas, which reaffirms that states have the obligation

and the responsibility to provide humanitarian assistance to protect the lives, integrity and dignity of people in situations of natural or man-made disasters.

In addition, the OAS emphasizes the need to strengthen regional and sub-regional organizations such as the Caribbean Agency for Emergency and Disaster Management, the Coordination Center for the Prevention of Natural Disasters in Central America, the Andean Committee for the Prevention and Attention for Disasters and the Humanitarian Information Network for Latin America and the Caribbean.

During 2012, the Inter-American Council for Integral Development, part of the OAS, approved the "Inter-American Plan for the Prevention, Attention of Disasters and the Coordination of Humanitarian Assistance". The agency also called for the implementation of a mechanism to gather experiences and good practices on the topic, from the database of the Inter-American Network for Disaster Mitigation (INDM), also part of the OAS.

At the sub-regional level, it should be noted the role of the Central American Integration System (CAIS) and its Coordination Center for the Prevention of Natural Disasters in Central America, which elaborated a Central American Policy for Integral Disaster Risk Management and represents the regional orientation of the highest level in this field (MELLA, 2013).

In this regard, some points are worth mentioning regarding the responsibility to protect, related to the international disaster response law and its balance with the issues of sovereignty and non-intervention

1) Countries must maintain a coordinated system that takes into account the models available in global, regional and sub-regional levels, and create a centralized mechanism that coordinates existing resources in an organized and fast manner;

2) The responsibility to protect is born from the Sovereign State's inability by not having conditions to respond to the challenges (human and socioeconomic) compared to the natural disaster.

3) The aid shall come from independent international organizations to prevent imperialist interventions from being carried out by countries that take advantage of catastrophes to provide assistance in order to take advantage of the fragile conditions of the rescued, imposing concessions;

4) The possibility of intervention or the obligation of intervention, regarding the responsibility to protect, through the use of force for humanitarian purposes, to send and receive international assistance in case of disasters, is the last resort and it is applicable only when the intensity of the disaster natural prevents the rescued State to provide its own reestablishment.

The compliance with these criteria, both in global legislation such as local legislation, would facilitate the decision-making in response to disasters, enabling a quick and effective aid, reducing harm to local population and respecting international principles of sovereignty and non -intervention.

## CONCLUSION

It is perceptible, in light of this paper, that the debate of a legislation on the subject and adoption of the IDRL is necessary at the international level, as well as standards to implement humanitarian aid, as the approach among the States and the rise of the individual to the outstanding level of subject of International Law. However, of course, such legislation cannot be used by States or assistant powers as an instrument of intervention or abuse of sovereignty to the rescued State.

It is argued that it is up to International Organizations operating responses to disasters, and more, the help of other states linked to its own internal cooperation and acceptance. This is because the affected State is in a better position to understand the needs of its citizens, knows the infrastructure, understands the habits and special needs of the population, and knows the help items that may not be appropriate to circumstances, this being a true demonstration of being a sovereign state.

In cases that the state is collapsing, it must be highlighted that there is the need for cooperation and not for imposition of measures and foreign aid. It is true that, in cases of impossibility of disaster management because of inability of the affected State on unjustified refusal, a middle ground must be sought for a foreign aid, or even as it is as is currently being developed, establishing a debate of such governments with non-governmental organizations to settle the limits of action.

Therefore, it is concluded that, in order for international principles to be respected and harmonized, aid and external intervention in the occurrence of a disaster must follow some principles, such as: the affected State must not be able to cope alone with the incident; as it must act jointly with other States and guide the assistance; moreover, the help must come from non-governmental organizations. And once again the need to avoid imposing measures is highlighted, which obviously would violate the State sovereignty.

Finally, Brazil is a country that currently seems to direct its operations to disaster responses, it is a country with financial conditions to deal with its occurrence, needing, however, to apply the measures that are present in established plans and legislations. The case of drought is a good example to be noted, that there are still barriers for the adoption of effective public policies, thus, debates before the international community in search for help seem to be more connected with the observation of policies that succeeded externally, mainly with the adoption of new technologies.

# REFERENCES

BRASIL. *Constituição da República Federativa do Brasil de 1988.* In: Vade Mecum Rideel, 15th ed. 2012. (original text in Portuguese)

_____. *Law 12,608, April 10, 2012.* Available in: http://www.planalto.gov.br/ccivil_03/_Ato2011-2014/2012/Lei/L12608.htm. Access in: August 1, 2013. (original text in Portuguese)

BECHARA, Fábio Ramazzini. *Cooperação jurídica internacional em matéria penal:* eficácia da prova produzida no exterior. São Paulo: Saraiva, 2011. (original text in Portuguese)

CAMPOS, José Nilson B.; STUDART, Ticiana Marinho de Carvalho. *A Seca no Nordeste do Brasil: Origens, Causas e Soluções.* Available in: <http://www.deha.ufc.br/ticiana/Arquivos/Publicacoes/Congressos/2001/Secas_no_Nordeste_do_Brasil_08_de_junho_def.pdf>. Access in: June 8, 2013. (original text in Portuguese)

CRIPPA, Stefania Dib. *Os Princípios Constitucionais das Relações Internacionais Estado, Direitos Humanos e Ordem Internacional.* Dissertação (mestrado) – Faculdades Integradas do Brasil – UniBrasil, Mestrado em Direitos Fundamentais e Democracia, 2011. Available in: <http://www.unibrasil.com.br/_sitemestrado/_pdf/stefania_final_19.pdf>. Access in: July 5, 2013. (original text in Portuguese)

EM-DAT – Emergency Eventes Database, The OFDA/CRED International Disaster Database. Available in: http://www.em-dat.net/ Access in: February 2, 2014.

FISCHER, Horst. *International disaster response laws, principles and practice: reflections, prospects and challenges. International Federation of Red Cross and Red Crescent Societies, Geneva, 2003, pp 24-44.* Available in: < https://www.ifrc.org/PageFiles/41194/idrl-book- c2.pdf>. Access in: June 9, 2013.

FONSECA JR., Gelson e BELLI, Benoni. Desafios da Responsabilidade de Proteger. Available in: http://www.ieei-unesp.com.br/portal/wp-content/uploads/2013/05/Politica-Externa-21-04-Gelson-Fonseca.pdf. Access in: February 20, 2013. (original text in Portuguese)

HEATH, J. Benton. *Disasters, Relief, and Neglect: The Duty to Accept Humanitarian Assistance and the Work of the International Law Commission.* Available in: http://works.bepress.com/cgi/viewcontent.cgi?article=1003&context=jbenton_heath. Access in: June 9, 2013.

IFRC - International Federation of Red Cross and Red Crescent Societies. Available in: http://www.ifrc.org. Access in: July 7, 2013.

# THE POLLUTER PAYS PRINCIPLE AND ITS EFFECTIVINESS IN THE SCOPE OF INTERNATIONAL ENVIRONMENTAL LAW

Túlio Belchior Mano da Silveira[18]
Márcia Baião de Azevedo Ribeiro[19]
João Rezende Almeida Oliveira[20]

## INTRODUCTION

This study has as object of investigation environmental law in order to present the polluter pays principle and analyze its effectiveness within the scope of international environmental law.

Humans live and develop on the environment and often theirs activities cause deterioration in the various natural elements of the planet Earth, as for example, in the atmosphere, water resources, soil and other species of life, whether animal or plants.

The problems related to environmental protection were made known when the environmental aging began to influence not only the well-being of people, but in the preservation of life and the human race itself.

The environmental crisis is thus a planetary crisis of human civilization, and implies a reinterpretation of the way in which mankind has always thought and understood the relationship between humans and the environment. Social injustices translate into environmental imbalances and these, in turn, reproduce the conditions of poverty.

The protection of the environment and natural resources represents one of the main purposes of the Modern State, therefore, its entire structure must be oriented towards this purpose and must meet its achievement.

---

18 Master's Degree Student in Law from the Catholic University of Brasilia. Post-undergraduated in Public Law from the Catholic University of Brasilia. Specialization in Administrative Law. Lawyer.
19 Master's Degree Student in Law from the Catholic University of Brasilia - UCB. Post-undergraduated in Civil Procedural Law from Damásio College. Lawyer
20 Doctor of Law from the Complutense University of Madrid. Professor in the Master's Program in Law at the Catholic University of Brasilia. Lawyer.

However, environmental legislation usually presents itself fragmented, divergent, unsystematic, too abstract and generic and often confused, not only in Brazil but all over the world, which brings out the need to discuss the matter to find effective ways to terminate human acts, and its various forms, leading to environmental degradation.

Faced with the need to create effective mechanisms for protection, since the deterioration of the environment is generating negative consequences, severely threatening including and, especially, the survival of the human species, the purpose of this study is to analyze the polluter pays principle, one of the most important principles of modern environmental law, with the overall objective of verifying its effectiveness within the scope of international environmental law aiming to contribute to stop the planetary environmental crisis that is threatening the survival of living beings, especially humans, understood, for purposes of this study, the set of physical, chemical, biological and social elements that affect living beings and human actions, now known as "the crisis of contemporary civilization."

Environmental damages themselves and the damages against life, physical integrity and human health through the environment are defined as attacks on human rights and are given legal treatment based on general constitutional principles. This does not mean that there are no specific rules, but everything is so new and so difficult that the standards are, however, too specific and must be anchored in principles that are more abstract and have more prominent purpose.

Aiming to locate the subject in the time and legal context, are described in the presentation of the research object, five specific legal-constitutional principles aimed at the protection of the environment, to prevent risk of injury and damage to the environment: principle of sustainable development, the polluter pays principle, the prevention principle, the principle of participation and principle of universality / ubiquity. Later addresses the polluter pays principle, which aims to hold the polluter accountable for the damages caused to the environment, in order both to punish those who have caused the damage as well as to prevent further damage from being practiced in the future. Following it addresses the effectiveness of the polluter pays principle within the scope of international environmental law from the awareness that contemporaneous environmental problems are planetary and not merely local or regional problems.

The text is developed through bibliographic research in a broad sense, encompassing production of knowledge on the subject, interpretation by the courts and the law encoded both domestically and internationally.

Finally, it is concluded that the protection of the environment depends on the balance between the principles related to sustainable development and the precautionary principles, whose interaction should moderate economic growth and reform the illusory idea that progress and sustainable development are incompatible.

Most environmental law principles are accepted since a long time and to some extent in various international instruments, called "Soft Laws", which are those non legal standards and not mandatory that serve only to guide the actions of international law subjects, example of declarations, international organizations recommendations and regional conventions.

The codification of international environmental law principles in international conventions and international bodies decisions is very recent; it has developed from the Rio Declaration on Environment and Development of 1992 in charge of placing the principles of environmental law in international relations, although the first universal codification of environmental rights practice has happened before, even in the United Nations Conference on the Human Environment, held in Stockholm in June 1972. The purpose of this Declaration, which is not a juridical document itself obliging States, was to inspire governments to preserve and improve the human environment. The intention of this study is to verify how is in reality the effectiveness of these principles of international environmental law.

With the intent of building knowledge on the theme of environment law, it is possible to form some questions that are related to the matter such as: Do the principles of international environmental law have direct application in national law? Do they depend on express constitutional provision? In order for the principles of environmental law to have applicability and effectiveness is sufficient that they be provided for in the Constitution, regardless of special rules regulations, that is, require additional action by the legislature to make them operative through more specific national legal standards?

The polluter pays principle, in general terms can be understood as follows: the agent generator of contamination must be held accountable for its cost. Behind this simple definition hides a complex concept. It is very common to identify the principle with the idea that the one who causes the pollution must pay a sum of money for it. The cost of pollution should be borne by whomever benefits from it, whether it is taking all necessary measures to prevent it or reduce it, either minimizing or repairing in its entirety its effects once occurred. So to understand the polluter pays principle and discover its true dimension in domestic and international law, it is necessary to analyze it from its dual perspective: the preventive one and the remedial, which are explained later on as the theme is developed.

Despite the extensive application of the polluter pays principle few grant its true meaning and scope, the root, probably, of that there is much more widespread subdenomination than its content. This justifies the approach of the polluter pays principle and its effectiveness in the context of international environmental law in this study.

## PRINCIPLES OF ENVIRONMENTAL LAW

There are several legal and constitutional principles guiding the protection of the environment. In Brazil, as the 1988 Federal Constitution does not specify what literally are these principles, each performer or researcher on the subject ends up building his or her own terminology. For example, to Antunes (2001), the principles of constitutional and environmental law are: the principle of fundamental human rights, democratic principle, the principle of prudence and caution, the balance principle and the limit principle.

In the view of Machado (2004), the general principles of environmental law are: principle of the right to a healthy quality of life, principle of equitable access to natural resources, user pays and polluter pays principles, the precautionary principle, the prevention principle, the principle of compensation, the principle of information, the principle of participation and principle of mandatory intervention by the Government.

According to Milaré (2007), are constitutional principles of environmental law: the principle of an ecologically balanced environment as a fundamental human right, the principle of the public nature of environmental protection, principle of the control of the polluter by the Government, the principle of consideration of the environmental variable in the decision making process of development policy, the principle of community participation, the polluter pays principle, the prevention principle, the principle of social and environmental function of property, the principle of right to sustainable development and the principle of cooperation among peoples.

Finally, Fiorillo (2003) identifies as principles of constitutional environmental law the following: the principle of sustainable development, the polluter pays principle, the prevention principle, the principle of participation and the principle of universality / ubiquity.

Internationally the United Nations Conference on Environment and Development - UNCED, through the Rio Declaration on Environment and Development, 1992, known as "Rio 92" lists seven principles of international environmental law, namely:

a) principle of sovereignty over natural resources and the responsibility to do no harm to the environment of other States or in areas beyond national jurisdiction; b) principle of preventive action; c) principle of international cooperation and good neighborly relations; d) principle of common but differentiated responsibilities; e) the precautionary principle; f) the polluter pays principle; and g) principle of sustainable development.

In this study, only for teaching purposes, based on the highest incidence in the doctrine, are covered only five specific principles aimed at protecting the environment: the principle of sustainable development, the polluter pays principle, the prevention principle, the principle of participation and the principle of universality / ubiquity.

## Principle of sustainable development

Sustainable development seeks basically the socio-economic development without destroying the environment. This principle has as content the maintainance of the vital bases of production and reproduction of human beings and their activities, ensuring equally a satisfactory relationship between human beings and between them and their environment, so that future generations also have the opportunity to enjoy the same natural resources available today (FIORILLO, ibidem, p. 25).

According to the ideas of Gudynas (1992, p. 68), the current actions towards sustainable development "require a critical cautious approach" because:

> In them there is no renouncement of the old paradigm of development for economic growth; on the contrary, it is adjusted to an ecological dimension. Thus the spread of a new neoliberal policy, which emphasizes the market as privileged scenario of social relations, is also generating its own environmental policy (GUDYNAS, 1992, p 68-69).

Dealing with the matter the Brazilian Supreme Court considered the principle of sustainable development as factor of getting the right balance between the demands of the economy and the ecology (STF, MC in ADIn No. 3540 / DF, 2006, p. 14).

In short, the State and the general population have the duty to defend and preserve the environment for present and future generations, taking into account, therefore, the sustainable development.

## Principle of preservation

Another important principle is the protection of the environment itself, which is often named "preservation," "precautionary" or "protection" and in others are treated each of these terms in separate, as if they were variants or different concepts. As for terminology definition, they are treated as synonyms: caution, care, protection, prevention, preservation and prudence.

For Leite (2012, p. 200) the principle of preservation and the precautionary principle are two distinct principles. Proclaims that "preventive action is a mechanism for risk management, targeted specifically to inhibit the concrete or potential risks, and being these visible and predictable by human knowledge" while the precautionary principle "operates in the first moment of this anticipatory, inhibitory and protective function, in face of the abstract risk, which can be considered a risk of harm, as it is often difficult to visualize and predict".

On the other hand, Fiorillo (ibidem) considers that it is unnecessary to differentiate between these principles.

Despite the differences, by the doctrine, regarding the concept of each of these principles, what matters for this study is that for the practical application any distinctions do not produce significant effects, due to the structural importance of preserving the environment. And that the damage to the environment, in addition to the serious consequences and unimaginable extent, is usually impossible to repair, reason enough to avoid the most the occurrence of the damage or its aggravation.

According to Antunes (ibidem, p. 28), the prevention principle unfolds in three other principles: a) the principle of prudence and caution so that are not produced "interventions in the environment before making sure that they are not adverse to the environment"; b) the principle of the balance, which enforces environmental law and to its enforcers, the duty to "assess the likely consequences of adopting a measure so that it can be useful to the community and not turning into excessive harms to ecosystems and to human life", that is, conducting a "balance between the different designs of a project to be implemented" as regarding to the economic, social and environmental effects, so that the law is "applied according to the result of all considered variants"; and c) the limits principle whereby the Government has the duty to "control the production, marketing, the use of techniques, methods and substances which represent risk to life, the quality of life and the environment."

The principle of preservation is a fundamental precept and consists in one of "the most important principles that guide the environmental law", given that "environmental damages, in most cases, are irreversible and irreparable" (FIORILLO, ibidem, p. 36).

It is the principle of preservation that should inform both the environmental[21] licensing, which is a preventive instrument of environmental protection as its own environmental impact studies, which is the analysis of the effects of certain action on the environment to see if it affects the preexisting stability of ecological cycles, weakening it (negative) or strengthening it (positive).

The Rio Declaration on Environment and Development 1992 deals with the principle of prevention by providing that:

> 4th principle: to achieve sustainable development, environmental protection shall constitute an integral part of the development process and can not be considered in isolation from it. [...]. 8th Principle: to achieve sustainable development and a higher quality of life for all, States should reduce and eliminate unsustainable patterns of production and consumption and promote appropriate demographic policies.

The precautionary principle emerged in Germany to protect human health from the effect of certain chemical products, and over time its application was extended to the protection of natural resources and ecosystems, as well as to global problems. It is currently defined as one that prohibits any intervention in the environment without first making sure that any actions will not produce adverse effects on the environment. It is a way to anticipate any risk or danger to the environment and stop it before it takes place. In case of doubt, it is decided in favor of the environment, forbidding the action (*in dubio pro natura or in dubio pro salute*).

Regarding precaution, Principle 15th of the Rio Declaration on Environment and Development of 1992 prescribes that, *in verbis*:

---

21 "The environmental licensing is not a simple administrative act, but rather a chain of administrative acts, which gives it the status of 'administrative procedure'. Also, it is important to note that the administrative license constitutes linked act, which shows a great distinction in relation to the environmental license, because this is, as a rule, discretionary act "(FIORILLO, 2003, p. 66).

Principle 15th: in order to protect the environment, the precautionary principle shall be widely applied by States according to their capabilities. When there is threat of serious or irreversible damages, the lack of full scientific certainty shall not be used as a reason for postponing cost-effective measures to prevent environmental degradation.

This Principle 15th aims to prevent the irreversibility of the potential damage to the environment, that is, the return to the previous state, in case the damage occurs, since the chances of an environmental damage being irreversible are significant. In this case it is up to the author of the alleged actions to prove that he or she will not cause any harm to the environment.

Inspired on international environmental law, the domestic legislations have been gradually adopting this principle. Qualified by proportionality factors, of coherence and effectiveness, the criteria of prudence and prevention, which offers precaution, it is no more than citizens expect from public authorities in a situation of uncertainty, when are at stake legal property of great value such as health and the environment that enable and condition life.

It is because of the prevention principle and environmental precaution that exists the polluter pays principle. One acts prior to the damage, the other later, to hold accountable those who committed the act, legally prohibited, against the environment. According to the polluter pays principle the agents, those who use natural resources or have an impact on the environment, must be held accountable for the negative effects of their activities, in order to not transfer to the rest of society, represented by present and future generations, part of the cost to generate a unit of product or service.

When the precautionary principle is correctly interpreted it can not be presented as an obstacle to development, but rather as a powerful stimulus to the development of science and new technologies, which are essential to move towards a sustainable development.

So, regardless of the nomenclature used nowadays this principle should be defined as broadly as possible, encompassing concepts such as a precaution, protection, care, prevention, preservation; and should also guide all modern environmental policy, giving priority to measures that prevent the emergence of acts of negative environmental impact. This principle "prescribes that the standards of environmental law should always be directed to the fact that it is necessary that the environment is preserved and protected as public property" (THE LAWYERS ASSOCIATION OF RURAL WORKERS OF THE STATE OF BAHIA - AATR-BA, 2002, p. 05).

## Polluter Pays Principle

The polluter pays principle or responsibility is variant of the precautionary principle, to the extent that is this that authorizes the punishment of those who did not follow the precautionary principle. The polluter pays principle is not to mean that you can "pay to avoid contamination," "pollute by payment" or "pay to pollute". This principle does not allow to look for ways to circumvent the repair of the damage, turning polluter act into lawful act through payment (FIORILLO, ibidem, p. 28).

Also called "principle of reparation," the polluter pays principle follows from the prevention principle and states that "he who cause injury to environmental goods must be held accountable for his actions, repairing or compensating adequately for the damage" (AATR-BA, 2002, p. 05).

According to Fiorillo (ibidem), this principle determines the incidence and application of some provisions of the legal regime of civil liability for environmental damage, as for example, the objective civil responsibility, the solidarity to support the damages caused to the environment and the priority of the specific repairing of the environmental damage.

It implies, therefore, in the civil liability of the causative agent of damage to the environment, that is, the duty to financially compensate the damages caused to the environment by the damaging activity practiced.

As the name suggests, this principle states that the costs of pollution and contamination of the environment must be borne by those who gave cause. The meaning and precise content of this principle, as well as its application to particular situations, still depends on better definition, particularly regarding the nature and extent of costs, and the exceptional circumstances in which the principle would not apply.

The polluter pays principle, also called "contaminator pays principle" is a still open to interpretation precept. It is more of an economic policy postulated than a principle of law, but one can not deny the implications for the development of international environmental law. So it needs to be mentioned in international treaties related to civil liability for environmental damage caused by hazardous activities.

## Principle of participation

The principle of participation, also known as the "principle of cooperation," means that "environmental law makes the people come out of a passive status of beneficiaries by making them share the responsibility for managing the interests of the whole community" (MACHADO, ibidem, p. 80).

The 1988 Federal Constitution, in Article 225 *caput*, provides for the participation of the State and civil society in the environmental protection when imposed those duties to the Government and the community. From this, it is inferred that in the commitment to the protection of the environment there must be a joint operation between all individuals, members of the civil society and the State.

## Principle of universality

Most of the doctrine delas with the principle of universality or ubiquity as element of the principle of participation. But Fiorillo (ibidem) prefers to approach it separately, given its importance when designing the preservation of a healthy environment as a right that must be protected as a universal value. According to Fiorillo (ibidem), the principle of ubiquity means that:

> [...] The object of protection of the environment, located in the epicenter of human rights, should be taken into account every time a policy, action, legislation on any topic, activity, work etc. has to be created and developed. This is because, to the extent it has as a cardinal point of constitutional protection the life and the quality of life, all one wants to do, create or develop must first go through an environmental consulting to finally know whether or not there is the possibility that the environment would be degraded (FIORILLO, 2003, p 42-43).

With this thinking, the environment can not be conceived apart from the other aspects of society, because it requires a global and joint action, inclusively by the nature of the phenomena of environmental degradation and pollution, for example, that do not respect territorial boundaries or barriers. Therefore, we must "fight the causes of environmental damage and never just the symptoms, because, avoiding only these, the conservation of natural resources will be incomplete and partial" (FIORILLO, ibidem, p. 43).

In this sense thus expressed Silva (2002, p. 02.): "The environment is the interaction of the set of natural, artificial and cultural elements that provide the balanced development of life in all its forms."

The principle of universality or ubiquity is embodied in the idea of the ubiquity of the environment, since it is present in all terrestrial sphere, which is inferred that any damage to the environment reflects, to some extent, throughout nature, regardless of the geographic area where it occurs.

Presented the main guiding principles of environmental law, and in view of the line of research adopted to identify the effectiveness of the polluter pays principle within the scope of international environmental law, the next topic is dedicated to the analysis of the polluter pays principle in international environmental law.

## THE POLLUTER PAYS PRINCIPLE AND ITS EFFECTIVENESS IN THE SCOPE OF INTERNATIONAL ENVIRONMENTAL LAW

Environmental law is a branch of law that had a rapid evolution very conditioned by international law. Although integrates other areas of administrative law, constitutional, civil and criminal, there is a set of principles proper of environmental law. One of them is the polluter pays principle, inherent to the environmental theme, in which science and the law meet on a permanent and sometimes difficult dialogue.

The polluter pays principle, in general terms can be understood as follows: the agent generator of contamination must be liable for its cost. Behind this simple definition hides a complex concept. It is very common to identify the principle with the idea that the one who causes the contamination must pay a sum of money for it. The cost of pollution should be borne by who benefits from it, whether it is taking all necessary measures to prevent it or reduce it, either minimizing or repairing in its entirety its effects once it has occurred.

So to understand the polluter pays principle and discover its true dimension in domestic and international law, it is necessary to analyze it from its dual perspective: the preventive and the remedial, which are explained on the development of the theme.

## Polluter pays principle as a variant of the precautionary principle

The polluter pays principle is a principle of international environmental law and evokes the idea that one should avoid all damage caused by a human being that put at risk the sustainability, the renewability and regenerability of the environment. Who ended up producing a damage to the environment, invariably violated the precautionary principle, which operates in the time prior to the degrading action and thus should be liable. This is the essential meaning of the polluter pays principle: hold accountable the act of damage to the environment. According to Matos (2001, p. 63), "the entrepreneur, he who represents the activity performed, should bear the costs of mitigating the damage that your venture might cause because these costs in principle can not be passed on to citizens."

Such accountability stems from the fact that "any violation of the right implies the sanction of responsibility for breaking the law", and in the case of environmental degradation, the violation is increased, given that the consequences will be felt throughout the ecosystem, which contains the set of all relationships of living beings with one another and with the environment where they live (ANTUNES, 2008, p. 31).

The polluter pays principle, that is, he who pollutes pays, means that enterprises, institutions, organizations, political parties, countries and people who pollute the environment must bear the costs and expenses that imply that damage. We must avoid that the victims, the State and society bear the burden alone for the adverse effects of activities on the environment and people.

According to this principle, the expenses arising from the contamination should be charged to the polluter, meaning the person or entity, public or private, that directly or indirectly damages the environment or creates conditions for damage to occur. The contaminant agent must bear the full burden of the necessary measures, such as to eliminate contamination or reduce it to a level considered acceptable according to the environmental quality parameters adopted. According to Aragão (2002):

> [...] Payments arising from the polluter pays principle must be proportionate to the estimated costs for economic agents to avoid or prevent the pollution. Only then the polluters are "motivated" to choose between "pollute and pay" to the State or "pay to not pollute" investing in production processes or less pollutant raw materials, or into research of new Technologies (ARAGÃO, 2002, p. 20-21).

Whichever decisions taken by the economic agent will be advantageous to society: or prevents pollution or maintain it at acceptable levels. What cannot happen is to transfer responsibility to the taxpayers of the measures taken by public policies to protect the environment.

It should be noted that the polluter pays principle does not only refer to compensation or mitigation of damage to the environment, but also to invest to avoid contamination. This does not mean that the individual or company can choose to contaminate by the subsequent payment, but rather avoid the damage to the environment, paying to implement preventive measures. The principles of environmental law are all interconnected: next to the polluter pays principle is the principle of prevention and precaution.

In other words, the polluter pays principle does not authorize any "right to pollute", by contrast, it has in its core a preventive essence and other repressive in the design to prevent environmental damage from occurring, and if it happens, that it does not stay without repair. Moreover, environmental policies should be aimed at prevention, as in most cases the environmental damages are irreversible.

## Liability for environmental damage in international law

In the Brazilian legal system, the polluter pays principle is enshrined basically in paragraph 3rd of Article 225 of the Federal Constitution of 1988 and in Article 4th, section VII, of Law No. 6.938 of August 31, 1981, which addresses the National Environmental Policy, its purposes and mechanisms of formulation and application.

Pursuant to paragraph 3rd, article 225 of the Federal Constitution of 1988, "the conduct and activities considered as harmful to the environment shall subject the offenders, individuals or legal entities, to penal and administrative sanctions, independently of the obligation to repair the damages".

According to section VII of Article 4th of Law No. 6.938 of August 31, 1981, the National Environmental Policy aims to "impose, to the polluter and the predator, the obligation to recover and / or to compensate for the damages caused, and to the user, for the contribution for the use of environmental resources for economic purposes".

Within the framework of international environmental law, the polluter pays principle first appeared as an environmental regulator in Japan, in 1970.

Subsequently, the Organization for Economic Cooperation and Development - OECD, through Recommendation No. C (72) 128 of May 28,1972, formally adopted the polluter pays principle as analytical basis of economic instruments to regulate contamination.

Since then the polluter pays principle has been extended to European Community law, to finally be welcomed widely in international law, found expressly enshrined in the Stockholm Declaration of June 1972[22], which manifested itself favorably to institute accountability for environmental damages. In paragraph 7th, of its Preamble, states the following:

> 7 - Achieving this environmental goal will require the acceptance of responsibility by citizens and communities, companies and institutions, in equitable sharing of common efforts. Individuals and organizations, adding their values and their actions will shape the future of the world environment. Local and national governments will bear the greatest burden of environmental policies and actions of the broadest scope within their respective jurisdictions. Also international cooperation becomes necessary to obtain the resources that will help developing countries in carrying out their duties. A growing number of problems due to its regional or global scale or to affect common international fields, will require extensive cooperation from nations and international organizations sharing the common interest. The Conference calls upon Governments and peoples to engage in a common effort to preserve and improve the environment for the benefit of all peoples and future generations.

And also, the precautionary principle as follows:

> Principle 15th: in order to protect the environment, the precautionary principle shall be widely applied by States according to their capabilities. Whenever there is threat of serious or irreversible damages, the lack of full scientific certainty should not be used as a reason for postponing efficient and cost-effective measures to prevent environmental degradation (the precautionary principle).

---

22 INTERNATIONAL Legislation. Stockholm Declaration on the Human Environment of 1972. Developed at the United Nations Conference on the Human Environment in Stockholm, 05-16 of June, 1972. Retrieved September 2, 2014, from http://www.silex.com.br/leis/normas/ Estocolmo.htm

The polluter pays principle is listed as Principle 16th of the Rio Declaration on Environment and Development of 1992, as follows:

> Principle 16th: national authorities should endeavor to promote the internalization of environmental costs and the use of economic instruments, in view of the approach that the polluter should, in principle, bear the cost of pollution, with due regard to the public interest and without causing distortions in trade and international investments.

Further, the principle 22nd expresses the following:

> Principle 22nd: States should cooperate to further develop international law regarding liability and compensation to the victims of pollution and other environmental damages, that activities performed within the jurisdiction or under control of such States, may cause to areas located outside their jurisdictions.

In short the Stockholm Declaration of June 1972 basically shows the principle of national cooperation and the polluter pays principle. Therefore, it tried to recognize the protective guardianship and the improvement of the human environment as a key issue that affects the well-being of humanity and economic development around the world, an urgent aspiration of people from around the world and a duty of all governments.

Later, by virtue of the Single European Act, concluded on February 27 and 28 of 1986[23], the legal systems of all countries of the European Community and the Council of Europe welcomed the polluter pays principle in the shape drawn by the Organization for Economic Cooperation and Development – OECD[24].

In Europe, the polluter pays principle is enshrined expressly to a 1975 Recommendation of the Council of the Membering States and in the comunication of the Commission to the Council annexed to it; in all multi-annual action programs of the European

---

23 INTERNATIONAL, Legislation. **Single European Act of 1986.** Established between the Kingdom of Belgium, the Kingdom of Denmark, the Federal Republic of Germany, the Hellenic Republic, the Kingdom of Spain, the French Republic, Ireland, the Italian Republic, the Grand Duchy of Luxembourg, the Kingdom of the Netherlands, the Portuguese Republic and the United Kingdom of Great Britain and Northern Ireland, concluded on 17 and 28 of February, 1986. Retrieved September 2, 2014, from http://www.fd.uc.pt/ CI / EEC / pm / Tratados/ AUE/AUE-f.htm.

24 [7] "Article 25: [...]. 2 - The action of the Community in environmental matter is based on the principles of preventive action, reparation, prioritarily at source, of environmental damages and on the polluter pays principle. The requirements on environmental protection matters are a component of the other policies of the European Community. [...]" (European Single Act of 1987).

Community on the environment since 1973, in the Single European Act of 1986 and the Treaties of Maastricht, Amsterdam and Nice (ARAGÃO, 2002, p. 19).

After the Single European Act came into force in 1987, the Treaty of Rome of 1957 formally recognized the polluter pays[25] principle:

Article 130.o-R: [...]. 2. The Community policy on the environment shall aim at a high level of protection taking into account the diversity of situations in the various regions of the Community. It will be based on the principles of precaution and preventive action, of the correction, preferably at the source, of the environmental damage, and of the polluter pays. The requirements on environmental protection must be integrated into the definition and implementation of other Community policies. [...]. Article 130. o-S: [...]. 5. Without harm to the polluter pays principle, in cases where a measure adopted in accordance with paragraph No.1 involves costs deemed disproportionate for the public authorities of a Member State, the Council, in adopting that measure, will lay down appropriate provisions in the form of temporary derogations and / or - financial support from the Cohesion Fund to be set up by December 31, 1993 in accordance with Article 130.o-D. [...].

The European Community law is more evolved regarding the application of the polluter pays principle. In this region, it is understood that who contaminates the environment is the one that directly or indirectly cause a harm to the environment or who creates the conditions that can lead to this damage, and the standards that apply this principle allows to clearly identify who is the subject to whom is attributed the liability for the contamination in each concrete case.

In order to assess how countries had promoted environmental protection since the Stockholm Conference of 1972, it was held in Rio de Janeiro, between 03 and 14 of June of 1992, the United Nations Conference on Environment and Development - UNCED also known as the "First Earth Summit" and "Rio-92".

Among the main objectives of this conference, we can highlight the following: a) review the world environmental situation since 1972 and its relations with the current development model; b) establish transfer mechanisms of non pollutants technologies to developing countries; c) examine national and international strategies for incorporating environmental criteria into the development process; d) establish an international cooperation system to forecast environmental threats and provide relief in emergency

---

25 INTERNATIONAL, Legislation. Treaty that establishing the European [economic] Community (TEC) of 1957. Treaty of Rome. Integral Version. Done in Rome on March 25, nineteen hundred and fifty-seven. Retrieved September 2, 2014, from http://dupond.ci.uc.pt/ CDEUC/TRVRINT.HTM>.

cases; and e) reassess the organizational system of the United Nations Organization, creating new institutions to implement conference decisions when necessary.

At the time it was drawn up two documents of international reach: the Global Agenda 21 and the Rio Declaration on Environment and Development of 1992.

The Global Agenda 21, known as "ECO-92" is due to the idealization of the concept of "sustainable development" and brings with it, a model that seeks to meet present needs without compromising the resources necessary to meet the needs of future generations, looking to develop activities that work in harmony with nature and promoting, more than anything else, the improvement in the quality of life of the entire society.

Especially, the United Nations Conference on Environment and Development – UNCED of 1992 contributed significantly to the innovation of Agenda 21 by attributing to each country the commitment to promote the inclusion of environmental issues in its national agenda, that is, an effective commitment to the positivation of environmental standards in the legal and institutional framework of each signatory country.

Another very important document issued at the same conference was the Declaration on Environment and Development of 1992, which contains twenty-seven principles aimed at guiding protective actions towards the integrity of global environmental systems and human development in a sustainable manner. The Rio Declaration on Environment and Development of 1992 aims to establish a new lifestyle, a new kind of presence of man on earth, through the protection of natural resources and the pursuit of sustainable development and better living conditions for all peoples. As in the form of principle 13th:

> Principle 13th: States shall develop national law regarding liability and indemnity to the victims of pollution and other environmental damages. States should cooperate intelligently and more determined in the preparation of new international rules on liability and compensation for the adverse effects of environmental damages caused by activities performed within their jurisdiction or under their control in areas beyond their jurisdiction.

These international documents are important not only internationally but also in formulating Brazilian environmental policies (FLORIANO, 2005, p. 04).

The Kyoto Protocol of 1997 originated from the Third Conference of the Parties of the UN Convention on Climate Change, organized by the United Nations in Japan in

1997, which discussed measures against the global warming. It was ratified on March 15, 1998 and officially entered into force on February 16, 2005, with a term to end in 2012. Overall it sets targets for the reduction of gases pollutants that are believed to be linked to global warming and enshrines the principles of "common but differentiated responsibilities" and the "polluter pays" principle, according to which, despite being the environmental crisis a global problem, it would be the industrialized countries held responsible, historically, for environmental damages, and for bearing the liability and the burden to avoid its aggravation, receiving, therefore, the support of developing countries.

The 1997 Kyoto Protocol still in force is object of criticism also with regards to the polluter pays principle, not only because the United States of America, one of the main contaminant countries of the environment, did not subscribe to it, but also because the way it regulates the polluter pays principle.

Following, the 2002 Johannesburg Conference or "Rio plus 10 (Rio + 10)" is considered the largest international gathering ever held in human history on the planet's future. The so-called "Johannesburg Summit" was convened in order to establish an implementation plan to accelerate and strengthen the application of the principles approved in Rio de Janeiro in 1992 (LAGO, 2006, p. 19).

In turn, the 2009 Kopenhagen Conference, held between 07 and 18 of December 2009, had as main objective global warming towards sustainable development. The result was disappointing because it failed to draw up a document stating any legal obligation, just a "letter of intent" purely political in content, non-binding and full of common minimum and vague denominators.

These UN Conference on Climate Change or "COP's" are held every year. The COP-19 should have created the basic foundations for building a new global agreement to be signed in 2015 in Paris, which will replace the 1997 Kyoto Protocol, and will be effective from 2020, but did not fulfill such intent, frustrating the expectations of the participating nations. The main obstacle happened just around the dillema of how to apply the responsibilities _ be them historical, current or future, that is, how to turn the speeches into a reality.

Despite the difficulties due to the interests at stake, these events pass by landmarks that brought effective inspiration to legislators as to internalize the spirit of the premises highlighted in the principles of environmental law.

However, still prevails within the social mindset the conception of human irresponsibility in relation to the environment where we live. The way we are dealing with a collective problem, as is the environmental issue, the actions should be joint and interconnected. We all, administrators, producers or consumers, have a shared responsibility in the process of destruction of the planet.

At the end of this topic it is verified the formal acceptance of the polluter pays principle in international law, defended as important economic instrument of environmental policy which requires the polluter and the potential polluter the obligation to bear the expenses related to the prevention, repression and compensation for damage to the environment. However, this principle is still in maturation, lacking effectiveness.

## EFFECTIVENESS OF THE POLLUTER PAYS PRINCIPLE IN NATIONAL AND INTERNATIONAL LAW

The polluter pays principle is one of the most popular in matter of environmental law. It reflects both in international law as well as in domestic law. Despite its apparent diffusion and general understanding its meaning is often not well understood, or its application is restricted, which is why this paper presents an explanation of it, briefly exposing its consecration in environmental regulations.

Among the techniques of realization of the polluter pays principle stands out the use of economic and fiscal instruments to generate a more respectful behavior towards the environment. The main objective is the embodiment of all external environmental burdens occurring during the entire life cycle of the product, from source through production, the distribution and the use until its final disposal, so that environmentally friendly products are not at a competitive disadvantageous situation in relation to products that contaminate and generate waste (UN, [n.d.], p. 02).

For example, in the case of nuclear energy, if we aggregate all costs related to risks, in the event of an accident, and expenditures with maintenance of toxic waste cemeteries which can remain active for millions of years, if these expenses were incorporated into the cost of energy, would generate a situation of competitive disadvantage in relation to other types of technologies, such as renewable energy, not to mention the social risk that is transferred to future generations, as we have no idea of the effects on the long term. But while do not arise technologies with less polluting effects, there is no way to hold anyone accountable specifically as humanity still needs nuclear energy.

The application of this principle is problematic, especially regarding the identification of the polluter and the evaluation of costs. For example, in Europe the lifetime of a vehicle is limited by the polluter pays principle (Directive No. 2000/53 of the European Parliament), imposing on manufacturers an obligation to remove the vehicles at the end of life. However, the question that remains open is about who is, in fact, the polluter, the manufacturer or the user. In the case who ends up paying the bill is the buyer, since the manufacturer inserts into the final price of the automobile the cost which he will have upon its removal.

The invocation of this principle is usual under European Community law. Virtually all policies on matter of waste adopt it, especially the Directive "Environmental Responsibility" - DRA of 2004 adopted by the Member States of the European Union. The text of presentation of the Directive states, based on the "polluter pays" principle, that:

> [...] holds liable the polluters who cause the damages for the implementation of preventive action and compensation necessary and payment of the respective costs. As a general principle, the reparation should restore the damaged environment to the state it would be found if the damage had not occurred. The Directive "Environmental Responsibility" - DRA provides a framework for this evaluation of the damages and its repair (EC, 2004, p 01.).

According to the Directive "Environmental Responsibility" - DRA of 2004, it is not necessary to determine the existence of fault or negligence by the polluter / contaminated to be liable for the adoption of preventive and restorative measures, as well as the payment of their costs (EC, 2004, p. 02).

In the European Community space, any person or entity, that is, or may be, affected by environmental damages, or who for some reason is interested in the matter can notify a damage or an imminent threat to the environment, to the competent authority, through the presentation of relevant information to the statement of his observations. That person has the right to challenge the decision of the authority before a court or other independent and impartial public body, to the scope that ensures he acts in the public interest, to claim the repairing of the environment (EC, 2004, p. 02).

The Court of Justice of the European Union says that oil companies should pay for environmental damages caused by tankers wrecks as reported on "El País". The Court of Justice of the European Communities reaffirmed the "polluter pays principle" when deciding that oil producers are also liable for damages to the environment caused by oil tanker wreck. In summary, the Court of Luxembourg responded to the questions raised by the French Court of Appeals in the case of the oil tanker Erika. A French Court sentenced the oil company Total, the owner of the vessel and the Italian Naval Certification Society to pay a compensation of 192 million euros, in view of the accident that poured 20,000 tons of fuel off the coast of Great Britain. The oil company appealed to the European Court raising questions of Community Law. The European Court, however, held that the Community Directive raised by the oil company does not prevent that States establish obligations that fall on the producer of pollutant materials (CURIA, Case C-188/07, 2009).

To the Court of Justice of the European Union, the polluter pays principle ("*verursacherprinzip*") is the principle governing the allocation of costs corresponding to other language versions which - unlike the German version - do not use the concept of causality, determining that the polluter must pay (*poluidor pagador, pollueur-payeur*). In this sense, the European Union Court of Justice understands that the polluter pays principle is the expression of the principle of proportionality, which requires the Member States - and the Community legislature - not to charge anyone costs that are not essential in face of the circumstances involved (CURIA, Case C-188/07, 2009).

In Brazil, to the Federal Regional Court of the 1st Region, in the rapporteur of Souza Prudente, "the polluter pays principle seeks, above all, prevent the occurrence of environmental damages and only ultimately, the repair" (TRF1aR, AG No. 0018353-06.2012.4.01.0000 / MA, 2013, p. 384).

On another occasion, the same Court ruled that under the polluter pays principle and repair *in integrum*, in environmental demands is possible to perform simultaneous and cumulative sentencing in obligation to do, not do and compensate (TRF1aR, AC No. 0002496-09.2002.4.01.3802 / MG, 2012, p. 675). In the same view is the interpretation of the Supreme Court of Justice, as follows:

> Summary: [...]. The refusal to apply, or truncated application, by the judge, of the polluter pays principle and repair *in integrum* risk to project, moral and socially the harmful impression that the environmental illicit pays off, hence the administrative and judicial response not exceed acceptable and manageable "risk or normal business costs." Leave debilitated thus the deterrent character, the pedagogical strength and prophylactic purpose of environmental liability (= general and special prevention). real stimulus for others, inspired by the example of impunity in fact, even as not of merit, of the polluter awarded, to imitate or repeat his deleterious behavior (STJ, Resp No. 1145083 / MG, 2012).

The polluter pays principle, complex and controversial, mainly for adding spending to economic agents, is an essential principle for whatever modern environmental policy, both internally and internationally.

## CONCLUSION

The environment is the set of elements that allows for the existence of life in all its forms. Under the Federal Constitution of 1988, it is a public good of common use of the people whose guardianship is imposed on the whole community.

To discipline the relationships between people and the environment where they live, it was established the right to the environment. Its regulation occurs through a complex of principles and coercive legal rules. For this study we highlighted the specific principles of sustainable development, polluter pays, prevention, participation and universality.

The principle of sustainable development means that there must be a healthy balance between socioeconomic development and environmental conservation. As for the prevention principle, the State and civil society must protect and preserve the environment. According to the polluter pays principle, those who cause environmental damages should financially compensate for the damages they caused, especially, to reverse them. Regarding the principle of participation, citizens share responsibility in the management of collective interests. Finally, according to the principle of universality or ubiquity the environment is a universal good, belonging to all mankind, and as such needs to be cared for.

The polluter pays principle remains open to interpretation and although it is not denied its implication for the development of international environmental law, it is more of an economic policy postulate rather than any principle of law.

This principle was adopted by the Organization for Economic Cooperation and Development - OECD in 1972, not to make fall on those responsible for the contamination the obligation to pay compensation for the caused losses, but to make sure that the costs involved in preventing and fighting contamination are undertaken by those who produce it and thus ensure that the environment remains in acceptable condition and that the costs of such measures are reflected in the price of goods and services that cause pollution in production and consumption. The measures of incorporation of environmental costs can not be subsidized, as they would cause distortions to international trade and international investments.

As seen at the international level the main object of the polluter pays principle is not environmental, but economic, since the elimination of hidden subsidies is a necessary part of the process of economic liberalization and free trade in the industrialized countries. In this sense is the provision of Principle 16th of the Rio Declaration on

Environment and Development of 1992, which provides that the rational authorities should promote the internalization of environmental costs and the use of economic instruments, due to the understanding that the polluter should bear the burden of pollution, with special attention to the public interest and without creating distortions in trade and international investments.

Among the main barriers to the application of this principle, there are the difficulties in identifying and differentiating the authors of damages. Moreover, sometimes the damages are produced long after the human action.

In short, it is a principle of economic character whereby the costs for the use of environmental resources, especially the use of the so-called "common goods" are internalized by those who get economic profit from their extraction, and not by society. This principle manifests itself in two phases: a preventive, as an economic instrument generated by rule of law, in order to stimulate economic agents to value the use of environmental resources and thereby carry out their activities based on real costs. But in no way it can be interpreted as an authorization to pay a certain price to pollute; and other reparatory, through action for environmental damage, so that the environmental damage is repaired in its entirety and not only in its financial dimension.

Finally, it is concluded that in the international context the polluter pays principle is an economic or national policy criteria before being legal to belong to international law.

# REFERENCES

AATR-BA, Associação de Advogados de Trabalhadores Rurais do Estado da Bahia. **Direito Ambiental**. Salvador: AATR-BA, 2002.

AMBIENTE Brasil S/S Ltda. **Agenda 21 brasileira**. Disponível em: <http://www.ambientebrasil.com.br/composer.php3?base=./gestao/index.html&conteudo=./gestao/agenda.html>. Acesso em: 04 set. 2014.

ANTUNES, Paulo de Bessa. **Curso de direito ambiental**. 5ª ed. Rio de Janeiro: Lúmen Júris, 2001.

ANTUNES, Paulo de Bessa. **Direito ambiental**. 11 ed. Rio de Janeiro: Lúmen Júris, 2008.

ARAGÃO, Maria Alexandra de Sousa. **Direito comunitário do ambiente**. Coleção Cadernos do Cedoua. Almedina: Cedoua, 2002.

BRASIL, Constituição (1988). **Constituição da República Federativa do Brasil, de 05 de outubro de 1988**. Disponível em: <http://www.planalto.gov.br/ccivil_03/constituicao/constituicaocompilado.htm>. Acesso em: 05 set. 2014.

BRASIL, Legislação. **Lei nº 6.938, de 31 de agosto de 1981**. Dispõe sobre a Política Nacional do Meio Ambiente, seus fins e mecanismos de formulação e aplicação, e dá outras providências. Disponível em: http://www.planalto.gov.br/ccivil_03/leis/l6938.htm>. Acesso em: 05 set. 2014.

CE, Comissão Europeia. **Directiva nº 2000/53/CE**. Directiva do Parlamento Europeu e do Conselho de 18 de setembro de 2000 relativa aos veículos em fim de vida. Disponível em: <http://eur-lex.europa.eu/LexUriServ/LexUriServ.do?uri=OJ:L:2000:269:0034:0042:PT:PDF>. Acesso em: 05 set. 2014.

CE, Comissão Europeia. **Diretiva "Responsabilidade Ambiental" - DRA**. Adotada em 2004. Disponível em: <http://ec.europa.eu/environment/legal/liability/pdf/factsheet/ELD%20factsheet_PT.pdf>. Acesso em: 05 set. 2014.

CURIA, Tribunal de Justiça da União Europeia. **Processo C-188/07**. Conclusões da Advogada-Geral Juliane Kokott. Apresentadas em 13 de março de 2008. Commune de Mesquer contra Total France SA e Total International Ltda. Pedido de decisão prejudicial apresentado pela Cour de Cassation (França). In: InfoCuria,

Jurisprudência do Tribunal de Justiça. Disponível em: <http://curia.europa.eu/juris/document/document.jsf?text=&docid=70499&pageIndex=0&doclang=pt&mode=lst&dir=&occ=first&part=1&cid=471595>. Acesso em: 06 set. 2014.

FIORILLO, Celso Antonio Pacheco. **Curso de direito ambiental brasileiro**. 4. ed. São Paulo: Saraiva, 2003.

FLORIANO, Eduardo Pagel. **Políticas de gestão ambiental**. 2. ed. Santa Maria-RS: ANORGS; Universidade Federal de Santa Maria-RS, 2005.

GUDYNAS, Eduardo. **Ética, ambiente e ecologia**: uma crise entrelaçada. *In: Revista Eclesiástica Brasileira*, nº 52, fascículo 205. Petrópolis: Vozes, mar. 1992.

INTERNACIONAL, Legislação. **Ato Único Europeu de 1986**. Estabelecido entre o Reino da Bélgica, o Reino da Dinamarca, a República Federal da Alemanha, a República Helénica, o Reino de Espanha, a República Francesa, a Irlanda, a República Italiana, o Grão-Ducado do Luxemburgo, o Reino dos Países Baixos, a República Portuguesa e o Reino Unido da Grã-Bretanha e Irlanda do Norte, concluído em 17 e em 28 de fevereiro de 1986. Disponível em: <http://www.fd.uc.pt/CI/CEE/pm/Tratados/AUE/AUE-f.htm>. Acesso em: 02 set. 2014.

INTERNACIONAL, Legislação. **Declaração de Estocolmo sobre o Ambiente Humano, de 1972**. Elaborada na Conferência das Nações Unidas sobre o Meio Ambiente, em Estocolmo, de 05 a 16 de junho de 1972. Disponível em: <http://www.silex.com.br/leis/normas/estocolmo htm>. Acesso em 02 set. 2014.

INTERNACIONAL, Legislação. **Declaração de Estocolmo sobre o Ambiente Humano, de 1972**. Elaborada na Conferência das Nações Unidas sobre o Meio Ambiente, em Estocolmo, de 05 a 16 de junho de 1972. Disponível em: <http://www.silex.com.br/leis/normas/estocolmo.htm>. Acesso em 02 set. 2014.

INTERNACIONAL, Legislação. **Declaração do Rio sobre Meio Ambiente e Desenvolvimento, de 1992**. A Conferência das Nações Unidas sobre Meio Ambiente e Desenvolvimento, tendo se reunido no Rio de Janeiro, de 3 a 14 de junho de 1992, reafirmando a Declaração da Conferência das Nações Unidas sobre o Meio Ambiente Humano, adotada em Estocolmo em 16 de junho de 1972. Disponível em: <http://www.onu.org.br/rio20/img/2012/01/rio92.pdf>. Acesso em: 26 ago. 2014.

INTERNACIONAL, Legislação. **Declaração do Rio sobre Meio Ambiente e Desenvolvimento, de 1992**. A Conferência das Nações Unidas sobre Meio Ambiente e Desenvolvimento, tendo se reunido no Rio de Janeiro, de 3 a 14 de junho de 1992, reafirmando a Declaração da Conferência das Nações Unidas sobre o Meio Ambiente Humano, adotada em Estocolmo em 16 de junho de 1972. Disponível em: <http://www.onu.org.br/rio20/img/2012/01/rio92.pdf>. Acesso em: 26 ago. 2014.

INTERNACIONAL, Legislação. **Tratado que institui a Comunidade [econômica] Europeia (TCE) de 1957**. Tratado de Roma. Versão Integral. Feito em Roma, aos vinte e cinco de março de mil novecentos e cinquenta e sete. Disponível em: <http://dupond.ci.uc.pt/CDEUC/TRVRINT.HTM>. Acesso em: 02 set. 2014.

LAGO, André Aranha Corrêa do. **Estocolmo, Rio, Joanesburgo**: o Brasil e as três conferências ambientais das Nações Unidas. Brasília: FUNAG, 2006.

LEITE, José Rubens Morato. **Sociedade de risco e Estado**. *In*: CANOTILHO, José Joaquim Gomes; LEITE, José Rubens Morato (orgs.). *Direito constitucional ambiental brasileiro*. 5. ed. São Paulo: Saraiva, 2012.

MACHADO, Paulo Affonso Leme. **Direito ambiental brasileiro**. 12. ed., rev., atual e ampl. São Paulo: Malheiros, 2004.

MATOS, Eduardo Lima de. **Autonomia municipal e meio ambiente**. Belo Horizonte: Del Rey, 2001.

MILARÉ, Edis. **Direito do ambiente**: a gestão ambiental em foco (doutrina, jurisprudência, glossário. 5. ed. São Paulo: Revista dos Tribunais, 2007.

STF, Supremo Tribunal Federal. **Medida Cautelar na Ação Direta de Inconstitucionalidade n° 3.540/DF**. Tribunal Pleno. Supremo Tribunal Federal. Relator: Celso de Mello. Julgado em: 01 de setembro de 2005. Publicado no DJ de 03 de fevereiro de 2006, p. 14. Disponível em: <http://www.stf.jus.br>. Acesso em: 05 set. 2014.

STJ, Superior Tribunal de Justiça. **REsp n° 1145083 / MG**. Segunda Turma. Relator Herman Benjamin. Julgado em 27 de setembro de 2011. Publicado no DJ-e de 04 de setembro de 2012. Disponível em: <http://www.stj.jus.br>. Acesso em: 06 set. 2014.

TRF1ªR, Tribunal Regional Federal da 1ª Região. **AC n° 0002496-09.2002.4.01.3802 / MG**. Quinta Turma. Relator: Souza Prudente. Julgado em 20 de agosto de 2013. Publicado no e-DJF1 de 30 de novembro de 2012, p. 675. Disponível em: <http://portal.trf1.jus.br/>. Acesso em: 06 set. 2014.

TRF1ªR, Tribunal Regional Federal da 1ª Região. **AG nº 0018353-06.2012.4.01.0000 / MA**. Quinta Turma. Relator: Souza Prudente. Julgado em 20 de agosto de 2013. Publicado no e-DJF1 de 29 de agosto de 2013, p. 384. Disponível em: <http://portal. trf1.jus.br/>. Acesso em: 06 set. 2014.

UN, Universidad de Navarra. **El principio "quien contamina paga" y la regulación del daño ambiental**. [s.d.]. Disponível em: <http://www.unav.es/adi/UserFiles/ File/80963990/pcipio_contamina_paga.pdf>. Acesso em: 05 set. 2014.

# CREATION OF A NEW LEGAL FRAMEWORK IN BRAZIL FOR VOLUNTARY PARTNERSHIPS BETWEEN THE PUBLIC ADMINISTRATION AND CIVIL SOCIETY ORGANIZATIONS, MEMBERS OF THE THIRD SECTOR

**José Eduardo Sabo Paes**[26]

## INTRODUCTION

The term 'Third Sector' was first used in the 1970s by researchers in the United States. From the 1980s also came to be used by European researchers.[27]

In terms of Brazilian law, the Third Sector or NGOs comprises non-governmental organizations, non-profit entities of social interest such as associations and private foundations, with autonomy and self-administration, whose goal is to protect some social

need, or to defend diffused or emerging rights. Such organizations and social groupings cover a wide spectrum of activities, work fields or activities, either in defense of human rights, environmental protection, health care, support to needy populations, education, citizenship, women's rights, indigenous rights , consumer rights, children's rights, etc.

When introducing the concept of Third Sector, it is commonly referred    to member organizations, their nature and their fields.  For some time, I presented the "third sector as a set of nonprofit organizations, or foundations endowed with autonomy and self-management. Their main objective and function is to voluntarily  act with civil society for  improvement." [28]

---

26 José Eduardo Paes Sabo, Doctor in Law from the University of Madrid, Attorney of the Public Ministry of the Federal District and Territories - MPDFT, Master's Program Professor of Law at the Catholic University of Brasilia, Advanced Studies Center of the Third Sector (NEPats), coordinator of Third Sector and National and International Taxation research group: forms of integration impact on society coordinator, both at the Catholic University of Brasilia.

27 Simone de Castro Coelho, in thesis published and titled "Third Sector - a comparative study between Brazil and the United States", now in 2nd edition, São Paulo, ed.Senac. 2008 states, to the fl. 58, which, according to Seibel and Anheir, Americans would be Etzioli (1973), Levitt (1973), Nielzon (1975) and the Fiter Commission (1975) and the Europeans would be Douglas (1983), Reese (1987), Reichard (1988 ) and Ronge (1988).

28 Constant Concept of the work of José Eduardo Paes Sabo:Fundações, Associações e Entidades de Interesse Social. "Aspectos jurídicos, administrativos, contábeis, trabalhistas e tributáveis". 8ª edição, Rio de Janeiro, Forense, 2013 p. 87

It is known the Third Sector needs a standard of its own to regulate transparency and objectivity in its relationship with the State, for the purpose of encompassing all entities irrespective of its classification, title or given certification.

This cooperative relationship is accomplished with the use of budget- public resources, and ensuring the relevance of these organizations to the democratic process, especially respecting the autonomy of these entities and strengthening them to complement the execution of government policies and new rights.

The current tools are varied and come from different legal arrangements as agreements, transfer agreements, terms of cooperation, partnership contracts, management contracts, among others, and each of them have specific regulations. Agreements and transfer contracts are regulated by Law No. 8,666 / 93, art. 116, Decree Law No. 6,170 / 07, and by the Inter-ministerial Decree No. 507/2011 and the Law of Budgetary Guidelines. Terms of the partnership are relevant to the Civil Society Organizations of Public Interests - CSOPIS under Law No. 9.790 / 99 and Decree Law No. 3,100 / 99. Management Contract restricted to entities qualified as Social Organizations (OS), according to the dictates of Law No 9,637 / 98.

As a result and sensitive to the need to improve the regulatory environment of the Third Sector and its comprising entities, the federal government, instituted -by Decree No 7568 of 16/09/2011- the Working Group (WG) under the coordination of the General Secretariat of the Presidency. Its main goal was to assess, review and suggest improvements within the federal legislation concerning the implementation of programs, projects and activities of public interest as well as the transparency of federal funds through agreements, transfer agreements , terms of partnership or similar instruments.

The WG was composed of principal and alternate representatives of seven agencies of the Federal Government and 14 national civil society organizations.

The activities of the Working Group started on November 11, 2011 producing fruitful debates in the course of their meetings, which continued until July 24, 2012 , [29]emphasizing the interaction between the actors (members of civil society and government), and promoting the achievement of important new multi-perspective understandings.

---

29  On 24.07.2012 was the closure of the WG activities with the presentation of the final report in the Presidential Palace to the Minister Gilberto Carvalho.

In this regard, a resulting proposal was made to create a new legal framework of collaboration and promotion between the State and Civil Society Organizations (CSOs). It was entitled Agreement of Collaboration and Promotion.

In this article we will discuss about this new legal regime of voluntary partnerships with the institution of the Agreement of "Collaboration and Promotion," which it is worth mentioning was processed under the National Congress, inserted in the form of replacement in the Legislative Proposal (PL) No. 3887/2004[30] and Legislative Proposal from Brazilian Senate (PLS) No. 649/2011. It was enacted on July 31, 2014, as Law No. 13,019, of 31/07/14, which will come into force on January 23, 2016.[31]

## From the Agreement of Collaboration and Promotion - Introductory notions, principles and guidelines

The creation of a "Agreement of Collaboration and Promotion" today laid down respectively in Articles 16 and 17 of Law 13,019 / 14, proposed in the WG and later in replacement of the PL No. 3,887 / 2004, and in replacement of PLS No. 649/2011 (in the nomenclature of Collaboration Agreement). This agreement would establish a special legal regime to equip partnerships with associative and foundational entities

and the Public Power that involve funds from the fiscal budget or Social Security Union (including the Judiciary, Legislature, Prosecutor and Court of Auditors), or

any federal entity regardless of whether those non-governmental entities possess any capacity, qualification or certification.

It notes that the following entities can not enter into Agreements of Collaboration and Promotion : Political Parties and their foundations, federations or trade union confederations, trade association or professional category representation; mutual

---

30 The congressman Eduardo Barbosa, PSDB-MG, rapporteur of the PL No. 3887 of 2004 showed substitute that, approved on 05.12.2012, in the Committee on Social Security and Family of the House of Representatives, provides for general rules for the relationship of collaboration and promotion between Public Administration and non-profit private entities, establishing the "Collaboration and Promotion Agreement", consulted on 03/18/2013. Available at: <http://www.camara.gov.br/proposicoesWeb/fichadetramitacao?idProposicao=259499>

31 It establishes the legal regime of voluntary partnerships, whether or not involving transfers of financial resources between the Public Administration and the civil society organizations in a mutually supportive basis for the attainment of public interest objectives; it sets guidelines for development policy and cooperation with civil society organizations; it establishes the collaboration term and the promotion term; and its amendments the Laws in 8429, of June 2, 1992, and 9790, to March 23, 1999.

benefit organizations that meet only the narrow interests of its members, autonomous social services, social organizations, simpler societies, entrepreneurs and individual businesses with limited liability.

There should be observance on those principles such as autonomy, free functioning and independence of civil society and social movements; promotion of national and regional development, and inclusive and sustainable development; promotion and defense of human rights; and the proportionality, reasonableness, simplicity and promptness of procedures in the control mechanisms of the Agreements of Collaboration and Promotion.

The required guidelines of the legal framework for cooperation and promotion are as follows: the promotion and encouragement of civil society organizations to collaborate with the government to implement activities and projects of public interest; the project selection or private nonprofit organizations to collaborate and promote public procedures prior to the celebration, making use of objective criteria and equalization of opportunities to entities that favor the best choice for public interest; social control to evaluate and monitor the results of the Agreement of Collaboration and Promotion; and prioritization of results control in accountability.

Taking into consideration the proposals and discussions, the law ended up defining that the collaboration term should be adopted by the public administration in case of voluntary transfers of resources to achieve work plans proposed by the public administration in mutual cooperation arrangements with civil society organizations. It also should be selected through a public call, except as otherwise provided in this Act (art.16). It also sets the funding term should be adopted by the public administration in case of voluntary transfers of resources to achieve work plans proposed by civil society in mutual cooperation arrangements with the public administration, selected through public call, except as provided in this Act (art.17).

It is indeed a new effective concept in this relationship of state and society, and essential to monitor and strengthen social transformations. The Article prepared by the Civil Secretary Staff of the Presidency and presented at the VI Consad Congress on April 18, 2013, points out very well this fact.

"The partnerships between the state and CSOs must attend the political, social and economic transformations of Brazilian democracy; they must be based on democratic public management ideas and social participation as a method of governing, creating a legal framework that provides favorable environment for social initiatives and recognizing their autonomy and their own forms of organization."[32]

## The Public Call

The access to Collaboration and Promotion Agreement will be realized through so-called public call procedure (which is even longer used for hiring agreements and terms of partnership as Art. 4 of Decree No. 6,170 / 2007), and it is currently provided for in Articles 23 to 32 of the recent Law No. 13,019 / 14.

This public call procedure will be held by the public body at two different times, however subsequently. The first can be referred as "Preparatory Phase", when the Public Administration define the collaboration and promotion object that want to be accomplished; the indication of the public interest involved in making the call; the diagnosis of the reality that needs to be modified, improved or developed; the feasibility, costs, benefits, time of action execution.

It should be noted that the public call procedure, created by Decree Law No. 7,568 / 11, which amended Decree Law No. 6,170 / 07, is mandatory. In addition, the Working Group of the Presidency of Brazil very well pointed out the need to consolidate this obligation for the legal level, with appropriate exceptions, in consideration of transparency and equality in hiring.[33]

The second may be called "The Public Calling Notice." Thus, selection of entities or projects that best meet the pre-defined selection criteria will be made through widely publicized announcement.

The Notice should have minimal information (according with what is already required to conclude the partnership agreement, especially the Article 25 of Decree No. 3,100 / 1999 and the public call for signing the agreement, and the Art. 8, § 1, of Ordinance No. 507/2011). Thus, it is required at least the object to be executed; disbursement limits of funds, where appropriate; requirements for eligibility; place, date, conditions and form of presentation and evaluation of bids, with the forecast deadlines and appeals´ process conditions; designation of the Selection Committee; criteria for scoring and

---

32 [ "Colaboração e Fomento: uma nova proposta de parceria entre Estado e Organizações da Sociedade Civil" by Lais Vanessa Carvalho Figueiredo Lopes, Silas Cardoso de Souza, Diogo de Sant'Anna, Maria Victoria Hernandez, Evânio Antonio de Araújo Júnior, Aline Gonçalves de Souza, Ana Tulia de Macedo, presented at the VI Congress of Consad (National Council of State Secretaries of Administration) of 19 April 2013.

33 BRAZIL. Civil House of the Presidency of the Republic. Final report of the Working Group established by Inter-ministerial Ordinance No. 392/2012. 2012, p.13-17.

the selection of proposals, including the adequacy of costs; the draft instrument to be signed.

This selection will be made through committee or banking composed jointly by government representatives and civil society, with thematic and proven mastery of the topic buildup, observing the republican principles of impartiality, transparency and neutrality.

## The popular initiative through Social Interest Procedure

As a novelty and inserted into the principle of participatory democracy, a social participation instrument in the scope of public call for execution of terms of promotion is established.

This is called Social Interest Procedure and it is provided by Articles 18 to 22. It is an instrument through which the private non-profit organizations, social movements and citizens can submit proposals to the Public Power so it assesses the possibility of accomplishing a public call aimed at the celebration and partnership.

## Collaboration and Promotion Agreement resource. Management and use.

It is important to highlight that the projects and studies clearly point out two important elements. First, the transferred public funds should be used, respecting the criteria of economy and impersonality; and second, the mentioned resource should cover all the expenses related to any project presented. This will include:

• Team Remuneration integrated in the Work Plan, even those related to the entity's own staff. It can contemplate the cost of tax payments, social security contributions, guarantee funds for length of service, vacation, Christmas bonus, proportional wages, severance pay and other social charges, if such values:

a) correspond to the planned activities and are approved in the Work Plan and the object of adjustment;

b) correspond to the technical qualifications required for the execution of the function to be performed;

c) show compatibility with the regional market value where it operates, and do not exceed the limited wage (ceiling) of the Executive Branch;

d) show equal proportion to the working time actually devoted to celebrate partnership,

• Taxes levied on the planned activities in the approved Work Plan, excluding those of direct and personalistic nature that burden the entity;

• Daily Payments related to travel, lodging and meals where the execution of the celebrated partnership object requires;

• Remuneration of accounting, auditing and monitoring, and evaluation services, as well as operating costs related to compliance with the Agreement, if they have as object the work plan, the financial execution plan and accountability in value compatible with the market value; and

• Payment of fines and charges related to delays in the fulfillment of obligations under work plans and financial execution as a default by the Public Administration to release, in a timely manner, the agreed installments; **insolvency.**

It is also observed that Law No. 13,019 / 14 provides what it is prohibited:

• Perform expenditure under management fee, management or similar;

• Pay, for any reason, to public worker or public employee with funds linked to partnership, except in the cases provided for a specific law and in the law of budgetary guidelines;

• Modify the object, except for expansion goals, if previously approved the adequacy of the Work Plan by the Public Administration;

• Use, although on an emergency basis, funds for purpose other than established in the Work Plan;

• Perform expenditure prior to the enactment of the partnership;

• Make payment at a later date to the validity of the partnership, unless expressly authorized by the competent authority of the Public Administration;

• Transfer funds to clubs, public workers associations, political parties or any congener entities;

It is also observed that administrative costs[34] provided for the Work Plan may be

---

34 The provision for payment of administrative expenses is already authorized by art. 52, sole paragraph, of the Inter-ministerial Ordinance No. 507 of 2011. The sole paragraph seeks to

executed up to the limit set by the public body which may not exceed fifteen per cent of the value of the agreement object (Art. 22). Administrative expenses include those with Internet, transportation, rent, telephone, electricity and water, among others that would be necessary for the implementation, always proportional and able to comply with the corresponding object of the agreement.

It is important and necessary to note the inclusion in device law that allows payment of own entity's personnel, and even essential in a regulatory framework that is founded on transparency regarding the use of public resources, and responsible for results in the execution of projects or activities of public interest or social relevance.

The Law of the SCOPIS - Law No. 9.790 / 1999, art. 4°, s. VI, took a first important step to make possible, in an innovative way[35] , the establishment of remuneration for directors of entities acting effectively in the executive management, and to those that provide specific services, respected, in both cases, the economic values practiced by the market, in the region corresponding to their area of expertise.

Similarly, the Law of Social Organizations - Law No. 9,637/1998, in the implementation of the management contract signed between the Public Power and the qualified entity as SO, which aims at building partnerships between the parties, allows in its section II of art. 7 to remunerate directors and employees.

Moreover, it is notorious the difficulty of the institutions to afford expenditure on staff salary, social security, labor disputes, and other fixed costs for maintenance, sustainability and continuity of their work.

For a long time I have positioned myself in favor of an executive and paid management so that NGOs can carry out their constitutional mission to complement the public services provision.

Recently Law No. 13,151, of July 28, 2015, was enacted, which provides the possibility of remuneration of directors of foundations or tax exempted associations or considered of charitable social assistance.

Moreover, as Valéria Salgado perfectly teaches, "the goal of the Public Power, when establishes bonds of cooperation with civil non-profit organizations, is to expand the

---

indicate that an administrative expenditure can be considered.
35  Review the work developed at the time of the discussion held at the Solidarity Community Council.Ferrarezi, Elisabete. CSOPI - Civil society organization of public interest: the Law 9.790 / 99 as an alternative to the Third Sector / Elisabete Ferrarezi. Valeria Rezende - Brasilia: Comunidade Solidária, 2000. 108p.

state's capacity to guarantee social order, especially by increasing the supply of social services to the population and indirect holding of other public interest activities".[36]

However, it shall be stipulated limits and criteria in the law for the costs with remuneration of directors, employees and those who are hired, as well as the institution service providers, **in casu**, parties **in** the Collaboration and Promotion Agreement.

The first is the strict adherence to the object (activity or project) Collaboration and Promotion Agreement included in the Work Plan.

The second is that the remuneration received is consistent in terms of values with assignments/functions performed or charge.

The third is that they are compatible with market values prevailing in the region where it operates and not greater than the value established as ceiling by the Federal Executive Branch.

## The accountability

It is essential that, under the new regulatory framework, accountability be understood through a shared responsibility perspective. This means both areas of competence of the public body as well as the private entity should meet at the same time and verify the fulfillment of what was agreed upon and set out in the object of agreement. Therefore, if it is properly run, goals and expected results will give the expected effects.

Lais de Figueiredo Lopes and others rightly mention that "to prioritize the results control in the implementation of the partnerships as CSOs is one of the most important goals indicated in studies conducted by public bodies and organizations. It

is recognized the need that the focus control should be the verification of compliance with the object and scope of results (outcome control), notwithstanding the need for analysis of expenditure indicators to ensure the information accuracy on how the object was (media control) achieved".[37]

---

36 Salgado, Valeria Alpine Bigonha. Manual de administração pública democrática: conceitos e formas de organização / Campinas, SP : Saberes Editora, 2012,, p. 393.
37 "Colaboração e Fomento: uma nova proposta de parceria entre Estado e Organizações da Sociedade Civil" by Lais Vanessa Carvalho Figueiredo Lopes, Silas Cardoso de Souza, Diogo de Sant'Anna, Maria Victoria Hernandez, Evânio Antonio de Araújo Júnior, Aline Gonçalves de Souza, Ana Tulia de Macedo, presented at the VI Congress of Consad (National Council of State Secretaries of Administration) of 19 April 2013.

It is noteworthy that today is indispensable an accountability proof of results, which should be provided by the analysis of the Object Implementation Report. This is prepared by the entity as well as signed by its legal representative, with the activities demonstrating the fulfillment of the object, containing comparative proposal goals with the achieved results from the schedule already agreed. It would also require the attachment of documents supporting realization of actions, such as attendance lists, photos and videos, if any, and financial execution reports to be generated with the data already recorded in the electronic platform for monitoring the Collaboration and Promotion Agreement, signed by its legal representative and the responsible accountant, which will describe the costs and actual revenue collections.

However, it is essential to include the setting of deadlines so the entity includes in its archives the original documents that support accountability and as for proof of results, which may not be less than five years or greater than ten.[38]

Similarly, it is also fundamental to enclose the time limits for the Public Administration work on the accountability analysis and proof of income. This period may be fixed between ninety (90) and one hundred fifty (150) days, lengthened for the same period[39], after which it will be filed and can be reviewed in certain circumstances; for there is

---

38 The parameter can be set taking into account that according to art. 205 of the CC, "the prescription occurs in ten years, when the law has not set a shortest time"; and (ii) in the current Ordinance MPOG/MF/CGU No. 507/2011, which provides in its article.3, § 3, that "the contracting party shall keep the documents related to the agreement for a period of ten (10) years from the date the accountability was approved".

39 Art. 71.The Public Administration will aim to assess the final accountability presented within ninety (90) to one hundred fifty (150) days from the date of receipt, as stipulated in the partnership instrument.

§ 1 The definition of the term for consideration of the final accountability will be established, on reasonable grounds, according to the complexity of the partnership object and integrates the technical analysis phase of the proposition and celebration of the instrument.

§ 2 The deadline to assess the final accountability may be extended, at most, for the same period, if it is duly justified.

§ 3. In the hypothesis of noncompliance with the defined deadline under the terms of the caput and of the §§ 1 and 2 within 15 (fifteen) days of its course, the unit responsible for examining the final accountability will report the reasons to the Minister of State or State or Municipal Secretary, as appropriate, as well as the public policy council and corresponding internal control body.

§ 4. The course of the defined term under caput and of the § 1 without the accounts evaluated:
I -It does not mean impossibility of evaluation at a later date or veto to adopt remedial , punitive or intended measures to compensate damage that might be caused to public funds;
II - in cases where it is not found guile of the organization's partner civil society or its agents, not subject to inflation adjustment, it prevents the incidence of arrears of interest on debits eventually calculated, for the period between the end of the deadline referred in the head of this paragraph and the date it was finalized the evaluation by the Public Administration.

no justification for Public Administration (by any of its powers, institutions or bodies) and the prosecution not to meet its deadlines. Not meeting its deadlines leads to legal uncertainty and inertia to be the keynote of the monitoring and supervision of public covenants.

Notice that in the templates the Federal Audit Court passes its decisions, the evaluation of the public power must be to regulate the accountability, regulate with reserves, or non regulate the accountability under promotion terms.

It is important that the accountability be appropriate to the amount of the values involved in the Collaboration and Promotion Agreement. That is, there must be rules, requirements and forms of control and differentiated auditing, according to the value of the object. More specifically, it can be used the value of R$ 600,000.00 (six hundred thousand Brazilian reais) as a parameter in constant casts of the CSOPIS Law - Law No. 9,790/1999, which established, in its Art. 19, that above this value, an independent external audit will be mandatory.

## CONCLUSIONS

The Third Sector has a strategic character of the utmost importance in the context of any society that cares about social development and the consolidation of democratic, pluralist, committed values to human solidarity and a sense of community. In Brazil, despite the strong presence of the State, **its** inefficiency opens spaces for many other initiatives.

Noting the Third Sector trajectory, we can clearly identify the existence of a very traditional , marked by the old-fashioned welfare and epitomized by the paternalism and condescension of alms giving; and a more modern, dynamic, where social rights are now recognized as inherent in the concept of citizenship in a society that is to be civilized.

Now, the establishment of a legal framework for the Third Sector is necessary. Legislative Proposals are in the final calculation course for the establishment of clear relationships to the partnership of non-profit private entities with the Public Administration to be effective in the purpose achievement to meet social demands.

In this process, the proposal carried out by the Working Group set up by the Federal Government, at the request of organizations, social movements and networks of the Third Sector contributed significantly to improve the regulatory environment of civil society organizations in Brazil.

A new legal framework for collaboration and development for the Third Sector was created under the tonic of efficiency and transparency, and now with the enactment of Law No. 13,019/2014.

Within our participatory democracy, it will be essential to clearly and permanently equip  the necessary partnerships between civil society organizations and the Brazilian State.

242

# REFERENCES

BRASIL. Casa Civil da Presidência da República. *Relatório Final dp Grupo de Trabalho instituído pela Portaria Interministerial nº 392/2012.* 2012

BRASIL. Secretaria-Geral da Presidência da República. Relatório Final do Grupo de Trabalho sobre o Marco Regulatório das OSCs. 2012.

SALGADO, Valéria Alpino Bigonha. *Manual de Administração Pública Democrática: conceitos e formas de organização.* Campinas: Saberes Editora, 2011.

Simone de Castro Coelho, Terceiro Setor – um estudo comparado entre Brasil e Estados Unidos, 2ª edição, São Paulo, ed. Senac. 2008.

Paes, José Eduardo Sabo: Fundações, Associações e Entidades de Interesse Social. "Aspectos jurídicos, administrativos, contábeis, trabalhistas e tributáveis. 8ª edição, Rio de Janeiro, Forense, 2013, pag. 87

PL n.º 3.887 de 2004, dispõe sobre normas gerais para a relação de colaboração e fomento entre a administração pública e as entidades privadas sem fins lucrativos, institui o "Termo de Colaboração e Fomento", consultado em 18.03.2013. Disponível em: <http://www.camara.gov.br/proposicoesWeb/fichadetramitacao?idProposicao=259499>

O PLS n 649/2011, de autoria do Senador Aloysio Nunes Ferreira PSDB/SP, tem como relator o Senador Rodrigo Rollemberg PSB/DF.

Lopes, Lais Vanessa Carvalho Figueirêdo, "Colaboração e Fomento: uma nova proposta de parceria entre Estado e Organizações da Sociedade Civil", apresentado no VI Congresso do Consad (Conselho Nacional de Secretários de Estado de Administração), de 19 de abril de 2013.

Portaria Interministerial n.º 507 de 2011.

Ferrarezi, Elisabete. OSCIP – Organização da sociedade civil de interesse público: a lei 9.790/99 como alternativa para o terceiro setor / Elisabete Ferrarezi. Valéria Rezende – Brasília : Comunidade Solidária, 2000. 108p.

A Lei nº 13.019/2014 dispõe sobre o regime jurídico das parcerias voluntárias, envolvendo ou não transferências de recursos financeiros, entre a administração pública e as organizações da sociedade civil, em regime de mútua cooperação, para a consecução de finalidades de interesse público; define diretrizes para a política de fomento e de colaboração com organizações da sociedade civil; institui o termo de colaboração e o termo de fomento. Consultado em 23.07.2015. Disponível em: http://www.planalto.gov.br/ccivil_03/_Ato2011-2014/2014/Lei/L13019.htm

# THE RIGHT TO DIE
# THE APPROPRIATE FORUM FOR END-OF-LIFE
# DESICIONMAKING: COURTS AND CLINICAL SETTINGS
# THE STAGE IN BRAZIL, ARGENTINA AND COLOMBIA

Diaulas Costa Ribeiro, Ph.D[40]
Kelle Lobato Moreira, M.Sc[41]
Roberto Luiz d' Ávila, MD[42]

## INTRODUCTION

In *Illness as metaphor* – an essay in which Susan Sontag (1933-2004) gathered distinct cognitive and emotional perceptions that lead to diseases –, it is evident that the illness-metaphor is already another metaphor in itself: it is the metaphor of an always inopportune death, i.e. *(id est)* a *mors intempestiva.* The fact that the expression "morte tempestiva" [meaning a "timely death"] is not used in Portuguese bears witness to such metaphor. Jacques Pohier points out that the same occurred in the French language, which only kept the Latin adjective *intempestivus,* but not its opposite, *tempestivus,* in the sense of arriving at a desired time. Therefore, *mors tempestiva* would be: death arriving at the right moment, in the right measure.[43] "It happens as if as human beings, we were willing to do anything to avoid recognizing death as a normal and natural event; as if such recognition caused an exceedingly severe wound in the image we seek to cultivate of ourselves and of the human condition. This wound deeply 'disenchants' us".

If in the recent past, people avoided speaking about death, even if by metaphors, it is certain that one never spoke as much about dying as in recent decades. Not because life lost its primacy for medicine, law, philosophy and religion, but because after we set standards of human dignity based on the reflections that emerged from World War II, and introduced the concept of human rights in the universal mind frame of individual rights guarantees, post-modernity as put forward by Bioethics has allowed us to reflect seriously on death and dying.[44]

---

40 Senior Public Prosecutor of the Federal District and the Territories Dean of the Catholic University of Brasília Law School and Professor of Bioethics and Law at the Catholic University of Brasília Medical School.
41 Master in Law ELPIS – European Legal Practice, Erasmus Mundus Consortium:Catholic University of Portugal, Lisbon, and University of Rouen, France Lawyer at the Catholic University of Brasília Law School
42 Cardiologist, Master in Medicine, Former President of The Federal Council of Medicine (Brazil), Professor of Bioethics and Medicine
43 POHIER, Jacques. *A morte oportuna:* o direito de cada um decidir o fim da sua vida. Tradução de Gemeniano Cascais Franco. Editorial Notícias: Lisboa, 1999, p. 11.
44 DWORKIN, Ronald. *Justice for Hedgehogs,* Massachusetts: Harvard University Press: 2011, p. 32.

In spite of the philosophical controversy around the expression 'post-modernity', we consider the period of renewal and innovation of the past four decades as such. This period brought to the scene not only the opportunity, but also the need to expand the discussion on the right to life in order to include the right to a dignified death, which is also a fundamental right. We can say the foremost right post-modernity has rescued is the right to autonomy, i.e. to self-determination; the right to determine one's own dying is a mere consequence of this rescue. "The antagonism between technical and human values, which characterized medicine in the early decades of the 20th century, is disappearing. The explicit acknowledgment of the human capacity to decide about one's biological destiny started to occupy its due place in modern democratic and pluralist societies".[45]

If anyone can take a man's life – if no one can take a man's death, because all paths lead us to it [46] –, then a question must be answered: – Is there a fundamental right to immortality? If the answer is yes, then the State must create mechanisms against death. If the answer is no, then we must see death as the only certainty of human consciousness. In this case, living and dying will be instants of one and the same right: the right to *autonomy*.

The word *autonomy*, from Greek *autos* (from oneself) and *nomos* (rule, authority or law) was incorporated to bio-medicine in the 1970s – we take the *Belmont Report* as a reference –, meaning an empowerment to make decisions regarding biomedical issues. A person with full autonomy has the powers and guarantees of a State. In other words, he or she has self-determination.

The *Belmont Report: Ethical Principles and Guidelines for the Protection of Human Subjects of Research)*, issued at the *Federal Register* on April 18, 1979,[47] results from the work of the National Commission for the Protection of Human Subjects of Biomedical and Behavioral Research. The Commission was created in 1974 "with the aim of undertaking a full research and study to identify the basic ethical principles that should guide human experimentation in behavioral and biomedical sciences".[48]

---

45 CECCHETTO, Sergio. *Curar o cuidar: Bioética en el confín de la vida humana.* Buenos Aires: Ad-Hoc, 1999, p. 93-4.
46 SÊNECA, *Sobre a brevidade da vida* [*On the shortness of life*]. Tradução, notas e introdução de William Li. Nova Alexandria: São Paulo, 1993.
47 The *Belmont Report's* first version was published in late 1978: *National Commission for the Protection of Human Subjects of Biomedical and Behavioral Research, Belmont Report: Ethical Principles and Guidelines for the Protection of Human Subjects of Research (Washington, DC: DHEW Publication OS 78-0012).*
48 BEAUCHAMP, Tom L., CHILDRESS. James F. *Principles of Biomedical Ethics.* 7th ed. New York: Oxford University Press, 2002.

Tom L. Beauchamp, a member of the Commission, reported that a proposal of moral principles to be observed in biomedical research emerged during the seminar held on February 13-16, 1976 at the Smithsonian Institution's Belmont Conference, in Maryland. Three core principles were originally put forward: respect for persons and beneficence, proposed by H. Tristram Engelhardt,[49] and justice, proposed by Beauchamp.[50]

In the draft report of June 3, 1976 for the Commission's 19th Meeting – held on June 11-13, 1976, the principle of respect for persons was rather "surprisingly" treated as principle of *autonomy*, and the new concept was approved by the Commission.[51]

In the search for a formula to specify the meaning of each of these principles, Michael Yesley – also member of the Commission – presented a schema of individual guidelines in which the principle of *respect for persons* applied to guidelines of informed consent; the principle of *beneficence* applied to the guidelines of risk-benefit assessment; and the principle of *justice* applied to the guidelines of selection of subjects.[52]

As a guideline for informed consent, the principle of *respect for persons* was not originally conceived as an instrument of protection against risks, but as a guarantee of *autonomy and personal dignity*. As such, it was meant to include the dignity of individuals incapable of making autonomous decisions, which needed the informed consent of legal representatives.

As we know nowadays, the Belmont Report not only influenced biomedical research relations, but also had an impact on the relations between health professionals and patients. These relations had been previously built based on a paternalistic model and were affected not only by the *principle of autonomy*, but also by all other principles (beneficence and justice), including the *non-maleficence* principle *(primus non nocere; first, do no harm)*, which was incorporated to the other principles by the influence of Beauchamp and Childress' book, *Principles of Biomedical Ethics*, written simultaneously with the Commission's work.

The *principle of autonomy* had a direct effect on the previous physician-patient relations, which were built based on a paternalistic model. In Brazil, this transformation is not

---

49 The principle of *respect for persons* emerged from the following proposal by H. Tristram Engelhardt: *"Respect for persons as free moral agents, concern to support the best interests of human subjects in research, intent to assure that the use of human subjects of experimentation will on the sum redound to the benefit of society"*.

50 BEAUCHAMP, Tom L. The origins and evolution of the Belmont Report. In: Childress, James F. Meslin, Eric M. and Shapiro, Harold T. (Eds.), *Belmont revisited: Ethical principles for research with human subjects*. Washington, DC: Georgetown University Press, 2005, p. 12-25.

51 BEAUCHAMP, Tom L., *idem.*

52 BEAUCHAMP, Tom L., *ibidem.*

yet fully consolidated, but a rapid substitution of paternalism for free and informed consent is in full course.

One speaks nowadays of *empowerment health*; in other words, one speaks of the patient who conquered the power to make decisions in regard to his or her health and life. Thus, a passive subject has become a holder of a right. On their turn, from active subjects, physicians have become holders of an obligation. Physicians have thus ceased to be fully sovereign to make clinical decisions and became counselors of a frank dialogue with their patients.

Brazil's legislation recognizes respect for patient's autonomy, for instance, in article 15 of the Civil Code: "No person can be forced to submit to medical treatment or surgical intervention in case of life threat".[53]

According to the Constitution, this article must be read in the following way: No person – not even in case of life threat – will be forced to undergo a treatment or surgical intervention, in respect for his or her autonomy.

Autonomy does not dismiss a person's capacity to express it. There are situations in which a patient becomes incapable of making instant decisions, e.g. in states of unconsciousness in general, which justify resorting to *living wills* and *advance directives* as instruments to express a future wish, a prospective autonomy, with one's refusal or acceptance of general medical treatments.

These *living wills* – a term that does not meet with widespread acceptance among strict advocates of the Roman Civil-Law tradition – are used in cases of terminal care, whereas *advance directives* are used in cases of medical treatments in general, when a recovery is expected. Thus, both terms are contiguous and it is not necessary to distinguish among them.[54] We adopt *advance directives*, which can materialize in at least four different ways: by written public notice at a registry office; by written statement in private document, at best with notarized signature; by declaring to one's assistant physician, with a written report on the medical record and the patient's signature; or, if the patient is incapable, with two witnesses. In any case, a personal attorney can be appointed to make decisions not provided for in the directives. The Civil Code also allows appointing a curator for an ailing person:

53 BRASIL, Código Civil (Civil Code). Lei nº 10.406, de 10 de Janeiro de 2002.
54 GONZÁLES, Miguel Angel Sanchez. Um novo testamento: testamentos vitais e diretivas antecipadas. In: Bastos EF, Sousa AH, coordenadores. *Família e jurisdição*. Belo Horizonte: Del Rey, 2005.

Article 1,780. At request of the ill or physically disabled person, or if none of the persons mentioned by article 1,768 are capable of doing so, a curator can be assigned to manage his or her dealings or property as a whole or in part.

The fourth alternative relates to the patient who did not anticipate directives but declared to friends and relatives his or her rejection to therapeutic efforts in cases of permanent vegetative state or terminal disease: it is the testimonial justification of this will. However, this option demands long judicial processes, as in the *Karen Quinlan*, *Nancy Cruzan* and *Terri Schiavo* cases. As a matter of fact, in the *Terri Schiavo* case, a point of emphasis regarded the supremacy of the *right to live*, whereas the case actually indicated the need to debate *the right to die*, i.e. the autonomous right to deliberate about the time and place of one's own death. Similar processes are already in course in Brazil.

The right to live does not antagonize the right to die, but includes, in truth, two dimensions of one single right. «All interest in disease and death is only another expression of interest in life». (Thomas Mann, *The Magic Mountain*).

The right to live has actually been considered by the Catholic Church in the *Declaration on Euthanasia*: "(...) some people speak of a 'right to die', which is an expression that does not mean the right to procure death either by one's own hand or by means of someone else, as one pleases, but rather the right to die peacefully with human and Christian dignity".[55]

Also in the *Declaration on Euthanasia*, approved by His Holiness Pope John Paul II, the Sacred Congregation for the Doctrine of the Faith affirmed:

> When inevitable death is imminent in spite of the means used, it is permitted in conscience to take the decision to refuse forms of treatment that would only secure a precarious and burdensome prolongation of life, so long as the normal care due to the sick person in similar cases is not interrupted. In such circumstances the doctor has no reason to reproach himself with failing to help the person in danger.[56]

However, the permissibility of refusing extraordinary treatment measures was already mentioned in the speeches of Pope Pius XII since February 24, 1957:

---

55 VATICAN, Sacred Congregation for the Doctrine of the Faith, *Declaration on Euthanasia*, May 5, 1980.
56 VATICAN, Sacred Congregation for the Doctrine of the Faith, *Declaration on Euthanasia*, May 5, 1980.

Natural reason and Christian morality say that man (…) has the right and the duty, in case of grave illness, to take the measures necessary to conserve life and health. (…) But usually the obligation is limited to the use of ordinary means (according to the circumstances of person, place, era and culture), that is to say, means which impose no extraordinary burden on either oneself or another. A more severe obligation would be too heavy for most men, and would render the acquisition of more important higher goods too difficult. Life, health, all temporal activity, are, after all, subordinate to spiritual ends.[57]

Brazil's legal system guarantees the right to live and, within its apparent contradiction, does not formally recognize the right to die. As a consequence of this fact, juridical doctrine has mistakenly stated that such a right does not exist. Living life autonomously is a "potestative" right, which can be exercised without the acquiescence of others; no one needs another person's license to live his or her own life.

This reasoning does not preclude a reassessment of the right to live, which, as a "potestative" right, can only be renounced by its holder. If it could not be renounced, it would not be a right but a duty: the duty to live. As a duty to live, it would have different juridical consequences *vis-à-vis* the presently known consequences, ranging from punishment of suicide attempts to the prohibition of radical sports and risky activities in general. This could lead to a mechanization of life beyond life, with the imposition of inhuman and degrading treatments to ill persons, known as dysthanasia or therapeutic obstinacy.

## The (absence of) individual freedom in the Ancient City

The notion of individual liberty was not a result of the ancient State. Fustel de Coulanges (Paris, 1830-Massy, 1889) (*The Ancient City: A Study on the Religion, Laws, and Institutions of Greece and Rome*, 1864) pointed out that religion – which stood at the origin of the State – and the State – which, on its turn, sustained religion – supported each other mutually and formed one single body. These two interlinked powers constituted a superhuman force that subdued both body and soul. It is a basic mistake to believe that man in the *Ancient City* was free. Man did not even have a slight conception of freedom and did not judge himself capable of holding rights before the city and its gods. And even with the change in the system of government, from

---

57  Papa Pio XII. Allocuzione del 24/02/1957. *Acta Apostolicae Sedis* 1957; 49:146. Address to those taking part in the IX[th] Congress of the Italian Anaesthesiological Society, February 24, 1957: AAS 49 (1957), p. 146.

monarchy to aristocracy and to democracy, man had not yet attained true freedom, that is, individual freedom. Nothing in man was independent. His body belonged to the State and was meant to defend it. In the *Ancient City*, man never stopped being a slave of the State.

In such historical context, death was demarcated by the supreme hand of the State, which neither accepted interferences in its resolves, nor recognized the right to die. In Greece, for instance, "an individual could not kill himself without the community's previous consent, given that suicide was a blow against the community structure. Suicide was politically or judicially condemned. Customary burial practices were denied to an individual who committed clandestine suicide, while one's hand was amputated from the corpse and buried apart. On its turn, the State had the power to disallow or authorize a suicide, as well as to induce it. Socrates, for instance, was forced to ingest poison in 399 (b.C.)".[58]

Christianity replaced ancient politics and introduced the notion, inherited from Judaism, of life as a sacred gift received from God, and did not recognize an individual's right to decide about his or her own death, as living and dying only depended on God. Thus, "Christianity's emphasis on life's sanctity is part of the Hebrew heritage. Christianity ascribed immortality to the human person, whose life's singularity on Earth starts precisely at birth".[59]

For Canon Law, we are not owners but trustees of the life God has bestowed on us; thus, we cannot dispose of it. In this line of reasoning, the Council of Arles (452) established suicide as the most serious of all sins. The Council of Orléans (533) forbade religious funeral for suicides. The Council of Braga (561) established the absence of funeral rites. The Council of Toledo (693) ruled on excommunication in case of failed suicide attempts. The Decree of Gratien (1140) prohibited obsequies and burial in ecclesiastic cemeteries. The Synod of Nîmes (1248) reinforced restrictions for funerals of suicidal individuals.[60]

Based on these foundations, Saint Thomas Aquinas (1225–1274) followed the footsteps of Saint Augustine at the Synod of Nîmes (1248) and reaffirmed that a suicidal – even a furious madman – would not be buried in Christian lands. In the 20[Th] century, on its turn, the issue was categorized in the Code of Canon Law by Pope Benedict

---

58 SILVA, Marcimedes Martins da. *Suicídio – Trama da comunicação*. Dissertação de Mestrado, 1992, Psicologia Social, PUC-SP. Available from: http://www.avesso.net/suicidio.htm. Accessed: June 8, 2015.
59 SILVA, Mário Tavares da. *Eutanásia: alguns aspectos morais*, Lisboa: AAFDL, 2011, p. 62-3.
60 DURKHEIM, Emile. *O suicídio:* estudo sociológico. Tradução de Luz Cary, Margarida Garrido e J. Vasconcelos Esteves, 2ed. Lisboa: Editorial Presença/Martins Fontes, 1977.

XV in 1918 and suicidal individuals were punished with the denial of obsequies and ecclesiastic graves *(Canon, 1240)*, which is still observed in the Jewish religion. However,

the Catholic ban was revoked by the 1983 Code of Canon Law *(Canon 1183 to 1185)*, edited by Pope John Paul II.

In Brazil, as in most countries with a Catholic tradition, helping another person commit suicide is a crime punishable with a sentence of 2 to 6 years of prison. Depending on the victim's reason, age and resistance capacity, it is a qualified crime with a sentence of 4 to 12 years. There is not a juridical category of physician-assisted suicide.

The Brazilian legislation does not include the category of *homicide at the victim's request*, as in the cases of Germany and Portugal, which are two paradigmatic systems for Brazil. In both countries, homicide at the victim's request is punished by a symbolic penalty if compared to traditional suicide. In Portugal, a person who kills after a serious, instant and express request of the victim is punished with a sentence of 1 month to 3 years (CP, article 134) while qualified homicide can result in 25 years of prison (CP, articles 131 and 132). In Germany, a person who kills at the victim's request is punished with 6 months to 5 years of prison (StGB, paragraphs 211 and 216), whereas qualified homicide can be punished with life imprisonment.

Therefore, rejection to the right to decide about one's own death is based on religious values, and also on the State view of ancient civilization. Christianity removed the State's supremacy over man and propagated the separation between State and religion. Christ himself taught that his kingdom was not from this world and added: "Render unto Caesar the things that are Caesar's, and unto God the things that are God's".

Traditionally cited as a symbol of distributive justice, this expression was actually uttered in another context. Caesar was still the supreme pontiff, the chief and the leading institution of Roman religion, the guardian and interpreter of beliefs who held cult and dogma in his hands. With these words, Christ broke through the previous alliance that linked earthly and divine realms, proclaiming that religion was no longer the State, and that obedience to Caesar was no longer the same thing as obedience to God.[61]

Even if for Judaism and Christianity, only God can decide on death and dying, secular States certainly cannot adopt religious positions to limit individual freedom. Yet, these

---

61 COULANGES, Fustel de. *The Ancient City:* A Study on the Religion, Laws, and Institutions of Greece and Rome, 1864. *A Cidade Antiga.* Estudo sobre o culto, o direito, as instituições da Grécia e de Roma, 1864. Tradução de Jonas Camargo Leite e Eduardo Fonseca. São Paulo: Hemus, 1975, p. 182-5.

are the issues that reach our days and stand at the basis of the universal discussions regarding the right to die and the ways of exercising and expressing it.

## History of Resolution CFM 1,805/2006

In Brazil, the end-of-life issue has appeared in several act projects both at the House of Representatives and at the Senate. So far, technical inaccuracies and *confusio linguarum* have prevented us from reaching a humanized solution for the end-of-life issue.

As a contradiction, it is necessary to point out that approximately 56 thousand persons are killed in Brazil each year and that no effective policies have been implemented to tackle this "Vietnam War" of our days.

In such context, the Federal Council of Medicine undertook the effort to regulate the suspension of therapeutic efforts (orthotanasia) as an ethical priority for the professional practice of physicians, and issued Resolution CFM 1,805/2006 on November 6, 2006:

DECIDES:

> Article 1. A physician is allowed to restrict or suspend procedures and treatments that prolong the life of an ill person in the terminal stage of a serious and incurable disease, provided that the physician is respecting the will of the patient or his/her legal representative.
>
> Article 2. The ill person will continue receiving all necessary care in order to alleviate the symptoms that produce suffering. The provision of comprehensive care will be secured, along with physical, psychic, social and spiritual comfort, including the right to discharge.

According to this resolution, a physician is allowed to restrict or suspend procedures and treatments that may prolong a patient's life at the terminal stage of serious and incurable diseases, while securing the necessary care to alleviate the symptoms that produce suffering, from the perspective of comprehensive care, provided that the physician is respecting the will of the patient or of his/her legal representative.

This resolution was the result of a long process that lasted over 2 years, starting with the public presentation of the project and leading to a series of conferences that included professionals of several areas, among them medicine, philosophy and law in the final week of August 2006. The resolution was issued on November 28, 2006.

## The civil suit of the Federal Prosecutor's Office

On May 9, 2007, the Federal District's Regional Prosecutor for Citizen Rights filed a public suit against the Federal Council of Medicine and requested the resolution's abrogation. On October 23, 2007, the 14th Federal Court of the Federal District granted a preliminary injunction to suspend the effects of Resolution CFM 1,805/2006.

The public suit was dealt with according to the regular procedures. At the end, the federal Public Prosecutor's Office, represented by another Public Prosecutor, concluded that its proposal was mistaken and that:

1) The Federal Council of Medicine had the competence to issue Resolution CFM 1,805/2006, which does not regard criminal law, but, instead, medical ethics and disciplinary consequences in case of non-compliance;

2) Orthotanasia is not a homicide when interpreted in the light of the Criminal Code under the Federal Constitution;

3) Resolution CFM 1,805/2006 did not determine any significant modification in the daily routine of physicians assisting terminal patients; therefore, it did not lead to any harmful effect described in the public suit;

4) Resolution CFM 1,805/2006 encourages physicians to describe adopted and not adopted procedures with precision in relation to terminal patients, to increase transparency regarding procedures and the possibility of further control of medical activities.

On December 1st, 2010, the same Federal Judge of the 14th Court rejected the civil suit and revoked the preliminary injunction.

The sentence was judged. Resolution 1,805/2006 is now in effect and led to a unique situation in the world: the right to a dignified death, orthotanasia or suspension of therapeutic efforts was recognized in our juridical system by a federal judge's sentence with an *erga omnes* effect. This means the decision is valid in the entire national territory and has the force of a federal act approved by the National Congress (House of Representatives and Senate).

Differently from paradigmatic decisions of the US Supreme Court – or of Italy's Supreme Court of Cassation in the Eluana Englaro case, which only benefitted persons mentioned in their relatives' requests –, the Brazilian decision accepted and protected a right for all Brazilian citizens who request the right not to undergo therapeutic efforts.

The new Code of Medical Ethics, which is also a resolution of the Council and entered into effect in 2010, repeated the same orientation:

A physician is forbidden to:

Article 41. Abbreviate a patient's life, even at the request of the patient or his / her legal representative.

*Single paragraph.* In cases of incurable and terminal diseases, the physician must provide all available palliative care without trying useless or obstinate diagnostic or therapeutic actions. Physicians must always consider the patient's express will or, in cases of patient's inability, the will of his/her legal representative.

## Advance directives

The same process repeated itself when the Federal Council of Medicine approved Resolution CFM 1,995/12, which institutes advance directives. Advance directives are defined as the patient's previously expressed wish regarding the provision of care and treatments he or she wants or not to receive in case of becoming incapable of freely and autonomously expressing one's will.

Article 1. Defines advance directives as the set of wishes previously and expressly manifested by the patient regarding the provision of care and treatment he or she wishes or not to receive in case of becoming incapable of freely and autonomously expressing his or her will.

Article 2. When deciding about the type of care and treatment for a patient incapable of communicating or expressing his or her will in a free and independent way, the physician shall consider the patient's advance directives.

Paragraph 1. If the patient has appointed a representative to this end, his or her information will be considered by the physician.

Paragraph 2. The physician will not consider advance directives of a patient's or legal representative's wish if they disagree, in the physician's evaluation, with the Code of Medical Ethics' precepts.

Paragraph 3. A patient's advance directives will prevail over any other non-medical opinion, including the wishes of relatives.

Paragraph 4. The physician will report in the medical record in case of advance directives directly communicated by the patient to him or her.

Paragraph 5. If the advance directives of a patient's wish are not known, if no representative has been assigned and no relatives are available, or in case of lack of consensus among relatives, the physician will resort to the Bioethics Committee of the institution, or, in its absence, to the hospital's Commission of Medical Ethics, or to the Regional and Federal Council of Medicine, to substantiate his or her decision regarding ethical conflicts, whenever he or she evaluates that such measure is necessary and convenient.

The Federal Public Prosecutor's Office presented a new public suit challenging Resolution CFM 1,995/2012. Again, the Judiciary ruled that this regulation does not contain any illegal or unconstitutional aspect. The decision now has an *erga omnes* effect.

Differently from the paradigmatic decisions of the Supreme Court of the United States or the Italian Corte de Cassazione, the latter in the case of Eluana Englaro, which have only benefited the people nominated in the requests made by their relatives, the Brazilian decision embraced and protected the right to every citizen demanding the right for not being submitted to therapeutic effort (*erga omnes* effect).

Much similar to the case of the North-American Nancy Cruzan, Eluana Englaro was injured in a car accident in the early hours of January 18, 1992, and she was assisted when a frame of cerebral anoxia had already established. For 17 years she remained in a persistent vegetative condition. Her parents, Beppino Englaro and Saturna Englaro, have sought a judicial permit for suspending the hydration and feeding of their daughter. After ten years of a real juridical battle, the Italian Corte de Cassazione, finally, stood by the decision of the Court of Appeal of Milano, which, by their turn, stood by the decision of the Court of Lecco, the city where the Englaro family lived. On February 9, 2009, four days after the execution of the judicial decision which only validated the right to her autonomy, Eluana Englaro died.

It's worth noticing that on July 8, 2011, there were 3,360 people in persistent vegetative status in Italy, in a situation similar to Eluana Englaro, at the annual cost of € 165,000, supported by the public health services.

Four years prior to that, on March 2005, Terri Schiavo became symbol for such an extreme debate on the right to die as much as the one experienced by Eluana Englaro's parents. In both cases, the facts overtook the media for political reasons and not for their clinical nature. The American government used a private life tragedy as act of contrition of the state interest and passed a law that suspended the decision of the Florida Justice. It was necessary for the Supreme Court of the United States to enforce the prevalence of the state of rights, making it clear it wasn't willing to yield its credibility nor its independence to the night relations (the project was approved at night, on a weekend) of the Congress with the White house, standing in agreement to the precedent of the *Nancy Cruzan Case*[62] and assuring the patient's autonomy right: the right of her death not being postponed.

Something similar happened in the case of Eluana Englaro. Religious movements and right wing parties demanded that (the former) President of the Republic, Giorgio Napolitano, passed a decree in annulment of the Corte de Cassazione's decision. The President, as guardian of the Italian state of rights, didn't yield to pressures. Nor he could. The Judicial Power, which comprises the Public Prosecution Service, is independent in the terms of the article 104 of the Italian Constitution: *La magistratura costituisce un ordine autonome e indipendente da ogni altro potere.*

Another case, which also occurred in Florida, entailed the same constitutional and ethical principles. However, no opposition was granted from the public opinion. Georgette Smith, hit by gunfire shot by her mother, wanted to disconnect the machinery that was keeping her alive. In a sentence uttered by the Circuit Judge Richard F. Conrad, on May 18, 1999, it was obvious the Office of the State Attorney's public interest in interrogating her to establish evidence against her mother, but such an interest couldn't invalidate the option she made. Thus, the Judge established a deadline until 17 o'clock of the following day in order for the Prosecutors to interrogate her. After this deadline, the patient could choose the moment for the ventilator to be switched off. From that indication, the hospital, the Columbia Park Medical Center, should enable the patient's option. «Ms. Smith has made a difficult choice, a choice which she has the right to make. This Court has found that she is competent to make that choice. Regrettably, this Court finds it necessary do delay her exercise of that choice in the face of compelling state interest. However, this Court will employ the least intrusive means possible to accommodate the state's interest and to safeguard Ms. Smith's rights. In other words, the Court will give the state a limited window of opportunity to protect its interest. Therefore, the Office of the State Attorney shall have until Wednesday, May 19, 1999, at 5:00 p.m. to secure any testimony from Ms. Smith. At any time thereafter, Ms. Smith may choose to discontinue use of the ventilator. Defendant is directed do comply with Ms. Smith's decision».[63] The hospital respected that decision.

---

62 UNITED STATES OF AMERICA, Supreme Court of The United States – 497 U.S. 261. Cruzan, by Her Parents and Co-Guardians v. Director, Missouri Department of Health. June 25, 1990, Decided.
63 RIBEIRO, Diaulas Costa, Eutanásia: viver bem não é viver muito, Consulex, ano III, vol. I, n.º 29, pp. 17-20, Maio1999.

Different from that is the so called *Suspension of Therapeutic Effort*. In it, patients in terminal stage of incurable diseases give their permit for the interruption of futile treatments which only aim at postponing their death, instead of maintaining their life. The *Suspension of Therapeutic Effort* puts an end to the *therapeutic obstinacy*, the disthanasia, the technological insistence in postponing death, as if that was a good and possible thing forever.

With the evolution of medical technologies, each day there are more means of keeping the therapeutic obstinacy which cannot be considered as treatment, because it doesn't heal. It only supports primary vital activities and, for years and with great suffering, it can keep alive someone who is clinically terminated. With the *Suspension of Therapeutic Effort* the patient doesn't die from an overdose of potassium cyanide; the patient dies from his/her own illness, the natural end of his/her own life.

The *suspension of therapeutic effort* needs a manifestation of the patient's will, which must be done prior to his/her loss of civil ability, in the context of anticipated guidelines or previous instructions or life will, which are synonym expressions. In order to enable that, four alternatives are presented: a public record in a notary's office – where the

patient states not accepting therapeutic obstinacy, nor he/she accepts being kept alive by machinery, including the specification of the type of treatment he/she agrees with; a written statement on a private document – a simple signed paper sheet, preferably with notarized signature; a declaration presented to his/her doctor – recorded on his/her medical record, with his/her signature on it.

In those cases, we have previous guidelines, the living wills, biological wills or *testaments de vie*. It is evident that, in any of the systems where they are valid, explicitly or implicitly, the living wills don't have the requirements of a traditional will (to be carried out after death). Contrary to those, the decisions that are not comprised in its clauses should be kept open to the knowledge of the relatives, the doctors or a third party (a proxy) nominated by the patient.

## Final remarks

Brazil is not the only country where the *Right to Die* is regulated, albeit in a restrained way, by a judicial decision. In Colombia, the first legally authorized euthanasia took place on July 3, 2015 after a Constitutional Court decision with *erga omnes* effect. The sentence of Colombian's Court (C-239, of 1997) held that the fundamental right to live with dignity also implies the fundamental right to die with dignity. On December 15, 2014, the Court secured the right to euthanasia for patients with incurable and terminal diseases that generate intense pain, providing that this final procedure must be authorized by the patient's free, informed and unequivocal consent. The Court determined that the Ministry of Health should regulate this right while observing the following criteria:

*Prevalence of patient's autonomy*: subjects responsible for securing the right to euthanasia must analyze the cases considering always the patient's wish. Only in objective and impartial situations can it be possible to contradict a patient's expressed wish.

*Swiftness*: the right to die with dignity cannot be temporarily suspended, thus imposing excessive anguish to the patient. This right must be swift, quick and without excessive ritualism that could set the patient apart from enjoying this right.

*Opportunity*: in connection with swiftness, opportunity implies that the patient's wish must be immediately fulfilled without excessive prolongation of suffering, to the point of allowing death with the pain one intended to avoid.

*Impartiality*: Health professionals must be neutral when applying procedures aimed at fulfilling the right to dignified death. They cannot impose their personal views in terms of ethical, moral or religious contents as an attempt to deny this right. A physician who claims a consciousness objection in connection with these values is not obliged to implement euthanasia, but must appoint another professional to take it to effect.

On April 20, 2015, Resolution 1216/2015 of the Ministry of Health and Social Welfare regulated the right to die with dignity. The right was formally secured to a patient with advanced cancer of the throat, who died on July 3, 2015, and became a relevant step so that other countries may also secure the right to a dignified death.

One month after the euthanasia of Ovídio Gonzalez, the patient under scrutiny, the Attorney-General of Colombia, Alejandro Ordóñez, adopted a series of measures in order to suspend the right to euthanasia. None of them got the intended result.

Using emotional expressions, Alejandro Ordóñez stated that the defense of euthanasia is imbued with a "false compassion" and the "acting typical of Mafiosi". The Ministry of Health, Alejandro Gavíria, on his turn, answered those provocations by saying that the practice of euthanasia doesn't risk discarding people. On the contrary, those are – natural or assisted – imminent deaths parted by days or weeks. Finally, he stressed that this isn't assisted suicide, but protection of the dignity of the human person.

Still in South America, the Supreme Court of Argentina, in a decision on July 7, 2015, insured the respect for a patient's will and guaranteed the suspension of measures that, for over two decades, were artificially prolonging his life.

Some particularities marked that case: the first of them, this patient didn't leave any written instruction on the medical procedures to be adopted in situations like that one he turned to be involved in. However, the Court noted that by the time of the accident still wasn't valid the *Law of the Patient's Rights* (Law n. 26,529) which authorizes the elaboration, by public record in a notary's office, of previous guidelines on his own health.

Besides, by that time, twenty years before, it wasn't usual to talk about disability situations and the choosing of medical treatments. Even so, the patient had stated to his sisters that, in the eventuality of an irreversible disability condition, he desired to not having his life prolonged artificially.

The Court recognized that the *Law of Patient's Rights* contemplates the situation of those who are unable to express their informed consent, authorizing their relatives to give witness on the treatments those patients would like to be granted or not. In the concrete case, the Court assured the patient's self-determination, by explaining this wasn't a case of euthanasia and that:

*a)* The interruption of life support doesn't imply the practice of euthanasia, which is forbidden by law, unless when it expresses a permitted therapeutic abstention;

*b)* The law authorizes the request for the suspension of artificial hydration and feeding, which by themselves constitute ways of medical treatment, as it was recognized by the Committees of Bioethics which manifested on this case; by the Parliamentary debates on the *Law of the Patient's Right*; by the recent decision of the European Court of Human Rights in the case *Lambert vs. France*[64]; and by the jurisprudence of the Supreme Courts of the United States, Italy, France, United Kingdom, and India.

*c)* It was indisputable that the patient was still a person in the wide sense, that his fundamental rights should be protected without a single discrimination, and that, because of this, he enjoyed the right to a full self-determination of deciding to obtain the necessary assistance to his health, as well as ordering the interruption of the medical treatment.

---

64 Available from: http://hudoc.echr.coe.int/eng?i=001-155352#{"itemid":["001-155352"]}. Accessed: Sept. 7th, 2015.

The Supreme Court assured the suspension of the therapeutic effort. The patient died a few hours after such decision was decreed, which made it unnecessary to enforce it, although the precedent was guaranteed for other cases.

On the medically assisted death as an act of respect toward the dignity of the human person, we note that Brazil assures euthanasia to animals, and in this issue history is repeated. The pain of a guinea pig, according to the Brazilian legislation, deserves more respect than the pain of a man or a woman. A traumatized horse sees its dignity recognized and its right to a "humanized" death. A human being, in his/her deathbed, doesn't.

But that already "was the case on March 2, 1937, six months before Getúlio Vargas established the *Estado Novo* – which would establish an undisguised dictatorship. On that date, the memorable lawyer Heráclito Sobral Pinto issued a request for *habeas corpus* in the Court of National Security. He was basing his arguments on an article from the Decree of Protection and Defense of Animals. His purpose was not to save a horse from suffering, but a man: the German political prisoner Harry Berger, kept in subhuman conditions. The law favoring the animals had been signed less than three years before by the very Vargas."[65]

Today, another law assures a dignified death to animals. But it was the Judiciary Power that guaranteed citizens that same right in the mentioned public civil action. The National Congress still didn't legislate on that matter.

The Law n. 11,794 of October 8, 2008, which regulated the incise VII of the §1st of art. 225 of the Federal Constitution and established procedures for the scientific use of animals, stated that:

> Art. 3rd For the purposes of this Law it is understood as:
>
> **IV – death by humanitarian means:** the death of an animal in conditions that comprise, according to the species, a minimum of physical or mental suffering.
>
> **Art.** 14. The animal can only be submitted to the prescribed interventions in the protocol of experiments that constitute the research or learning program when,
>
> before, during, and after the experiment, it gets special cares, as established by the CONCEA.

---

65 EVALDO NOVELINI, Como um cavalo salvou a vida de um preso político. *Brasileiros.* Available from: http://brasileiros.com.br/2010/05/como-um-cavalo-salvou-a-vida-de-um-preso-politico/#. Accessed: Sept. 08, 2015.

§ 1ˢᵗ The animal will be **submitted to euthanasia**, under strict obedience to the prescriptions pertinent to each species, according to the guidelines of the Ministry of Science and Technology, whenever, being the experiment finished or at any of its stages, it is technically recommended such procedure or when intense suffering occurs.

## The last but not least

*The Economist* asked Ipsos-MORI to survey people in 15 countries on whether doctors should be allowed to help patients to die, and if so, how and when. «Russia and Poland are against, but we find strong support across America and western Europe for allowing doctors to prescribe lethal drugs to patients with terminal diseases. In 11 out of the 15 countries we surveyed, most people favoured extending doctor-assisted dying to patients who are in great physical suffering but not close to death.

The most determined people do not always choose wisely, no matter how well they are counselled. But it would be wrong to deny everyone the right to assisted death for this reason alone. Competent adults are allowed to make other momentous, irrevocable choices: to undergo a sex change or to have an abortion. People deserve the same control over their own death. Instead of dying in intensive care under bright lights and among strangers, people should be able to end their lives when they are ready, surrounded by those they love».[66]

---

66 Doctor-assisted dying. The right to die. *The Economist.*
Available from: http://www.economist.com/news/leaders/21656182-doctors-should-be-allowed-help-suffering-and-terminally-ill-die-when-they-choose. Accessed: Jun 27ᵗʰ, 2015.

# NEW STRATEGIC ALLIANCES TO TAIWAN: IMPORTANT PARTNERSHIPS IN A WORLD INCREASINGLY DRIVEN BY ECONOMIC AND TECHNOLOGICAL INTERESTS

**Wilson Almeida**[67]

## INTRODUCTION

The world of the XXI century is changing rapidly. Policies and economies structures that were built recently, from the end of the Cold War, are suffering major transformations. The Asian continent, is one of these regions. At the end of the Cold War the political situation in Taiwan over mainland China appeared to be difficult and threatening due to a possible reduction of US interest in the attractions of Taiwan. With the increase in Chinese GDP and the growing commercial interest of both China and the US, it seemed that Taiwan was in trouble.

The relations between the US and mainland China, have undergone transformations when China began to pose a threat to regional and even global hegemony for US interests. In this complex world that we have today, where middle powers such as Brazil, India, South Africa and Mexico have been important in many decisions, this project aims to analyze the possibilities for Taiwan to pursue strategic economic alternatives to keep their secured interests. Taiwan today is very important for many regions of the world, especially in terms of economic and technological development. The purpose of this study is to point out these opportunities and help with some suggestions to the authorities of this country, or this economic region, to reflect on its position in this new world.

### Summary of the main ideas

a) History of relations between Taiwan and the United States in the context of the Cold War;

b) With the end of the Cold War, the importance of Taiwan has been reduced for geo strategic purposes and there was the threat of reduction of the US interest to continue defending militarily this region;

---

[67] Professor at Catholic University of Brasília.

c) The growth of world trade and the economic growth of China in the 1990s and early 2000s, in terms more than proportional, led the United States to increase interest in closer and closer to China which can be understood as a threatening the survival of Taiwan as autonomous unit;

d) John Measrsheimer and other American authors, argue that China can not rise peacefully. And the US can not allow any country to be hegemonic in its region of influence. Arises again the US ability to get back in geo strategical interests in Taiwan;

e) Considering the influence that emerging countries have in the world today, including Brazil, India, South Africa and Mexico, probably increasingly diverse alliances can ensure Taiwan important partnerships for the maintenance of its position as autonomous unit can plan their future condition in Asia in more favorable conditions.

## Development

The modern phase of Chinese history began with the fall of the Ching Dynasty (Manchu) in 1911 and the establishment of the Republic of China the following year. During the first two decades of republican system, the country was plagued by internal turmoil, while military regimes competed to take over. In 1927, get through-the national unification, after the defeat of regional military leaders by General Chiang Kai-shek. Soon after, however, the Japanese invasion led the Chinese to a resistance war that lasted eight years until the victory over Japan in 1945, with the support of allied nations.

That year, the winners of the Second World War gave Taiwan the Republic of China. In 1949 with the military defeat of the Kuomintang by the Chinese Communist Party, Mao Zedong took power in Beijing and proclaimed the People's Republic of China.

As a result, followers of Chiang Kai-shek refuged in Taiwan, where, until the early 1990s, defended the existence of "one China", represented by the "Republic" installed "temporarily" on the island, with the firm intention also to regain the mainland, by force. The Taipei authorities then unilaterally decided in 1991 to waive the "sovereignty" on the other side of the narrow, limiting its jurisdiction to the archipelago of Taiwan and the small islands of Penghu, Kinmen and Matsu.

Taiwan presents aspects of modernity that cause envy the Asia-Pacific. The local political system provides electoral democracy and free press.

There are conditions for any future scenario to think for its 23 million inhabitants. These are: the insular condition of the territory they occupy, to 145 km. The coast of a country with 1.3 billion people; the fact that this giant neighbor considers Taiwan a Chinese province; the existence of shared culture that persists in putting together the civil societies on both sides, in terms of values, habits and even family ties; and increasing economic integration, which strengthens the trend towards the formation of a "Greater China".

With the onset of the Age Deng Xiaoping in the late 1970s, Beijing abandoned its release Taiwan by force policy, and formulated a new guideline of "peaceful reunification". Triggered, then a series of Taiwanese approach initiatives. In January 1979, the Standing Committee of the National People's Congress sent "a message to compatriots in Taiwan".

On September 30, 1981, Ye Jianying, Chairman of the Standing Committee of the NPC, announced nine-point proposal to resolve the problem of Taiwan, to include: free trade and communications between Taiwan and the PRC; autonomy for Taiwan and maintenance of the Taiwanese armed forces; taiwanese participation of representatives in the political system of the PRC; preservation of Taiwanese capitalist economy; financial assistance from the central government to Taiwan, if necessary; freedom to that Island residents are established on the Chinese mainland; profit participation for Taiwanese capitalists in the PRC modernization program; Conversations between the Kuomintang and the Chinese Communist Party with a view to reunification; and acceptance of proposals from the "masses" on the reunification should be realized.

Two years later, Deng Xiaoping reiterated the possibility of direct talks between the CPC and the KMT, since there they would configure as dialogue between the Central Government, Beijing and the provincial, Taipei. On February 22, 1984, Deng has proposed "one country, two systems", which came to be applied to the reunification of Hong Kong in 1997, but it was intended originally to Taiwan.

It appears, therefore, that, from the end of the 1970s, the Chinese bet that with the establishment of diplomatic relations between Beijing and Washington, the Taiwanese would undergo crisis of confidence that would lead easily to give the designs reunification of the PRC. Moreover, with the beginning of its modernization process, there would be new incentives for taiwanese people were interested on the participation of China with vigorous economy, trade expansion and advantageous opportunities for investments.

The US, the same year that transferred diplomatic recognition to Beijing, however, enacted the Taiwan Relations Act, keeping the island strongly inserted in the Cold War confrontation structure. During the 1980s, little progress has occurred through the narrow, while remaining in effect the proposal of one country, two systems already mentioned.

After the death of Chiang Ching-kuo in January 1988, Beijing considered initially, you would expect that Lee Teng-hui continue the negotiating process established with the Chiangs. It is recalled by the way, father and son, to govern the island between 1949 and 1988, held the position that Taiwan was part of China's territory, just as the continent. They considered, moreover, that there is only "one China" represented by the "Republic of China" - not the "People's Republic of China."

Lee, however, gave prompt start changing direction. In the late 1980s, the new leader also stated that: "one China is the supreme principle." By the beginning of the following incorporated the new speech that through the strait, there was actually "one China, two governments". From September 1990, the Taiwanese have gone to the initiative and established a National Council for Unification. When launching the Guidelines for National Unification, in February 1991, the Taiwanese maintained that there was "only one China," but presented the concept of the innovation "one China, two equal political entities".

By requiring the return to the policy of "one China", Beijing declared that President Lee had given "an extremely dangerous step" toward China division and warned that "was playing with fire." They reiterated the Chinese, too, who had not renounced the use of military force if the island follow the path independence. According to the newspaper South China Morning Post in Hong Kong on July, 14 (1999), citing Chinese authorities, "Lee had taken the people of Taiwan and their foreign sponsors toward their own destruction with its separatist and suicidal adventure."

There was broad speculation about the possibility of a prompt armed reaction. Chinese military exercises - apparently already programmed - were reported as preparations for an invasion. Editorial newspapers in the PRC criticized the theory of "two states". It was stated that China would not hesitate to attack even in the face of US resistance.

Record worthy, too, was the US reaction, through the spokesman of the State Department, only reiterated the known position of Washington with respect to the "three no's" - the independence of Taiwan; the "two Chinas"; and Taiwanese

participation in international organizations reserved for states. From this perspective, the US and the PRC seemed at that moment have identical positions on the provocation of President Lee.

Similarly, Japan has pledged to maintain the same policy of adhering to the principle of "one China." Other Asian countries were against the initiative of President Lee, to proclaim the existence of "two Chinas".

To some extent, the new framework presented by the Taiwanese translated leader, only the actions triggered by the diplomacy of the island since 1993, when they started the efforts of admission to the UN. That is, the Charter of the United Nations requires statehood to its participants. The Taiwanese, therefore, to plead access, had been advocating the thesis that they meet the requirements set, they occupied a clearly defined territory, with a population identified 23 million, with a government able to implement domestic policies and assume and fulfill international commitments. Thus - by Taipei - only there would be political arguments and not "legal" so that the Chinese opposed the admission of Taiwan in the United Nations.

In this regard, the defenders President Lee's initiative still remember that there was greater flexibility as, for example, the two Germanys and the two Yemens were UN members. Two Koreas continue to integrate it.

It is recalled that the unofficial relationship between Taiwan and the United States is governed by: Taiwan Relations Act (TRA), who turned 36 in April 2015; and the three "Joint Announcements": the Shanghai (28 February 1972); which established diplomatic relations between Washington and Beijing (January 1 1979) and on sales of arms to Taiwan (August 17, 1982).

Prior to the transfer of diplomatic recognition to Beijing the United States had with the "Republic of China" a treaty of mutual defense against possible attack from China (PRC). The US Congress has therefore decided to present the consolidated legislation in the Taiwan Relations Act, containing defensive articles. The proposed legislation was, therefore, to stop and prevent the annexation of Taiwan by China by means which were not peaceful. They would thus preserved US strategic interests in this region.

President Clinton, on a visit to mainland China, out beyond the expected, for example, the Taiwan Relations Act (TRA), April 1979, was establishing, among other things, that "the future of Taiwan will be determined by peaceful means ". Twice during his visit, however, the president said that "reunification will be determined by peaceful means". To the watchful Taiwanese, of course, your future room for maneuver had been reduced to reunification, as a matter of time without alternative.

The idea that citizens of the island should benefit from a "free choice" or self-determination, however, would be central to the relationship between the US and the PRC. This concept is not only enshrined in the "TRA" but also outside reiterated on many US presidential speeches, especially Ronald Reagan, the day when, in 1982, signed the second joint statement with the Chinese. "The Taiwan question is a matter for the Chinese people, on both sides of the Taiwan Strait, to resolve," he stated then that former president.

"We will not interfere in this matter or prejudice the free choice of, or pressure on, the people of Taiwan. At the same team, we have an abiding interest and concern that any resolution be peaceful. I shall never waver from this fundamental position ".

Such a stance differed from that came then to be adopted by Clinton administration that, among other initiatives, proposed the creation of a "second track" to deal with the Taiwan issue through alternative channel, managed by academics. Search they would thus new formulas for possible reunification. The problem is that, according to Taipei's view, the suggestions passed to be more influenced by Chinese recipe of "one country two systems", than by Taiwanese "one country, two governments".

In general terms and with regard to the interests of Taiwan, as could be seen in Taipei, these would be some aspects of the "strategic partnership" between Washington and Beijing, which prevailed on the question through the narrow, during the Clinton Administration.

In another development, in early 2000, the PRC published a new "White Paper" on Taiwan. According to the policy, established thereafter, it was introduced an additional element to the two already provided as cause for a Chinese military action against the island. Previously, as mentioned, would be sufficient independence movement or foreign invasion.

This evolution in thinking about the Beijing Taiwanese occurred less than a month in an electoral contest that would define the future of the Kuomintang that had fifty years leading the destinies of the "Republic of China" (as we know, in March 2000, really the Democratic Progressive Party defeated the KMT in the elections for president of Taiwan). Fortunately, for those who stood in just four minutes of Chinese missiles, the most exalted spirits were controlled mainly as a reaction to moderate inaugural address of Chen Shui-Bian.

With the election of George W. Bush in November 2000, the US began to express a much more explicit, with respect to the defense of Taiwan. From then on, it would be appreciated in Washington, the fact that the 21 million islanders "have evolved towards a democratic regime, while Beijing stored naval and air forces able to attack the Taiwanese."

It was estimated at that time that in the previous ten years, the PRC would have installed over three hundred missiles against Taiwan.

Dong Feng-type 6:07, would reach less than 400 km, but would be capable of carrying nuclear device. If fired only with conventional weapons would cause immense destruction on the civilian population of the island.

## A new Cold War?

In recent years, an American organization - Foreign Policy in Focus - evaluated the proposed military budget the White House found that the report's details had not intended the fight against terrorists or supporters States networks. Included is "the purchase of 40 F-22 super-fighter (considered" the most advanced aircraft of today's combat "), for US $ 4.1 billion; building a new type of aircraft carrier (CVN-78), which shall initiate will replace the Nimitz class ships and is equipped, for example, with the new nuclear engine model, an electromagnetic system to launch aircraft, advanced radar and other innovations; and the launch of new classes of destroyers and submarines. "In short, for the group at all these expenses are reflected in the war against terrorist networks but to face" a new cold war, "forward to" a capable power to pose a threat to the US military.

If the United States works to increasingly improve its military complex, the People's Republic is not far behind. At the end of 2010, an important US official in the Pacific Ocean warned his government on a missile being completed by the Chinese, able to sink an aircraft carrier George Washington - ultimate symbol of naval power in the country. The DF21D is controlled by satellites and can hit a target a1.500 kilometers away. Considered by experts as "a new wall," (Wall of China reference) Beijing seems willing to challenge US hegemony in that ocean, unprecedented in the geopolitical context in the post World War II - as analyzes journalist Rodrigo Bocardi, "the first time [the waters of the Pacific Ocean] are being disputed by another power, given the growing number of Chinese submarines in the region."

On the cover of SCO China is building an alliance with several intents and purposes to the Asian center, some of them are: mount the Energy Club of the Shanghai Cooperation Organization - as called Richard Morningstar; stabilize the region geopolitically and consolidate the supremacy of Asian giants (China and Russia), and especially and most importantly, undermine the US intention to put together a solid foundation of his power there. Assertively diagnosing the actions of Chinese diplomacy over the said place, the Chinese Yan Xuetong, director of the Institute of International Studies, categorically stated that "We created the SCO in order to resist the US strategic intention to extend its military control of Central Asia. The US intention to Central Asia under its sphere of military influence was aborted. With the SCO, relations between China and countries in the region have improved a lot. "

When the great fastest growing economy in the world and the largest exporter of energy come to some agreement, the thing is always much broader than simple matter of bilateral cooperation. Today nothing is more alarming to Americans that the Beijing-Moscow alliance. The largest country in area in the world, Russia, and the most populous, China, have never been honed your steps in the political and diplomatic scene - even at the time of the Soviet Union, when both, at least in theory, spoke in name of communism.

## New strategic alliances to Taiwan

With the new XXI century world order characterized by the appearance of military powers like China and Russia and other emerging countries like Brazil, India, Mexico and South Africa, the world approaches the new power balance setting. The possibility of continued economic growth in China and the emergence of other forces challenging the US hegemony create something new that can be equated to a new Cold War. In addition there is a constant terrorist threat that demands attention and many resources, reducing the comfort of the main US allied powers. This new point provides the Taiwan new opportunities to take advantage of the situation with the support of some of these global payers. Partnerships that make Taiwan part of a major economic and technological network can be set for a new era of international cooperation.

# REFERENCES

KORNAI, Janus. *From socialism to capitalism. Paper, num 4, Center for Post-Collectivist Studies, Londres, 1998.*

NAUGHTON, Barry. *Growing Out of the Plan. Chinese economic reform 1978-1993.* Cambridge, Cambridge University Press, 1995.

NAUGHTON, Barry. *The China Circle: Economic and Technology in PRC, Taiwan and Hong Kong, Washington, DC, Brookings Institution Press, 1997.*

ZELIKOW Philip. *The United States, the cold war, and the post-cold war order* in Paul Kennedy, William Hitchcok, editores (2000). From war to peace : 174. New Haven : Yale University Press.

UNITED STATES DEPARTMENT OF STATE, The Taiwan Straits Crises: 1954–55 and 1958 Office of the Historian, Bureau of Public Affairs.

Fillipe Leal Leite Néas[68]

## INTRODUCTION

Science of Law has largely discussed whether there is a single source of law or whether there may be other(s). It is the dialectic clutter among the schools of legal positivism, for which every right emanates from the State, positivism or sociological realism, which attributes to the social group the only source of rules of law.

However, first it is appropriate to understand the meaning of *source of law*. The word *source*, which comes from the Latin word *"fons"*, leads us immediately to the idea of water gushing out of the land, indicating the origin of something.

Indeed, the first necessary questions are: where does the Law come from? How does it materialize or manifest? These questions have been strengthened since the beginning of the movement of Law Codification, which started in the European systems, as of the nineteenth century, in which significant value is given to the legislator (FERRAZ JÚNIOR, 2011, p. 194).

In the midst of these debates, the doctrine has come to a definition of what source of law is, with subdivisions in the concept it proposes and, further, it has evaluated the various existing autonomous legal systems in order to find what their sources of positive law would be. We anticipate in saying that we disagree with this classic definition, which requires a conceptual suggestion that will be made in the course of this work.

From the *sources of law*, the customs as a manifestation of Law is of our interest, notably the international customs and the possible (or not) interference in an essential state activity to the exercise of its own sovereignty: taxation.

---

68  Lawyer. Attending Masters in Law from Universidade Católica de Brasília - UCB. Post-graduated in Tax Law from Instituto Brasileiro de Estudos Tributários - IBET. Bachelor in Law from Centro Universitário UDF.

In this context, the first chapter will have as object of study the meaning of *sources of law*, both national and international. This will be an opportunity to offer a different definition of what is classically spread by the doctrine.

In the next chapter, general considerations about the customs will be done in order to outline the still conceptual considerations on international customs and customs in the Brazilian Tax System.

Finally, given the particularities of the referred national system, whether it is possible for the international customs to interfere in the Brazilian tax audit activity will be investigated.

## SOURCES OF LAW

Although this is an introductory subject for the study of Law that has been debated for a long time by the legal doctrine, it is still far from achieving appeasement concerning the definition of *Law source*.

In a perspective focused on the Italian legal system, it is appropriate to bring up the inexorable lesson of BOBBIO (1999, p. 45) in the sense that *"sources of law are those facts or acts that generate the production of legal norms, as posed by the legal system."* He precisely says that the knowledge of a legal system starts by listing its sources and, at the same time one recognizes that there are facts on which the production of legal norms depend on (the sources, for the author). The legal system also regulates the way the rules must be produced. These are the denominated norms of behavior (for the first, those regulating people's behavior) and structure norms.

The subject is classically explained from a didactic division, from which the first two subdivisions of sources of positive law have been created: the material and formal sources.

According to DIMOULIS (2011, p. 166-167), material sources are the factors that create the law, giving rise to valid mechanisms, which would be composed of all the authorities, persons, groups and situations that influence the creation of the law in a given society.

Similarly, KÜMPEL (2007, p. 59) defends that the material sources of the law are all factors that influence the formation of legal norms, affecting the content of the formal sources. Moreover, all human reasons established the making of a specific law, of a certain custom or a general principle of law, such as economic, sociological and political reasons etc.

Indeed, the study of the material sources is linked to the study of the society itself in order to find out the events that could motivate the creating activity of positive law.

In turn, the formal sources would be entrusted to study the way the Law is articulated to its recipients, that is, how law is manifested – still in the intellection line of DIMOULIS (2011, p. 167).

In this group, the doctrine makes up a new subdivision of what would be proper formal, direct or pure source; and improper, indirect or unclean source.

The firsts would be those genuinely dedicated to the production of Law, from which the subjects of the State could get direct assistance in search for the righteous. They would be the laws, in a broad sense (in the Brazilian legal system: the Federal Constitution, complementary laws, ordinary laws, delegated laws and provisional measures[69]), the customs and the general principles of law.

The second would be the sources of law as exception, such as the doctrine, the jurisprudence and the customs, commonly used in the interpretation activity and in the integration of the laws in a general sense.

There is also another subdivision in the framework of the formal sources, which would be state and non-state sources, that means, when they derive from the State action (for the first) or when they have a particular origin, as it happens with the customs and with the doctrine. The classification suggested by VENOSA (2003, p. 42-53) is similar. According to him, the sources are primary when they are strong enough to generate the legal rule or secondary when they do not have the strength of the first, but they are able to clear up the spirits of the law enforcers and serve as a valuable substrate for a general understanding and application of the law.

The last subdivision within the formal sources we intend to expose is the main sources, which represent the laws in general and broad sense, that is, with little or no room for the judge/law enforcer to resort to other sources to resolve conflicts and establish what is righteous. And complementary sources, used only in cases of express legal omission,

---

69  We understand that it is not possible to fit the infra-legal acts such as decrees, resolutions, ordinances, etc. into this qualification, once they derive from the regulatory power of the State (in the figure of the Executive Power). As they are authoritative by law in strict sense that precedes it and gives specific authority of the producing agent of infra-legal act does not create genuinely rights but describes those already provided.

when the judge/law enforcer is empowered to decide or declare the subjective law based on customs, doctrine, jurisprudence and general principles of law.

It is usual to notice in the framework of the Brazilian Positive Law the doctrine to resign the article 4 of the Law of Introduction to the Brazilian Norms of Law - Decree-Law No. 4,657 (BRAZIL, 1942) in order to describe the formal sources of law. The law establishes in Article 4: "When the law is heedless, the judge will decide the case according to the analogy, customs and general principles of law."

The identification of the formal sources under the Public International Law (in the conceptual terms previously exposed), depends on the examination of international practices, as well as on the processes accepted by most components of the international community as a means of generation or revelation of legal rules.

As pointed out by CUNHA and PEREIRA (2000, p. 212), this investigation is now much easier because we can find plenty of such processes in certain texts of positive International Law. Because of the general acceptance they deserve, those texts may be considered the expression of a common view and form the basis for drawing up the list of International Law sources.

A significant part of the doctrine, perhaps unanimously, remits the analyst to Article 38 of the Statute of the International Court of Justice, incorporated by the United Nations Letter of June 26, 1945, in the investigation of their sources. They are:

a) General or special international conventions, which establish procedures recognized by the disputing parties;

b) International customs: as evidence of a practice generally recognized as Law;

c) The general principles of Law: recognized by civilized nations;

d) Under the provision of the Article 59, judicial decisions and the doctrine of the most qualified jurists from various nations, as subsidiary means for the determination of the legal rules.

Although they also refer to Article 38 of the Statute of the International Court of Justice, CUNHA e PEREIRA (2000, p. 211) affirm that under the International Law, only those sources denominated as formal can be considered as sources in the General Theory of Law, what we agree with, as discussed below.

The term sources of Law in the International Law, as well as in the general theory of Law, is likely to have the meaning of causes of social order that determine the need of the norm (material sources, creating sources, real or deep sources), or of modes or of processes of establishment, manifestation or revelation of the norms in social life (formal sources).

Although the investigation of the first is essential for a complete understanding of the positive international norms, which from a technical point of view show more interest and can be considered in strict legal-positive sense as the only sources of International Law.

After these considerations, we point out the first problem to be faced by the classical doctrinal qualifications, notably in defining a formal source of Law, national or international: legislation in broad sense is the way by which the positive Law is manifested. How could be the source of Law its expression language, namely its own product?

Before proceeding, let us return to the analysis of the conception of materials sources, which – as we viewed lines above – would deal with the facts of social reality that would require or justify the production of new prescriptive propositions to integrate the affirmed law. If legal facts are nothing more than hypothetically described facts in the supposed normative (CARVALHO, 2011, p. 84), i.e., events occurred in society, for which it was agreed in the State activity to standardize it in order to adjust the social behavior, describing it in the hypothetical field of the legal norm, which once occurred, would initiate effects also prescribed in the norm.

We cannot deny the relevance of the social events that require legislative action of the State. However, we believe it is credible to assert that the social fact that originated the normative plexus that compounds the Positive Law system would also compound the foundation of the validity of the latter. That is, a retrospective persecution, starting from the affirmed norm towards the reason of its origin, we will encounter social events and subsequent creating human activity of normative requirements, in the patterns of the power conferred by the society (theory of the social contract in the vision of John Locke[70]).

---

70 For him, the civil power is established in order to ensure better the enjoyment of natural rights (such as life, property, freedom). Therefore, it is originally born limited by a pre-existing right. In reverse, Thomas Hobbes defended the contractualism as a complete renunciation to all rights of the natural state by the individuals who compose a society, and the civil power is born without limits (any future limitation will be a self-limitation)

The Studies on what the material sources are, while not provided in legal mechanisms, are subject to be studied by the legal sociology, and anthropology, among other fields of study of the human being.

Resuming the critical analysis of the current meaning of the formal sources, one must have in mind that the Positive Law is a complex of legal norms valid in a given country. It is translated into a language, which is its way of expression. In addition, that language layer, as a man construction, turns to the discipline of human behavior, in the context of his inter-subjectivity relations. Its language is prescriptive, propagated by laws in a broad sense, which is nothing more than the physical support of the norms (CARVALHO, 2011, p. 34).

Following this reasoning, it is indicated that both doctrine and jurisprudence are not sources of Positive Law, because of its descriptive and not prescriptive speech, being the latter an inherent feature to the Positive Law language. Both only help to understand the prescription of legal texts that have foreseen them, but they do not modify them or dictate obligatory, permitted or prohibited actions/omissions. They just declare the meaning of the text affirmed and the possible effects that may be radiated from it when the event happens, in the phenomenal level, from the fact described as sufficient to normative incidence.

The general principles of law are, in turn, commands of greater abstraction that are conveyed or recognized in normative provisions contained in the system, in an implicit or explicit way, which indicates they are also a product of positive law, just like the law in a broad sense.

Concerning the customs, we will reserve the next chapter to analyze them.

The analysis of the Positive Law sources should rely on how laws are created, as they are the way it is manifested.

Indeed, as highlighted above, to assert that the law is the source of positive law does not mean more than postulating that norms create norms, law creates law, in an evident circular proposition, which leaves the first term as an unexplained residue (CARVALHO, 2011, p. 84).

In this context, CARVALHO (2011, p. 420) teaches that we must understand the sources of law as the ejector focus of legal rules, i.e., the organs empowered by the system to produce norms, in a staggered organization, as well as the activity developed by these entities, aiming the creation of norms.

Reviewing the lessons of BOBBIO (1999, 47-48) highlighted above, it is also important to spend some time in the so-called norms of structure, as far as no individual will be able to produce any legal imperative without holding expressly granted powers given by the legal system to do so. This competence is also conferred by norms of structure whose possible contents would be (i) to order the legislator to order, (ii) to prohibit the legislator to order, (iii) to allow him to order, (iv) to order prohibiting (v) to prohibit prohibiting, (vi) to allow prohibiting, (vii) to order allowing, (viii) to prohibit allowing and (ix) to allow allowing.

It is easy to notice that such norms, although predicting behaviors, will always be pre-arranged in the legal system. In addition, they have specific recipients and proper purpose: to establish limits to State activity of regulating its subjects' behavior.

Therefore, it would be correct to say that the norms of structure, for previously qualifying the producer of laws in a given system, would eventually be the sources of norms of behavior, delimiting the legislative process and the authority for the production of laws.

In this relentless retrospective analysis in the pursuit of what may be the source of what, in the Brazilian legal system we will find the Federal Constitution of 1988. Nevertheless, as a legal instrument, the regression would continue. Moreover, in order to establish the character of uniformity that every science claims for, it could be set as a methodological cut from the fundamental norm, conceived artificially to make the constituting activity a legally skilled *factum* to establish a new order of positive law. The system would be closed, having remained for the dogmatic jurist only the norms already affirmed, through which the facts and legally regulated behaviors are reached.

However, a new reflection has to be done on the wise teachings of KELSEN (1998, p. 134-142), regarding the notorious fundamental norm.

According to the long-standing jurist, there are no self-evident norms, in other words, every norm searches fundament of validity in another norm that is superior to it, forming a pyramid of normative hierarchy in a given system. However, the recurrence cannot be infinite. At one point, a norm can be found that does not depend of another norm to validate it, nor is there a norm that precedes it in a higher hierarchy. This norm cannot be affirmed because it would require the work of an agent and, therefore, a norm that authorizes them to do so and force others to obey his stated decision. Such norm must be assumed, without, however, an arbitrary imposition (the system must need of its existence, running the risk of being infamous). On the other hand, it must not require acceptance of its existence. For this reason, the fundamental norm is a presupposed norm that stands as a valid fundament for all affirmed norms of a legal system.

Nevertheless, the fundament of validity of the norm cannot be confused with its source, as there is patent semantic discrepancy between the words. For the sources, the recurrence must be interrupted as soon as the authority that produced the legal act and procedure is identified. These subjects are traditionally regulated by the constitutions.

In short, a source of positive law is considered as the organs that produce legal acts (in the broad sense) in a particular legal system, as well as its activity, creating the expression formula of the Law. However, every norm depends on another figure, called fundaments of validity, whose search is made from a receding analysis, in which we will encounter norms of higher hierarchy until reaching the Constitution. Before the Constitution, we would have a constituent assembly that originated it and that is seen as legitimized by means of the famous Kelsen fundamental norm, which would be the fundament of validity of the entire legal system.

Thus, we understand that the laws in a broad sense are a vehicle of expression of the Positive Law and, therefore, its own product. We will lend them the designation of "source of subjective rights", for the individual seeks the recognition of what is righteous in them: their rights.

It is true that in the *common law* system, the subjective right of the individuals is the result, primarily, of legal decisions in full compliance with the guidelines of that particular system. Its sources of law would reside in the norms that predict the competence of the judicative organs and the performance procedures, though. Decisions are also products of the system and are in subsequent time to the sources.

The sources of law, in our view, refer to the competent authorities in the production of the vehicles of Law expression and to the procedure predicted in each jurisdiction to do so. The product of such entities will be source of subjective law of the state subjects, then.

## CUSTOMS

In a proper approach from Sociology, customs mean social rules arising from a repeated practice in a widespread and prolonged manner, resulting in a certain conviction of obligation, according to each specific culture and society (RODRIGUES, 2006, p. 18-19).

In a historical context, greatly elaborated by MATA-MACHADO (2005. p. 234), one realizes that the custom "went through an easily noticeable evolution." Until the nineteenth century, the influence of the custom was dominant; after the French codification (1804-1810) it was almost abolished, particularly from the Civil Law; but in the last century, by virtue of the controversy between Thibault and Savigny, the tension between law and custom keeps the attention regarding the role of the latter.

BOBBIO (1998, p. 38-39)[71] has predicted the possibility of pointing out a sort of recognized source of Law (for us, source of subjective law) in modern political systems in which the direct and superior source is the Law. He has also glimpsed at the possibility of the normative force of the custom to derive from the authorization of the organ itself/Legislative Power, delegating to the State subjects the ability to issue norms. The author explains:

> When the legislator expressly adheres to the custom in a particular situation or hangs on expressly or tacitly to the custom in matters not regulated by Law (it is the case of the so-called 'consuetudo praeter legem', that is, custom beyond the law), he welcomes legal norms already produced. He also enriches the legal system with a set of norms produced in other jurisdictions, which can also be considerable, and perhaps before the constitution of the state system.

Naturally, one can also think of using the custom as a permission for citizens to produce legal norms through their own uniform behavior. That means to consider the custom among the delegate sources, assigning users the qualification of state agencies allowed to produce legal norms with their uniform behavior.

It is clear that any cogent force to be given to customs depends on a previous legal provision that allows it or enables the society to create its own norms directly, which will obviously be customary.

The customs, meaning social rules, arising from a repeated practice in a widespread and prolonged manner producing a certain conviction of obligation, according to each specific culture and society, are originated in society itself and its practices are repeated and accepted. Nevertheless, to possess legality and consequently relevance to the Positive Law, they depend on the legislative state act to impose so.

---

71  BOBBIO asserts that "the complexity of a legal system derives from the fact that the need for rules of conduct in a society is so great that there is no power (or organ) in a position to satisfy it by itself. To satisfy this requirement, the supreme power generally refers to two expedients: 1) the reception of norms already made, produced by diverse and precedent systems. 2) The delegation of power to produce legal norms to powers or lower organs." (1998, p. 38).

Given the strength that the positivation of Law has acquired, as observed elsewhere, both in the current Brazilian legal system, initially by means of the Law of Introduction to the Brazilian norms of Law, and in the international order, through the Statute of the International Court of Justice, the customs have been conferred such legal relevance, being elected as source of subjective law of individuals.

In States marked by the *common law* regime, structure is mostly used by countries of Anglo-Saxon origin as the United States and England, in which the Law is more based on the Jurisprudence that binds future decisions (*stare decisis*), the customs have stronger legal relevance, as they represent the most expressive form of Law expression in this system.

It is evident the importance of a state entity that recognizes the existence of such custom, providing it with typical prescriptive force of legal norms. In the States submitted to the previously mentioned non-coded system, this entity is the Judiciary that, *in casu*, is truly the source of law, which strongly underlies its manifestations in the customs, representing, for this reason, the fundament of validity of those decisions.

In the *civil law* system, in fact, there are no doubts that the customs only have prescriptive force of rights if there is a prior legal provision that authorizes so.

It is our matter, then, to evaluate the customs in the international and domestic legal systems, especially for the subsystem of the Brazilian Tax Law.

## CUSTOMS IN INTERNATIONAL LAW

The international custom, also identified as an "international practice", "non written International Law" (*jus non scriptum)*, among other terms, is the oldest tool that prescribes behaviors or, as agreed elsewhere, the earliest source of subjective law in the international sphere.

Its importance comes from the fact that an integrated center of normative production in the International Law field does not exist, despite the current trend of codification of international norms of customary origin ((MAZZUOLI, 2009, p. 101).

In the language of the Statute of The Hague Court, the custom results from a general practice accepted as being the law.

REZEK (2005, 118), following the line of countless precedents of international courts[72], readily identifies the subjective and material elements of the custom from the referred statement. They are, respectively: "repetition, over the time, of a certain manner of proceeding regarding a specific factual situation" and "the conviction to proceed not without reason, but because it is necessary, fair, and therefore legal."

Regarding the material element, REZEK (2005, 119) also asserts that the action or omission from which may emerge an international custom will emanate from the subjects of Public International Law. They are revealed as sovereign States and, in a modern sense, as International Organizations able to set up precedents and modulate conducts, whose repeated practice over time can make it an internationally recognized custom.

Moreover, we identified a third subject: the individual. Because of his assiduously participation in the social and economic evolution process, he demands from the public international law not only its protection in the international scenario, but also its participation in the Law creating and in the evolutionary process, as a recipient of the International Law norm, especially if we consider the Declaration of Human and Citizen Rights[73].

Indeed, the possibility of individuals to celebrate international contracts with States or international Organisms would enhance the possibility of emergence of international customs. We can mention, for instance, a case of 1950 in which a contract celebrated by *Anglo Iranian Oil Company* with the government of Iran was analyzed and through which the company was nationalized.

In fact, the origin of the international custom occurs spontaneously by the repeated practice of certain conducts coming from the coexistence of the States in response to wishes and needs of the various existing people in the world. They do not emanate from a central organ with competence to impose behaviors, despite that it may be recognized by international organisms and Courts and, very often, positivized in international treaties.

---

72 The most evident was cases were the Continental Platform at the North Sea, in 1969, the Continental Platform between Libya and Malta, in 1985, and the Military and Paramilitary Activities in Nicaragua and against it (Nicaragua v. United States of America ) in 1986.
73 In this line of intellection, MIRCN (2002), citing Peter James Nkanbo Mugerva justifies the possibility of the individual to act as a subject of public international law because the fact that the man has "the ability to establish contractual relations, or any other legal ones, with other legal entities recognized by the legal system in question".

The custom is slow to develop and is often inaccurate in its prescriptions, raising difficulties to ascertain whether a certain conduct has elapsed long enough to be considered an international custom. Otherwise, it would be a mere usual phenomenon without legal force.

From this perspective, Paul Guggenheim distinguishes the customs from simple uses when he asserts that, in order for a legally relevant custom to exist, its violation must be followed by a penalty, which, in our view, is a crucial element for it to be configured as legal norm - customary rule, in this case (CUNHA; PEREIRA, 2000, p. 287).

The validity or enforceability of the customary norm, in turn, rests on the consent, expressed or not (it may appear in the form of silence or entry into official relations with other States, assuming the tacit agreement, hence).

Furthermore, it is also important to highlight the difficulty to prove the existence of an international custom and its obedience by a determined subject of international law. REZEK (2005, p. 122-123) teaches that its proof may happen by the investigation of the State acts, not only those from the executive, but also in legal texts and judicial decisions that have as topics of interest the law of nations. At this point, we realize the extreme importance of joint investigation of the international norms, always in comparison with the domestic legal system of each country.

After having seen the nuances of the international customs, it is very meaningful to investigate the customary norms in the Brazilian legal system, especially with regard to Tax Law.

## CUSTOMS IN THE BRAZILIAN TAX LAW

We have already mentioned above that the Brazilian Law honored the custom and positivized it initially in the Decree-Law No. 4,657, of September 4, 1942 (LINDB), enabling its use by the judge on a scenario of inexistent laws or legislative gap (BRAZIL, Article 4, 1942)

The Brazilian Civil Procedure Code (Law No. 5,869, of January 11, 1973) followed the same line in its scope:

> Art. 126. The judge is not exempt from sentencing or deciding alleging gap or obscurity of the law. At the trial of the case, he is supposed to apply legal norms; in case they do not exist, he will call on analogy, customs and general principles of law. (BRAZIL, 1973).

It is, then, a normative integration tool (or a normative gap) used when the magistrate finds no rule when trying to solve case, and he is not able to subsume the fact to any existing provision in the legal system. That means there is a lack of knowledge about the legal *status* of certain behavior, due to a malfunction of the system, which is the gap - absence of norm (DINIZ, 2010, p. 332).[74]

However, the customs have their own and peculiar aspects in Tax Law, once it was not listed in the National Tax Code (Law No. 5,172, of October 25, 1966) as one of the possible integration methods. Confer below:

> Art. 108. In the absence of an express provision, the competent authority to enforce the tax laws will use successively in this order:
>
> I - the analogy;
>
> II - the general principles of tax law;
>
> III - the general principles of public law;
>
> IV - equity. (BRAZIL, 1966).

In effect, the National Tax Code (CTN) elected customs as "complementary norms" of the tax legislation, whose role is "to make explicit the content of the laws in order to standardize its interpretation by the tax authorities" (MACHADO SEGUNDO, 2009, p. 203). The Code disciplines, with particular attention to item III:

> Art. 100. They are complementary norms of laws, treaties and international conventions and decrees:
>
> I - the normative acts issued by the administrative authorities;
>
> II - the decisions of singular or collective organs with administrative jurisdiction to whom the law attributes normative effectiveness;
>
> III - the practices repeatedly observed by the administrative authorities;

---

74 The celebrated doctor states that the gap may also consist of the presence of unfair statutory provision or in disuse, with what we asked *venia* to disagree, because the existence of legal precept demands its application, making use of interpretative methods, or not (for reasons of unconstitutionality, in which the legal provision is cut off from the system by judicial act). In the latter case, the dependence on previous act recognizing the unconstitutionality of the presumed unconstitutional law prevents the immediate use of integration methods.

IV - the covenants celebrated among the Union, the states, the Federal District and the municipalities.

Sole paragraph. The compliance with the norms mentioned in this article do not exempt the imposition of penalties, the collection of interest arrears and the updating of the the monetary value of the tax calculation basis. (BRAZIL, 1966)

It is clear that the general law of the Brazilian Tax Law has not assigned prescribing force to the customs, but it has given it the power to describe complementarily the content of the so-called tax legislation, where the source of the subjective law of the individuals will be based on.

In addition, the Brazilian Tax Law did not assign this power to any custom, but only to those arising from the practice of State organs that guide all their activities on the principle of legality (Articles 5, II, and 150, II of the Federal Constitution of 1988). They have the competence to compel the interpreter to seek prescriptive sentences exclusively among those introduced in the positive system by means of law or another diploma that has the same status (CARVALHO, 2011, p. 299). In the recurrent analysis of the repeated practices of the State Tax Administration, we will fatally encounter a generic and abstract normative act (law in the broad sense).

In this same scenario, the character of subsidiarity the CTN assigned to customs makes it clear that they are not allowed to extrapolate the content of the laws and, therefore, the regulatory power conferred by the Constitution to the Executive Administration. [75]

By the way, the compliance with administrative authorities' practices, which are contrary to the legal provisions, has no strength to overcome the cogent force of law. It only "excludes the imposition of penalties, the collection of interest arrears and the updating of the monetary value of the tax calculation basis" (BRAZIL, Law No 5.172, 1966, Article 100, sole paragraph) as a means to protect the principles of legal certainty, confidence, good faith, morality and rationality. It would not be lawful to the administrative authority, after having oriented the passive subject to behave in a certain way, to defend the unfeasibility of those same norms and punish the taxpayer who obeyed them. Then, the descriptive language that customs have in the Brazilian Tax Law is reinforced.

---

[75] "Art. 84. It is incumbency of the President of the Republic: IV - to sanction, promulgate and order the publication of laws as well as to issue decrees and regulations for its faithful executiont." (BRAZIL, 1988).

Thus, we realize that only the customs produced by the administrative tax authorities can interfere in the national tax field. In a contrary case to an express legal provision, they do not have enough power to repeal it. They can only exclude the penalty that the taxpayer would have for noncompliance with his obligations with the State. All this radiates from the principle of tax legality, which restricted the origin and the use limits of these customs.

Nevertheless, we have seen that international customs do not emanate from a specific central organ, although the international community elected them as source of subjective law. We will thus investigate them in comparison with the national tax system.

## THE INTERNATIONAL CUSTOMS IN THE BRAZILIAN TAX LAW

It is known that the regulation of relations and the activities of the subjects of international law are objects of the International Law. According to SEITENFUS and VENTURA (2003, p. 24), its functions can be defined as (i) Jurisdiction sharing among sovereign States, each one with its territorial delimitation, over which they exercise their jurisdiction; (ii) setting of obligations to sovereign States, so that their freedom of acting is delimited; and (iii) conducting relations among international organizations.

It is evident that the International Law is often opposed to the sovereignty of the States, concepts that, as remarked by VALADÃO (2000, p. 192), are evolving, dictated by the constant changing of the international conditions and the commercial and cultural exchanges among the States. In addition, there is also the elevation of problems that are common to all, going beyond territorial boundaries, for example, issues related to the environment, use and pollution of water, of the atmosphere, the preservation of animal and plant species in extinction. Those subjects were not even mentioned in the dawn of the last century.

However, it is necessary to make it clear that, in Brazil, the State activity of instituting taxes, denominated taxing competence, is closely linked to its sovereignty and emanates from the legislative activity, resulting from the State empowered organs.

Notwithstanding, we are not only talking about state sovereignty, but also about fiscal sovereignty. As taught by BORGES (1992, p. 40-43), the latter is part of the first, although they not always coincide. This is what happens with the existence of own tax systems of non-sovereign states and with the European Union. The fiscal sovereignty can thus be understood as the power to establish an autonomous tax system.

In this context, VALADÃO (2000, p. 196) synthesizes that "the tax competence arises from tax sovereignty and tax sovereignty is derived from the state sovereignty, although one does not necessarily coincide with the other."

Given the importance that the International Law has acquired with direct interference in the internal legal systems, especially on issues correlated to the economic activity, closely linked to the Tax Law, specific fields of legal knowledge arose: Tax International Law and International Tax Law.

The first one has as an object International Law norms that regulate the relations among the States with regard to tax activity, while the second one consists of materials norms from the Domestic and International Law aimed at limiting the international tax competence of the States (VALADÃO, 2000, p. 144).

Given the relevant object of the knowledge fields above, phenomena such as double international taxation of income[76], for example, have received special attention from the most renowned jurists and hence from international organizations and States. This is in order to standardize the possible economic events regarding to the problems coming from the internationalization of relations.

Well, we observed that among the normative framework aimed at regulating relations among States and delimitating tax competences, the International law conferred normative force to international customs, which also borrowed the definition of international source of subjective law.

We have affirmed and reiterated, with the support of the doctrine of Francisco Rezek, that the own existence of an international custom can be proven by investigating the internal State acts, which exalts the importance of the Domestic Law of each country in understanding the International Law.

We have also asserted that the Brazilian Tax Law has restricted the power of the customs in the Article 100 of the National Tax Code, differently from what the Introductory Law to Brazilian Law Norms did, giving the custom the constitutional principle of strict legality.

Given this scenario, the question is: what would be the legal force of an international custom in the Brazilian Tax Law?

---

76 As defined by the Fiscal Committee from the Organization for Economic Cooperation and Development — OECD: "The phenomenon of international double legal taxation may generally be defined as the result of the reception of similar taxes in two - or more - States on the same taxpayer, for the same enforceable matter and for the same period of time." (OECD, 1977, p. 15).

Despite the International Court of Justice exercises jurisdiction over Brazil (BRAZIL, Decree No19.841, 1945) and, although the customs are of extremely relevance in other issues such as international trade, directly involved in the taxation activity, they differ from the international treaties as they do not have normative relevance in the Brazilian tax Law.

It is appropriate strongly reiterating that although the international treaties are currently the most significant international source of subjective law, this article is not intended to ascertain their normative force in the Brazilian Tax System. The National Tax Code denominated them as "tax legislation"[77], giving them normative force.

Out of curiosity, the statement highlighted by VALADÃO (2000, 244-245) regarding the role of the international treaties in the tax activity is valid:

> The relevance of the matter is to know whether the international treaties are able or not to institute or increase taxes or, on the other hand, to establish hypotheses of tax relief. As it has already been already stated, treaties are incorporated into Domestic Law with the status of ordinary law, and the principle of legality remains preserved. The creation of a tribute by a treaty still seems to be a distant reality, possible in the scope of economic integration processes. However, the increase of taxes by treaty is not that distant, although what predominates in the treaties is the exemption.

However, despite the study of treaties is of remarked importance, we will only consider the international customs in comparison with the national tax system, once its interference has long been the subject of investigation by the Legal Science.

Indeed, the submission of Brazil to the International Court of Justice and therefore to its Statute, induces to conclude that in the National Tax System the normative force attributed to the international customs would have to be repeated and respected. That is an example of what the Law of Introduction to the Brazilian Norms of Law and the Civil Procedure Code prescribed.

Nevertheless, we note that Brazil's fiscal sovereignty enables this State to establish an autonomous system of taxation, with its own rules, as predicted by the Federal Constitution, Title VI, Chapter I.

---

77  "Art. 96. The expression 'tax law' includes the laws, treaties and international conventions, decrees and the additional norms that apply in whole or in part, on tax and legal relations concerning to them." (BRAZIL, Law No 5.172, 1966).

The definition of international customs is quite broad, whereas the Brazilian Tax System, following its constitutional guidelines (Article 146, III[78], in particular) explicitly delimited the customs that have legal significance, as well as their degree of enforceability.

International customs are not the result of repeated acts of the State organs or international organisms, focused on the tax inspection. Allowing customs to intervene in the fiscal activity of the Brazilian state could be considered a harassment to its own fiscal sovereignty.

For that reason, a certain foreign company could not try to justify noncompliance with complementary tax obligations by offering simplified tax income declarations that do not match to those determined by the Brazilian law, for example, alleging the use of a determined international custom against the Brazilian Finance Administration. Nor can it justify certain suppressive conduct in international custom focused on trade relations.

It is clear that if such international custom has been positivized by an international treaty, to which Brazil has been a signatory, and internalized by means of its own legislative process, acquiring legal status of ordinary law, as a rule[79], its enforceability would be legitimate. However, the source of the subjective right would no longer be the custom, but the national legal act, added to the treaty. The custom would only become the fundament of validity of the treaty.

Therefore, we conclude that to enter Brazil and carry out economic activities, any foreign activity should pay attention to the Brazilian regulatory provisions, even when they are contrary to international customs, given that the latter are not accepted by the national legal system concerning the Tax Administration.

---

78 "Art. 146. It is in charge of the complementary law: III – to establish general norms concerning tax legislation, especially about: [...] ." (BRAZIL, Federal Constitucion, 1988)

79 If they concern about human rights and are internalized with typical procedure to approve constitutional amendments, the treaties now hold legal nature of constitutional norm. Otherwise, if they relate to the same subject, but are not subjected to that specific and rigorous rite of approval, they will possess the so-called *supralegal* force..

## CONCLUSIONS

We realize that what the doctrine has currently defined as sources of law, expression to which we can still apply various subdivisions, does not effectively reveal the source of Positive Law. In fact, it is the concept that mixes realities that are relevant to Law.

The laws, in a general sense, are not sources of Positive Law, but the vehicle that introduces the norm, the hardware of the normative enunciation, and hence does not come from itself. Its source depends truly on the legislative activity and on the agents that produced it.

The customs in the Brazilian legal system only have legal significance when predicted in a legal act that enabled its use by the Law enforcer.

The international customs have equal or greater legal relevance, because of the obvious lack of organ or entity that produces enforceable laws to the nations, despite the large production of international treaties for the same purpose (to regulate relations among states, as a rule), turning them essential in resolving conflicting relations.

Although the international customs are enforceable against Brazil, they may not be so regarding the national tax activity, exactly because of its state and fiscal sovereignty. In other words, our autonomous taxation system has not enabled every custom as a complementary norm, primarily for purposes of tax avoidance, but only those produced by the Brazilian tax authority.

Therefore, international customs can never be enforceable against Brazil by foreign entities to refrain from obeying any obligation under the Brazilian law, due to its irrelevance to the National Tax System.

# REFERENCES

## ELECTRONIC REFERENCES

BRASIL. Constituição Federal de 1988. Available at: <http://www.planalto.gov.br/ccivil_03/constituicao/constituicao.htm>. Access on: June 18, 2014.

BRASIL. Código Tributário Nacional. Available at: <http://www.planalto.gov.br/ccivil_03/leis/l5172.htm>. Access on: June 18, 2014.

BRASIL. Decreto n.º 19.841, de 22 de outubro de 1945. Available at: < http://www.planalto.gov.br/ccivil_03/decreto/1930-1949/D19841.htm>. Access on: June 18, 2014.

KELSEN, Hans, Teoria Pura do Direito, 1998, p. 134-142. (traduzida por João Baptista Machado) ed. Martins Fontes, São Paulo 1999 - Available at: <http://www.estig.ipbeja.pt/~ac_direito/HansKelsenTeoria.pdf>. Access on: Access on: June 11, 2014.

MIRON, Rafael Brum. O indivíduo como sujeito de Direito Internacional Público. In: Âmbito Jurídico, Rio Grande, III, n. 9, maio 2002. Available at: <http://www.ambito-juridico.com.br/site/index.php?n_link=revista_artigos_leitura&artigo_id=4019>. Access on: June 11, 2014.

## BIBLIOGRAPHIC REFERENCES

BOBBIO, Noberto. Teoria do Ordenamento Jurídico. trad. Maria Celeste C. J. Santos. 10ª Ed. Brasília: UNB, 1999.

BORGES, Antônio Moura. Convenções sobre Dupla Tributação Internacional. Teresina: EDUFPI, 1992,

CARVALHO, Paulo de Barros. *Curso de Direito Tributário*, 23ª ed. São Paulo: Saraiva. 2011.

CARVALHO, Paulo de Barros. *Direito Tributário Linguagem e Método*, 4ª ed. São Paulo: Noeses, 2011.

CUNHA, Joaquim Moreira da Silva e PEREIRA, Maria da Assunção do Vale. Manual de Direito Internacional Público. Coimbra - Portugal, Almedina, 2000.

DIMOULIS, Dimitri. Manual de introdução ao estudo do direito: definição e conceitos básicos, norma jurídica, fontes interpretação e ramos do direito, sujeito de direito e fatos jurídicos, relações entre direito, justiça, moral e e política, direito e linguagem, 4. ed. rev. atual. e amp. - São Paulo: Editora Revista dos Tribunais, 2011.

DINIZ, Maria Helena. Dicionário jurídico universitário, São Paulo: Saraiva, 2010.

FERRAZ JÚNIOR, Tercio Sampaio. Introdução ao estudo do direito: técnica, decisão, dominação. 6ª ed. - 3 reimpr. São Paulo: Atlas, 2011.

MATA-MACHADO, Edgar de Godoy da. Elementos de Teoria Geral do Direito. Líder. 2005.

MAZZUOLI, Valério de Oliveira. Curso de Direito Internacional Público. 3.ª ed., São Paulo: Editora Revista dos Tribunais, 2009.

REZEK, Francisco. Direito Internacional Público: curso elementar, 10. Ed. Ver. e atual. São Paulo: Saraiva, 2005.

RODRIGUES, Joelza Ester. História em documento: imagem e texto (1. ed.), A História do passado e do presente. São Paulo: FTD, 2006.

SEGUNDO, Hugo de Brito Machado. Código Tributário Nacional: anotações à Constituição, ao Código Tributário Nacional e às Leis Complementares 87/1996 e 116/2003, 2ª ed. São Paulo: Atlas, 2009.

SEITENFUS, Ricardo Antônio Silva e VENTURA, Deisy de Freitas Lima. Introdução ao direito internacional público, Imprenta: Porto Alegre, Livr. do Advogado, 2003.

VALADÃO, Marcos Aurélio. Limitações Constitucionais ao Poder de Tributar e Tratados Internacionais. Del Rey : B. Horizonte, 2000.

# THE TAX CONSCIOUSNESS AS NA INSTRUMENT TO COMBAT THE TAX AVOIDANCE AND THE TAX EVASION

Amanda Madeira Reis[80]
Celso Antonio Pires Ferreira[81]

## INTRODUCTION

This article addresses the perennial and necessary search for justice in all branches of the legal system, bringing more specific notions to its application to the Tax and Fiscal Law. The taxes enable the entire social fabric to remain integrated because through them are held all structures that allow this connection.

The main purpose of the work is to show the importance of information gathering by citizens-taxpayers in relation to the meaning and systematization of taxes that surround them, because by being aware of the importance of all the macro tax system in which he appears and having awareness of its integration, he would be able to take action in order to enhance their status and the community within this system. It is believed that a more accurate understanding, coupled with a harmonization and balance within this social-tax net, the possibilities of fraud or scams to the State's fiscal activity would be minimized.

Preliminarily, a theoretical framework on the notions of justice, citizenship and individual/collective consciousness as forms of harmonious integration of an honest and balanced social structure will be presented. Demonstrating how all these concepts are interrelated and could hardly subsist isolated. By connect them it is possible to get a workable pattern of fiscal justice, thus achieving an approximate ideal the alleged common desire to any modern society: proceed fairly and suppress actions that are illegal or, even legal, are immoral and harmful to society.

---

[80]    Master's Degree in Law at the Catholic University of Brasília (in progress). Specialist in Civil Law and Civil Procedural Law (UCDB, 2008). Law graduate (CEUT, 2006). College Professor at CESVALE and IFPI.

[81]    Master's Degree in Law at the Catholic University of Brasília. Master in Business Administration (MBA) in Business Management - Getúlio Vargas Foundation (FGV). Researcher at the International Policy Laboratory of the Catholic University of Brasilia (UCB). Secretary of Economic Affairs of the State of Piauí Industrial Association (AIP). Taxpayers Board of Directors' State of Piaui.

After a overall discussion, it will be questioned its involvement in the taxation sector. With the conviction that the fair distribution of the tax burden among taxpayers citizens passes by their consciousness and encouraging the effective exercise of their fiscal citizenship. With such references the works exposes how to implement such theoretical frameworks relying on Brazilian constitutional guarantees in order to motivate a solid foundation to evolve and give support to a conscious Fiscal State, organized and taking the fiscal justice as its main purpose to be achieved. The Brazilian Constitution of 1988[82] provides means for perpetrating what is suggested throughout all its text and more specifically in its article 150, § 5.[83]

Conclusions are drawn about the progress of this slow but necessary change of social and legal paradigm as a mean to achieve a tangible fiscal justice. In the legal context, inquiring which laws have been created or are in the process of creation, scanning his duties as stimulating debates on social framework. Such questionings urge society to move when it is imperative or to rebel when they feel wronged. It brings up yet the conceptual contours of Tax Avoidance and Evasion, concluding with an ideal horizon in which to rise a more integrated and participatory society with effective glimpses of fiscal justice. Against this background, the practices that tend to be fiscal behavior deviations, illegal or immoral, would naturally be repelled by the community.

There is no doubt that the road to social paradigms transformations is quite complex, however, as said by CALAMANDREI (1995, p. 4) "To find justice, one must be faithful to her. She, like all deities, manifests herself only for those who believe in her".

## GROUNDS OF JUSTICE AND ITS FISCAL TAX EXTENSION.

Historical and ideological contours of the conception of justice.

The questioning around the conceptual definition of justice and its application boundaries date back to the origins of law. Its notion varies by time and culture, but its ideal of social justice remains since ancient times. This happens since the pre-history of law, even before the appearance of writing and consequent appearance of the first

---

82  Enacted on October 8, 1988.

83  "The law shall determine measures for consumers to be informed about taxes on goods and services".

legal texts. Such compilations around the ideal of justice emerge at different times, varying according to each civilization.

The right thing to say, without exacerbated digressions, is that institutions of public law existed even before the writing as a form to regulate life in these primitive societies and those relatively developed organizations that are difficult to study, in their "archaic law", already sought notions of justice. Emphasizing, however, that the conceptual abstraction of its content varies by time or social context of its interpretative perspective. We cite here the historical analysis performed by Gilissen (2003, p. 36):

[...] It is therefore accepted that there is no universal and eternal notion of justice, and this notion may vary over time and space. In archaic systems of law it is just everything that matters to maintain the cohesion of the social group, and not for what tends to respect for individual rights; thereof a great severity in relation to any anti-social behavior, that is contrary to the interests of the group, and on the contrary, a tendency to seek conciliation to resolve any conflict within the group; the function of judge is not to resolve a dispute according to pre-established rules, but trying to get the agreement of the parties by mutual concessions; where, the importance of the negotiations that can last for days, and also the absence of any notion of authority of res judicata.

This conceptual variation of the conception of justice is the result of a current transfer within human social relations. Examples of this are the legal elements introduced by Roman law, which brought the notions of values such as "all are equal before the law" and "everyone has equal rights"; having as utmost symbolism justice depicted as the statue "blindfolded" and with a "sword in hand". The Catholic Church contributed to the formatting of the ideal of justice by having it as one of its four cardinal virtues, consisting of a "constant and firm will to give to others what is their due"[84]. The transformation process can be slow, but it is perennial.

Within this evolution varied conceptions of justice were theorized. RAWL (1971), one of the most influential, conceptualized justice as equity, resuming the "social contract theory" proposed a similar hypothetical situation to the state of nature in which certain individuals chose principles of justice. They were thought to be "rational" and "balanced" and still subjected to a condition called by him as "veil of ignorance"; it is

---

[84] Compendium of the Catechism of the Catholic Church, No. 381.

defined as situation of lack of knowledge on the advantages and disadvantages of life in society (class system, education, moral beacons, etc.).

In these categories they were considered "free and equal", thus choosing principles of justice, in the perception of Rawls would be: principle of freedom, whereby each person should have an equal right to equal basic liberties that are compatible with one another and the principle of equality, in which economic and social inequalities must be sorted in order to be considered advantageous for all within reasonable limit (the principle of difference) and linked to positions and offices accessible to all (the principle of equal opportunities). These principles exercise the function of judging the standards of "justice" in society, regulating the allocation of collective rights and duties.

Another important jurist to dedicate himself to the complex conceptual borders of justice was Ronald Dworkin85. His theorizing report on two fundamental premises: the distribution of social wealth should envision people's preferences, so that an equal division would not be necessarily fair (equal concern) and material inequality would not be justified if they could not be attributed to people's choices or were beyond their control (special responsability). Equality for DWORKIN (2000) manifests in the resources that people have to reach their choices and not in the welfare they could possibly get with these resources. The government, in this conception, would have a key role to provide a "substantive equality" which he calls "distributive justice".

Another perspective on what can be analyzed justice is economic, having as its its greatest exponent Richard Posner86. . In his theory, the normative basis for the concept of justice involves the maximization of wealth, which occurs at the time when material goods and other sources of satisfaction are distributed so that its added value is maximized. This maximization can be facilitated by three categories of fundamental rights: personal security, personal liberty and private property. The state, in view of POSNER (1972), not only distributes wealth, but can also create it through their

---

85 He analyzed the work of John Rawls on the concept of justice in two books already considered modern classics: "The Sovereign Virtue," originally published in 2000 and "Justice for Porcupines", originally published in 2011. Only as a curiosity, we inform you that, unfortunately, Professor Ronald Dworkin died in February 2013.

86 His classic book is entitled: "Economic Analysis of Law", originally published in 1972.

institutions and benefits to the population. The understanding of justice arising from this approach uses the maximization of wealth as critical judgment to analyze the existence of justice in deeds and institutions. For him, this insight would admit to harmonize utility, freedom and equity approaches. The intent of this study is not to discuss the theories of justice that have developed throughout history; because of this, these brief comments were limited to lift general ideas of those who have proved most important.

We close this topic highlighting the general notions of justice developed here, namely: A deliberation with plenty of abstraction charge, referring to an idealized state of social interrelation, where there is a plausible stabilization and to some impartial point among interests involved and varying according to the time and culture in which they arise. Such elements that trace the contours of justice, despite the polysemy of this term, are notable for guiding the plans to be achieved in a Democratic Rule of Law.

## Consciousness and Citizenship under a Tax Perspective

There is no doubt that consciousness is a very complex structure, through which we explore the world around us. As stated by PINKER (1971), no one can be aware of anything in the first contact with this thing, at most can reference it with other close records, allowing us to conclude that the thing is like this or that of another domain.

The implementation of this first contact to the citizen has historically been denied; with him without knowing the justification for the payment of taxes. With the evolution of the democratic processes that was turning up to be considered in our times essential to establish a tax consciousness to measure the degree of social development of a State. In the precursor lines of Baleeiro87 (2002, p. 196):

Most of population, under the regressive weight of taxes of sales, consumption, stamp, etc., assumes that the taxes fall on the shoulders of large taxpayers or do not think at all about these matters. They believe that their interests are not compromised by financial measures.

---

87 Professor Aliomar Baleeiro showed his worry about the "fiscal anesthesia" (according to his own words) and the tax consciousness of the citizen-taxpayer since the first publication of his book An Introduction to Science of Finance. That was way back in 1955, in other words, for 60 years now, such an important topic has not been of our concern.

For the full functioning of a State it is imperative that its citizens feel responsible for it and that responsibility comes from a knowledge of the reasons why make them qualify as taxpayers. Even the etymology of the word in portuguese ("contribuinte") brings the notion to contribute, in other words, participate with something. To feel like a "contribuinte" the citizen has to be aware of the need to contribute, he needs to know why.

This tax consciousness should be brought to the citizen-taxpayers, but shall not in any case be missed. In didactic remarks of Machado (2012, p. 284):

So that all citizens feel "contribuintes", actually, it lacks the so-called tax consciousness, the consciousness that the tax burden weighs not only on the shoulders of those who have a legal duty to pay of taxes, but also on the shoulders of those who, buying goods or hiring services, pays a price in which are embedded taxes.

The innovative aspect presented by him is using the taxpayer consciousness as a mean to limit the power to tax. Covering a subjective concept that can never be overturned. Machado asserts with precision (2012, p 286):

The tax consciousness is the most important of limitations of the power to tax. More important because it is a substantial limitation, and, therefore, their removal by the ruler is virtually impossible. While the formal limitations of greater range, such as the principles of legality and prospective application of taxes, may eventually be removed from the Brazilian Constitution, tax conscience can not be removed and may even prevent the removal of those formal limitations.

The tax consciousness generates greater participation of the citizen-taxpayer in his social environment, participating more actively in the search for improvements to the quality of life of community, proving to be very effective in the full range of Human Rights. It raises questions including related to the State's size and mainly, to its cost for citizens; in other words, it serves as reflection for the analysis of real obligations of increase of tax revenue.

The exercise of civil, political and social rights and duties established in the Brazilian constitution will be used as an instrument for the full conceptualization of citizenship. The consciousness and citizenship should always walk together, since only when he approaches the consciousness does it become possible for citizens to legitimize the decision-making of their representatives and the State. Since they interfere directly in the life of society, these decisions necessarily have to be legitimized for all of us (the citizens).

## The Fiscal State and the Fundamental Duty to Pay Taxes

Disregarding exceptional cases of States that do not use ingresses and primary revenue on an ongoing basis and we can cite as an example countries with large natural reserves of oil or gas; governments over time have used some universal means to support themselves financially, such as taking from other people or receiving donations, producing income through state properties and enterprises, taking or forcing loans and ultimately, coercively establishing taxes. In the teachings of Valadão (2000, p. 21):

To earn the revenue necessary for the performance of functions that are inherent to the State it uses the power to tax, which is intrinsic to it. Of course, the evolution of the concept of State was accompanied by changes in the form of raising funds and, over this evolution, tax claims not always were the main sources of the States' revenue.

Modern States are mostly considered fiscal, in other words, they use taxes as a source of funding for their entire organization and operation, invoking a power of imposition before its citizens and legitimated by them to collect taxes. For Hensel (2005, p. 117):

La palabra poder tributario designa, de acuerdo com la moderna concepción del Estado, la soberania estatal general aplicada a una concreta materia de la actividad estatal: la imposición. El objetivo de estas líneas es clarificar qué particularidades presenta esta manifestación de la soberania del Estado.

Counterbalancing the state power with more defining criteria of their application in the context of taxes, teaches Nabais (2012, p 687):

[...] all citizens are assigned to fulfill the duty to pay taxes, and uniformity, to demand such duty to be assessed under the same criterion - the criterion of ability to contribute. Thus, this implies equal tax for those who have equal ability to pay (horizontal equality) and different tax (qualitative and quantitative) for those who have different capacity of contribution in the proportion of this difference (vertical equality).

The imposing state activity of the duty to pay taxes arises from the sovereignty. There is no doubt about it. What has to be clarified is the imperative need of democratic legitimacy, as the suport of these modern States. This legitimacy emanates from its citizens, and it is only validated through consciousness (exploring/asking/studying) of these citizens, referring to what is happening in their social environment and the exercise of their citizenship.

In a legitimate and democratic fiscal State it is important the perception of rights protection, but rather, can not excuse to exercise the duties. Liberalisms that only recognize rights no longer fit in modern societies. The citizen's responsibilities should be encouraged as a way to balance between personal liberties and community needs. This balancing of interests is critical to stabilize the State's social relations.

This is not about to denying rights to citizens, such rights are already protected in the Brazilian constitution as a defense against the imminent aggressions of the fiscal State. What is sought is an assumption of responsibility by the citizen-taxpayer, as a way of balancing in society, stipulating the end of that social rejection towards the tax. The tax is not pure power of the State, or mere sacrifice of the citizen; the tax should be seen as a fundamental duty, part of a virtuous cycle of consciousness to stimulate citizenship. It thus legitimizes the State actions to guarantee fundamental and social rights of the citizen-taxpayer. Costa ponders (2012, p. 24):

It is worth noting the existence of another strain, permanent, observed between the imposition of taxes and the exercise of fundamental rights. If, on the one hand, the demand of those may, improperly, hinder or even derail the exercise of these, on the other hand, it seems clear that many of the rights guaranteed in the legal system depend, for their protection, on the proceeds from the tax revenue.

Citizenship and taxation ideas should go together, the act of a citizen to contribute to public expenditure represents an externality of citizenship.

## The Organized State as a Guarantor of Human Rights

Successive grouping of humans in various parts of the world gave rise to cities and later came the idea of the State as maximum aspect of human conglomerate, transcending it only the modern conception of the international community. Coulanges teaches (2000, p. 134):

Thus, human society, in this race, did not expand from a circle spreading gradually, from one place to another, but rather by joining small groups, already established long ago. Many families formed the phratry, many phratries the tribe, and many tribes the city. Family, tribe, city are therefore perfectly analogous societies and born from one another by a number of federations.

[...] This was how the State was created among the ancients; its study became necessary to fully elucidate the nature and institutions of the city.

After this brief social historical description we enter the area of our responsibility, stating that the support base of this state organization goes through the tax. These legal provisions that rule life in society, guaranteeing and ensuring the rights of its citizens, asserting civil liberties, individual and social rights, consider tax as indispensable. Through this it is organized the social system and all its costs are solved. Didactically, Valadão says (2000, p 221):

The State, to meet social demands, there included the guarantee of human rights, incurs various expenses, such as paying employees, maintaining control structures, public investments, etc. Such expenditures are state costs that should be paid with state revenues. Hence the need of financial activity of the state in which it is included the assess of these revenues, among these there is the taxation.

It is evident that taxation does not limit individual rights, but it actually functions as a necessary precondition to achieve these; without taxes "[...] there would be no State and without State would not exist the very right". (VALADÃO, 2000, p. 206) Considering their conditions, it is imperative the contribution of citizens to the financial support of the State. A State concerned with the welfare of those who are part of it can only be achieved with the accountability of them for this support. We must put an end to this exaggerated liberal conception around the requirement only of rights, that even has reason to exist because of traumas caused by historical troubled periods. The respectable thought to spread is that with the maturing of democracy theories that preach the defense of citizens' rights only no longer fit. It is important to add to this theoretical context, the intellectual foundation around the need to fulfill the duties of citizens.

To the State tha seeks to accomplish justice it is appropriate to theorize the understanding of these duties to the citizen-taxpayer. It is the duty of all to cooperate, guaranteeing their rights through the assumption of his duties; we can speak, in medio virtus, in a fundamental duty to pay taxes in order to finance the State and guarantee fundamental rights. Cardoso explains (2014, p. 147):

It can be said, therefore, that there is a right of all individuals and society, that each one fulfills the duty to collect taxes. That is so because of the fulfillment of this duty is directly linked to concrete possibility of realization of the fundamental rights guaranteed to Brazilian citizens. Instead of a right x duty duality, there is actually an interface, in which a duty to contribute to each one corresponds to a right of others. It is a real social responsibility, and no more than simple duty towards the state apparatus.

The tax can not be interpreted by citizens as something bad anymore, an action to be rejected, a sacrifice without return. In a conception always current, no taxation without representation, it is about the conception of taxes as consensual in a Democratic Rule of Law; they are legitimized by its citizens, who are not allowed to deny them, but rather to question them when presented to society as unrighteous.

When objectionable, every citizen must fight for justice and not accept unrighteousness and passively complain facing the tribute as a purely arbitrary representation of the state power; or as mere unilateral sacrifice of the citizen as a taxpayer. The idea of the tax as a legal power serving the citizen and not the other way around is consolidated.

## DUTY OF INFORMATION ABOUT THE TAX BURDEN, ITS CONSTITUTIONAL BASIS AND LEGAL IMPLEMENTATION

The tax burden in Brazil is considered heavy, but if this statement is analyzed more acutely, it remains clear that the disproportion between the invested by way of taxes and its return as improvement of life in society is high. There is a vast gulf between investment and return.

As a type of social progress, the search for an ideal of tax justice is defended throughout this work showing that the scope of this need is related to the exercise of fiscal citizenship, and its obtaining is understood only after an awareness among citizens. Therefore, the indispensable duty to inform is the turning point for achieving tax consciousness.

The definition of "information" refers to the effect of data manipulation and processing, such that imports a transformation both quantitative and qualitative in the person who receives those data.

Under the Tax Law the duty of information on taxes is the primary contour that lead to fiscal justice. Through it the citizen-taxpayer becomes aware of why the need for taxation imputed to him, and therefore he consent to it. As a result, the entire normalization of the tax legislation is legitimized. The Brazilian Federal Constitution of 1988 contains an article that, once properly implemented, can do much to reinforce all the theory on fair taxation brought here.

The article 150, § 5, of the Brazilian Constitution says that: "the law shall determine measures for consumers to be informed about taxes on goods and services" This rule defend the transparency of the tax burden mainly on goods and services (indirect taxation); when we analyze the phenomenon of financial impact, we find that such taxes are paid by the final consumer of goods and services to which the taxes are imposed. What happens routinely is the fact that most citizens do not even realize this burden. But, based on this constitutional article, the integral tax burden of the final price of the goods and services must be explained to the consumer, actual taxpayer.

The preference of the Brazilian legislature for indirect taxes prevents the identification by the taxpayers of the tax portion that is being imposed to them, which does not occur with direct tax, whose taxation system allows the taxpayer to have a more accurate notion of what he is actually paying. Didactically explains Pitten (2012, p. 338):

And the legislator, aware of the taxpayer's ignorance of the tax burden that supports, explores it, opting to establish and raise indirect taxes, whose economic burden is supported by passive and uninformed final consumer, at the expense of the institution or raise of taxes that burden directly. With this, the legislator gets the approval of onerous tax laws through the passivity of citizens indirectly affected by the measure, who normally believe that the issuenot even concern them.

This determination brought by article 150, § 5, of the Brazilian Federal Constitution, is fundamental to the fiscal justice purpose, since it aims to educate the citizen of the economic burden assigned to him. We take the opportunity to expose enlightening lessons Calmon (2005, p. 395):

The desired goal is the awareness of the citizen-taxpayer. We know well the amount of taxes levied on our patrimony and our income to when we do a financial investment, enter into a contract, formulate a statement of income, receive our salaries and so on. Social security contributions, income tax, Urban Land and Building Tax (IPTU), Tax on Rural Property (ITR), Tax on Property of Motor Vehicles (IPVA), the tax on inheritances and gifts, the *inter vivos* real estate property inheritance tax (ITBI) offer no problems. However, there is a list of 'indirect' or 'market' taxes that often go unnoticed to the consumer of goods and services due to the financial phenomenon of 'impact' or 'translation' tax burdens. Who collects the tax, in other words, the *de jure* taxpayer', is not necessarily who financially supports the financial burden, but the 'in fact taxpayer'. Must people do not know that while buying a tie, a shoe, a shirt, food, a refrigerator, is paying tax on merchandise circulation and service (ICMS), or even tax on manufactured products (IPI). People should know that there are taxes in the price of fuel (tax on sales and retail - IVV and ICMS) and in the electricity and telephone bills, sometimes the t installments of the lease, the rent, a bus ticket, tax installments are included in the price. To clarify this phenomenon, the taxpayer decided to force the political people to clarify the taxpayers. It is a complete and unwavering determination, not a mere empty recommendation. It applies to taxes whose nature includes the legal repercussions. [...] (Our emphasis).

Given the importance of the duty of information about the tax burden as a way to materialize constitutional rights and duties in a society of democratic rights and committed to the welfare of its citizens, we must go further. This loyalty and openness of the government with the taxpayer has to be extended to all taxes, rising to an ideology of general duty of information, as Pitten elucidates (2012, p. 339.):

The general duty of information is not limited to non-cumulative taxes, applying to all the tax species. Therefore, is necessary to clarify to the in fact taxpayer about the legal and economic repercussions, and also the only economic repercussions. It requires that they are informed, as much as possible, what is the tax burden effectively supported by the in fact taxpayer. (Emphasis in original text).

In practical terms there is no doubt about the difficulty of decomposing the price of certain goods and services, in view of the complexity of the tax system of replacements, for example; though not possible the provision of an accurate indication, it will be likely possible to provide the consumer-taxpayer a general sense of the contours of the tax burden, duly established by law. Greco criticizes (2013, p. 1664):

However, with this range, the device presents difficult operation due to the complexity of taxation, particularly the contributions. Though apparently simple to say that the contributions should also be highlighted object so that the population could directly know the load of the burden that supports, that runs conter to the system adopted by the legislation establishing – for exemple, in the case of COFINS - three taxation regimes: not cumulative, single and cumulative with different rates, in different moments of charge depending on the type of activity or negotiated product. How clearly determine case by case what burdened the goods or the service?

It is evident that in the ideal of isonomy the direct taxes should be taxed more strongly, using the progressive technique. In this system, the taxation would be diferente for those who are in a different economic situation, according to the premise that must pay more who can pay more. It is important to remember that the actual his global income. The criticism that is made relates to the terrible practice of our representatives legislators who mostly prefer to see us alienated in relation to heavy tax burden we bear in indirect taxes, leaving us to wander in theur fiscal insensitivity; than meet the constitutional precept and clarify the situation of the tax implications within the repercussion phenomenon. However, this is changing.

Within the concepts about the duty of information on the tax burden as a tool to reach an effective participation of the taxpayer, giving rise to consciousness and the tax citizenship related to the fiscal justice, we have the example of the complementary law No. 107/2005 of the State of Paraná - Brazil, which addresses in its article 2 and § 5, *in verbis*:

Article 2. The institution or increase of tax will meet the principles of economic efficiency, administrative simplicity, flexibility, responsability and justice. (...)

§ 5. The tax must be and seem fair, given the criteria of isonomy, ability to pay, equitable distribution of its burden, generality, progressivity and non-confiscation. (Our emphasis).

This pioneering legislation of Paraná State allows law operator to demand the application of universal justice ideals, applied to tax theory. The intent of the law to meet these ideals was so strong, that it even determines that the tax should not only be, but also seem fair. In addition, it is clear the purpose to make possible the achievement of the intention imposed by the constitutional provision by requiring relevant measures to the demand for transparency and elucidation of the tax burden. Following the same guidelines, the complementary law of Senate No. 646/1999, called "Taxpayer Protection Code", which in its article 2 states:

Art. 2. The institution or increase of taxes will comply with the principles of tax justice.

Sole Paragraph. It is considered fair the taxation that meets the principles of isonomy, ability to pay, equitable distribution of the tax burden, generality, progressivity and non-confiscation.

Once again the compliance of these provisions leads to ethical and legal boundaries for tax justice, establishing principles for the operator of the law to have application outlines the conduct him to this ideal. This association with fair taxation leads to the acceptance of the constitutional principles of isonomy, ability to pay, equitable distribution of the tax burden, generality, progressive and non-confiscation. The most important factor in putting such concepts expressed in the law, is bringing to the citizen-taxpayer the assurance that justice can not be away from taxation.

Continuing with the implementation of the ideal of fiscal justice, we highlight the Law 12,741/2012[88], which provides clarification measures to the consumer referring to how much taxes influence the price formation of goods and services. The law expresses in its article 1:

Article 1. In fiscal or equivalent documents issued at the time of sale of goods and services to the consumer, throughout the national territory, it must convey the information of the approximately amount corresponding to all the federal, state and municipal taxes, whose incidence influences the formation of the respective price sale. (Our emphasis).

According to this law, the adequate and clear information about the taxes on products and services should be included in the fiscal document to be delivered to the consumer-taxpayer. The taxes to be disclosed according to law 12,741 / 2012, are[89]: ICMS, ISS,

---

88  Law No. 12,741 of December 8, 2012. Provides for the clarification of measures to consumers, referred to in § 5 of article 150 of the Brazilian Federal Constitution; amends item III of article. 6 and item IV of article 10ₐ of Law No. 8,078, of September 11, 1990 - Code of Consumer Protection.

89  Article 1, § 5° of the Law No. 12,741/2012.

IPI, IOF, PIS / PASEP, COFINS, CIDE, II, PIS/PASEP - IMPORT and COFINS - IMPORT. It is clear the intention of the ordinary legislator to seek the ideals of fair taxation brought by constitutional rule, making its implementation through this law, which may become a milestone in the constant search for justice that should guide the legal operators.

The most important factor in this law was to be able to ascend to the federal level the possibility of adding more objectively to the tax law an element that should be intrinsic to Law: justice. Thus, it stimulates effective popular participation to legal-tax relationship, unveiling a realization of citizenship and tax consciousness. Related to the law operator, establishes clearly defined points os reference for the implementation of tax justice. Tipke says (2012, p. 13):

In a Rule of Law all should occur fairly as much as. This is the highest requirement that can be done before. This requirement can not be canceled in its essence or offset by other requirements. Hence also emerge constitutions that expressly invoke Justice or Tax Justice.

Thus, a proper taxation is a taxation accepted by all citizens as fair. A taxation necessary to maintain the public interest, that shows good faith, proportional and reasonable.

## THE CONCEPTUAL CONTOURS OF TAX AVOIDANCE AND TAX EVASION

Taxes are guaranteeing means of the State and serve as support for fundamental rights, given that they are used as maintainers of the state structure. There is no doubt that the citizen-taxpayer is always looking for ways to try to minimize fiscal costs, particularly in societies where the return perception of this "investment" is not noticed. It lacks understanding of consciousness, citizenship and fiscal justice.

When the tax planning done by the citizen-taxpayer is conducted under the compliance of the law, however much he seeks means to reduce or suppress the payment of all taxes, he does not harm the legal system. Its legality is full and perfectly covered by legal form; but this vision of fiscal self-preservation is too individualistic and simplistic. The taxpayer's point of view that enjoys these actions, its only to pay less taxes, but this spectrum lacks a macro sense, which at its base is the State Tax, based on financial demands required to meet their tasks through taxes. Without taxes and taxpayers there is no way to build a State, much less a Rule of Law guarantor of the rights and duties of its citizens. Montesquieu already stated long ago (2000, p. 221):

State revenues are a portion of his property that every citizen gives to have the security of another or to enjoy it nicely. To properly establish this revenue, one must consider both the State needs as the needs of citizens. One should not take the real needs of the people to give the state's imaginary needs. (Our emphasis).

As a result of the State Tax, we see an organized State with its strong institutions and guarantor of the fundamental rights of its citizens. For this, dodging exaggeratedly liberal principles, it is evident the need for a balance between rights and duties, in which the "duty" is equivalent to "right" in a continuous balance in the search for values of Justice. We highlight at this point the fundamental duty to pay taxes, in which the citizen guarantees his rights through the fulfillment of their duties. According to this balance emerges to the taxpayer the duty to not excuse his tax obligations, either through simulated legal transactions containing deviations of purpose, either through tax fraud with the intention of not paying his taxes. Such conduct lack legitimacy and sin by inciting social destabilization.

In an ideal society, tax justice would be achieved through a process in which citizens informed of their rights and duties, would be aware of both, participating and legitimizing the payment of their taxes through their citizenship. This payment would happen fully, because the citizen-taxpayer participated, consented and led the whole process about the information, awareness, citizenship exercise, legitimacy and consequent tax justice.

However, this is not what happens, hence the need to define two forms usually employed in order to avoid paying taxes: Tax Avoidance and Tax Evasion. Objectively, tax avoidance is a tax planning that uses legal methods to decrease the incidence of the tax burden of a given taxpayer.

Before the triggering events of tax liens, the taxpayer uses previous choices that respect the legal system, allowing a mitigation or complete elimination of the tax impact on their accounts. The avoidance prevents the occurrence of the, and since it does not occur, the tax is not due. In the lessons of Xavier (2009, p. 351) on tax avoidance:

It is, in short, to avoid the application of certain standard or set of standards by actions or sets of actions, aimed at preventing the occurrence of the triggering event of the tax duty in certain (less favorable) or produce the occurrence of this fact in another (more favorable).

The most favorable characteristic of the chosen legal order does not necessarily translate into a lack of taxation, the objectives of the taxpayer can be satisfied with a more moderate taxation.

In the case of tax evasion the system is diverse, considering that the taxpayer use illicit means to avoid paying the tax due. We can mention among the usual tricks to evade taxes: data omission, false statements, production of documents containing false or altered information, use of false or altered invoices. In evasion, the triggering event occurs and yet the taxpayer does not pay the tax, meaning that such conduct is unlawful. In the words of Torres (2012, p. 123):

[...] the tax evasion issue is ambiguous: a) it can mean the pure tax saving, by the absence of the triggering event, as is the case in which the taxpayer quits smoking in order to not pay tax; b) or it can have the meaning of unlawful evasion (tax evasion), which also constitutes a crime against the tax system, as, among others, in cases of simulation, evasion and fraud against the law.

Evasion is a tax saving occurred from the possibility of avoiding an act or na emergence of legal facts that would lead to the triggering event of the tax. Quit smoking in order to not pay taxes on cigarettes is an example of lawful evasion because the taxpayer acts in a field not subject to the incidence of the law. (TORRES, 2012, p. 10). In the case of unlawful evasion, the taxable event came and the taxpayer hide it in order not to pay the tax due.

In tax planning, tax avoidance is widely used by companies in cases of international transfers of funds. They look for different tax designs in different countries in order to direct their financial values where the tax law is less costly, in order to reduce the tax burden. Is very common, in transfers of values between branches and head office, where the first need to transfer resources to the second. The big head offices are usually found in countries where moral discussions about tax avoidance are more mature; thus combating abusive tax avoidance or inconsistent tax planning are much stronger than in countries that have not woken up to this reality.

Legitimate tax planning has to be the paradigm of analysis to identify precisely the aspects of these two figures exposed here. Calmon says (2006, p. 60):

There is avoidance that the law neither prohibits nor allows. But since it does not expressly prohibit, implicitly allows. The rule is freedom. The exception is that has to be expressed. It is not prohibited by law to choose instead of wage labor over provision of services by third parties (typists, calculators, consultants, etc.), to avoid taxation on the payroll, then this kind of avoidance is lawful.

Everything that is not forbidden is allowed. Everything that is allowed is not forbidden, it can be done.

The negotiating freedom and the right to self-management areallowed.

Illegal evasion is prohibited by law (fraud, deceit, simulation).

Within this exposé by Sacha Calmon we conclude that the taxpayer has full freedom to conduct his business the way he believes is best for him. The question that arises is: within a fiscal State there is a space for a self-limitation of that individuality and freedom? The legality, in order to maintain the institutional and sponsor of individual and collective rights and guarantees structures can oppress freedom of the taxpayer?

The citizen taxpayer has full freedom to conduct his business structuring his business in order to allow you a tax saving, the freedom of initiative can not suffer unnecessary interferences by the State. However, the tax is (or at least it should be) legitimized by the taxpayer, and this can not exacerbate the legitimate tax planning and use fraud, deceit or simulation to evade the payment. As a result we defend the power of fiscal State to enter the individual field of the autonomy of the citizen-taxpayer and disregard those legal transactions that meet the real purposes of the instruments for which they were created. When the purpose of the transaction is simply the mitigation or annulation of tax payment, a detailed analysis of tax administration and the judiciary would be indicated.

It is important to emphasize here that we agree with this situation in an ideal state in which the premises proposed here are fully observed. In a State where the tax is not legitimized by its citizens (duty of information is not except), the Executive Branch establishes the tax by provisional measure and the tax law is so complex and extensive that even the law operators feel lost, consistent tax avoidance can not be criticized.

## TAX CONSCIOUSNESS AS MEAN OF COMBATING PURPOSE DEVIATIONS AND TAX FRAUD

Throughout this study notions of justice, citizenship, and tax consciousness were exposed. It was commented on purpose deviations that despite the taxpayer using a "veil of legality" he actually exacerbates his moral duties and aim defraud the tax authorities. We addressesed still legal forms that conceptualize the trick in its full form, in which the taxpayer objectively deceives the tax State.

Justice has to be the cornerstone of the whole social system. From the moment in which citizens do not feel citizens or socially inserted, he begins to isolate himself in small groups creating a fragmentation of the social cluster. These parallel "social states" within the formal State begin to create endless conflicts with on another; all aspects of social life are reached by this fragmentation. And what are the reasons for this social breakdown? Many. Impunity, the feeling of not participating of the whole, injustice, lack of a faster response of the State in relation to the demands of its citizens. All this social balance can be fine, but can be achieved through a stronger social pressure regarding their representatives by education or a provision by the State to its citizens of more optimized conditions of formal education at all levels which would be more difficult. Current major countries rebuilt from completely adverse conditions through education. Such is the case in Germany after World War II and South Korea.

And what does this have to do with taxes? Everything. The Contemporary State Tax is structured by the collection of taxes from its citizens-taxpayers, these citizens want their fundamental and social rights to be guaranteed by the State; being fundamental to them the understanding that the fundamental duties structures are part of this plexus of guarantees. It is necessary to abolish an extremely liberal view, with the citizens realizing that there is a special significance to the community passive and collective legal positions as they bring balance to the social system. Nowadays, fundamental rights and duties are considered an expression of state sovereignty based on human dignity.

The fiscal State, to provide quality education, needs to be structured; tu be structured, it needs to collect tax. Citizens must agree on what they are paying by way of tax, because only then it will be legitimate. To agree citizens nust have information and consciousness of what they are paying and its return through quality of life for society. With the tax consciousness integration will occur fluidly through what we commonly call citizenship. This participation prevents the breakdown of the social fabric and legitimate the requirement of fiscal State; this strong, balanced and supervised state has to meet the demands of its citizens, resulting in the only scope of a Democratic Rule of Law: Justice. The financial phenomenon is manifested "[...] especially in the activity of obtaining funds entry and carrying out expenditures. It is located in the intervening context of public entities both in legal transactions and in economic activity "(BASTOS, 2001, p. 5); it is really important in business dynamics of entries and exits of capital among countries of this great globalized world economy.

The both internal and external struggles, the countries against figures such as the tax evasion and tax avoidance are, indeed, complex. Human creativity when it comes to getting forms and stratagems to pay less taxes seem endless. As an example there is a very complex trick of tax avoidance known "the double irish and dutch sandwich"[90]. In it, major multinational companies attach all profits earned outside their home country to a subsidiary in Ireland, this subsidiary transfers the profits as dividends to another subsidiary in the Netherlands, not paying taxes because they are two countries of the European Union, and from the Netherlands the money is transferred to another subsidiary in Bermuda (tax haven). It is necessary to go through the Netherlands because if there were a direct transfer from Ireland to Bermuda there would be payment of taxes, which does not happen due to the inclusion of the Netherlands in the scheme. Important detail, the Dutch subsidiary of the companies participating in this diagram, often does not have any employees. Arriving at Bermuda, the money is totally unencumbered beacause of its characteristic of a tax haven.

It is evident that all this is due to a lack of harmonization of fiscal legislation among countries and the existence of tax havens, that have that name because of the no taxation of their financial transactions. On the subject, Borges teaches (2006, p. 9):

Today, the tendency of state governments to create mechanisms of minimization or elimination of the tax burden is strong, setting tax concession policies to attract business investment and business activities to the territory of the respective States. In a

---

90 Such avoidance strategy is quite complex and difficult to characterize. In practice, apparently, it does not contradict any fiscal/tax law of the country in which it occurs; but it has rather dubious moral, mainly because it comes from companies whose worldwide advertising preach values completely opposite to these practices. The social damage of this type of action undertaken by these companies is incalculable. The more correct attitude would be the same use of their financial and political power to stimulate fiscal citizenship of the people of the States that supports them.

competitive and more open global market, the so-called 'international tax competition' has produced beneficial effects, such as reducing tax rates and broadening the tax base. However, as in any contest or competition, tax competition becomes prejudicial or harmful when not observed such requirements and especially when measures are taken to encourage the non-compliance with tax laws of other States.

As highlighted by the author, it is currently very common incentives for States with sole purpose of mitigating tax obligations and encourage the establishment of businesses; the problem arises when lack transparency, honesty and mainly a collaboration among the tax laws of those States. The "legal" can not supplant the "moral" every time the purpose of a particular action is detrimental to the community, it must necessarily be disregarded. We can not let the negative points of this international tax competition outweighs the positive ones through acts that outrage a common moral. The solution is international cooperation towards a balance of cohesive, transparent and interconnected tax systems. For this to happen there must be among them a certain degree of "intellectual maturity", which can only be achieved with the compliance with the concepts, all the time, here emphasized. This connection that must exist among the tax laws of the States for mutual support, can only be realized more consistently if the perception of diversity on the tax State is lower.

This is not an attempt to standardize States, aiming that all are equal. It is more about perception of the taxpayer regarding the main reason for the purpose of the tax State. Each state has individuality related to their social, cultural, political, economic and legal characteristics. Regardless of his personality, he may have a current awareness of the essential purpose of the modern fiscal State. The main objective of this work is, through the concepts of fair taxation, eliminating reckless practices as, for example, the double irish and dutch sandwich. Borges continues its teachings (2006, p. 10):

[...] greater international cooperation - is a feasible and appropriate action to respond to the pressures of globalization. Indeed, with the adoption of this last form, each State remains with the power to set its tax system in the way that suits them, in response to their own interests, but always taking into account the internationally imposed constraints, especially in relation to agreements that would have to be made to establish acceptable and not acceptable practices in tax matters. [...].

With so many possibilities of tax evasion and tax avoidance it is necessary battle them constantly; a battle that most often is repressive, punishing people who have been identified with the behavior, but it can be preventive, through legislation to inhibit such actions. The proliferation of numerous possibilities can not be done topically. The problem of excessive legislation (though fundamental) is approaching a vicious and empty cycle that does not eliminate the problem at its core; at this point we emphasize, once again, the need for change in citizen's behavior, which must face the tribute not as a loss, but as an investment that will return in the form of quality of life.

For Tipke (2002, p. 19):

Since justice is the most fundamental concept of Law, it is also the most abstract. As a highly indeterminate evaluative concept, it is a constant temptation for lovers of pompous rhetoric and empty forms of expression. [...]

It is perceivable that we can not get lost in ineffective legislation that works as an embarrassment, to solve case by case. A paradigm shift is imperative, a radical transformation in the way in which citizens-taxpayers interact with the fiscal State that represents them. For more utopian that such mutations may seem we need to start them, because only through them this impulse that nowadays tempt taxpayers in order to avoid taxes assigned to him will be permanently solved. No legislation is more efficient than the change of social behavior, a change in the perception of the citizen-taxpayer regarding the return given by the tax State. This State is a reflection of its taxpayers, it is so by the approvals or omissions of those who compose it. The change of contours of the tax State depends on a real obsession of its citizens-taxpayers in developing and regulate a solid dogmatic construction in the pursuit of education, consciousness, citizenship and fiscal justice.

Through proper understanding of these fundamental concepts for structuring the fiscal State, we present a very realistic way to eliminate various types of fraudulent actions, essentially with a self-centered nature, that harm to society so much. It is widely recognized and perfectly acceptable for the parties in a free society to have the right to conclude the legal transactions the way that suits them within the legal permissiveness. This stems from a basic principle of law that legitimate transactions are admitted and protected. However, even if lawful, if these legal transactions assault the purpose for which those legal instruments have been created, they must be disregarded. Jarach says (2004, p. 164):

What is relevant to the tax law is the economic fact, the *intentio facti*, or, to use an expression used in American jurisprudence, the business purpose. If the legal forms correspond to a *intentio juris*, which influences the discipline of private law guiding it to a different direction than, without expression of will, had been given the natural law, the elected legal forms are indifferent to the tax law; admitting otherwise would clash with the nature of the enforceable fact, which is economic and not legal, and moreover against the source of imposing relationship, which is exclusively the law and not the expression of will of the parties.

The legal transactions, not only in tax field, must be guided by a principle of good Faith, in this regard it is essential that there is no abuse of forms or deviations of purpose within these transactions. The tax avoidance and tax evasion must be analyzed within this perspective, questioning what are the real intentions of the parties in that legal transaction. It is clear that the "business purpose" was not that for which they have used given system, it is disregarded, and interpreted for the real reasons. Synthetically and far from exhausting the topic, these notions would be needed to deal with this important issue. The purpose of implementing a virtuous cycle of tax justice is complementary to the understanding of how a claim to a just and better society is possible; with the translation from a reality seen as imaginary to a perfectly feasible one, through behavior, indeed absent in our social environment: the assumption of responsibilities by citizens, trying to overcome at least partially their subjectivity and focus on community. The idea of human dignity goes through this delicate balance between individualismo of rights and collectivism of duties.

## CONCLUSION

The most exciting on the issue of tax justice is the belief that through theoretical frameworks can pursue its operation in practical life. In a world that rulers' decision-making revolves around economic issues, and, as always, throughout history, the great revolutions and transformations occurred due to fiscal/tax demands, it is imperative the spread of a environment conducive to fair taxation. For Ferguson (2007, p. 78) "The best way to understand the history of the tax is to see in it the intangible search for a just measure: a system that maximizes its income and at the same time minimize the inhibition of growth of the economy, [...]". The eternal quest for balance and justice.

Addressing the issue of justice, we wove its contours through influential thinkers. Explanations have been made about tax consciousness and its fundamental importance in the development of citizenship. It was considered essential the use of information about the tax burden as a promoter of consciousness and subsequent fiscal citizenship. Defining fiscal State as being the one which through the tax derives its maintainance and through it the State prepares to ensure rights and duties of its citizens, it was shown that, among the fundamental duties of citizens, there is the one to pay taxes as a way to provision the organized and guarantor State.

The conceptual outlines of tax avoidance and tax evasion are related to the issue because of the perennial creation of means to avoid the incidence of taxes. We highlighted the constant need for interconnection among States to battle these practices. Although utopian, it is defended the position to avoid legislation created for occasional confrontations of emerging issues, seeking a more lasting change of social paradigm through education, consciousness, citizenship and fiscal justice. Through the effective integration of these concepts in society we will achieve a reality in which figures created for the sole purpose of defrauding community development will not exist.

According to Becker (2002, p. 85), "The Law does not exist to moralize the man, but to be practical instrument that promotes a Common Good (true or false) achievable (not only ideal or utopian)". Because of the importance of the issue, the present work is not intended to exhaust the subject, but to promote a debate in search of positive changes for the development of the whole society.

## REFERENCES

BALEEIRO, Aliomar. **Uma Introdução à Ciência das Finanças**. (Updated by: Dejalma de Campos). 16th ed. Rio de Janeiro: Forense, 2002. (original text in Portuguese)

BASTOS, Celso Ribeiro. **Curso de Direito Financeiro e de Direito Tributário**. São Paulo: Saraiva, 2001, 8th ed. (original text in Portuguese)

BECKER, Alfredo Augusto. **Teoria Geral do Direito Tributário**. São Paulo: Lejus, 2002. 3rd ed. (original text in Portuguese)

BORGES, Antônio de Moura. **Considerações sobre o Combate à Concorrência Tributária Internacional Prejudicial**. In: GICO JÚNIOR, Ivo; BORGES, Antônio de Moura (Coords.). **Intervenção do Estado no Domínio Econômico**. São Paulo: Aduaneiras, 2006. (original text in Portuguese)

CALAMANDREI, Piero. **Eles, os juízes, vistos por um advogado**. 1st ed. São Paulo: Martins Fontes, 1995. (original text in Portuguese)

CARDOSO, Alessandro Mendes. **O Dever Fundamental de Recolher Tributos**. Porto Alegre: Livraria do Advogado, 2014. (original text in Portuguese)

COÊLHO, Sacha Calmon Navarro. **Comentários à Constituição de 1988 – Sistema Tributário**. Rio de Janeiro: Forense, 2005, 9th ed. (original text in Portuguese)

COÊLHO, Sacha Calmon Navarro. **Evasão e Elisão Fiscal. O Parágrafo Único do Art. 116, CTN, e o Direito Comparado**. Rio de Janeiro: Forense, 2006. (original text in Portuguese)

COSTA, Regina Helena. **Curso de Direito Tributário – Constituição e Código Tributário Nacional**. São Paulo: Saraiva, 2012, 2nd ed. (original text in Portuguese)

COULANGES, Numa Denis Fustel de. **A Cidade Antiga**. São Paulo: Martins Fontes, 2000. (original text in Portuguese)

DWORKIN, Ronald. **O Direito da Liberdade – A Leitura Moral da Constituição Norte-Americana**. São Paulo: Martins Fontes, 2006. (original text in Portuguese)

DWORKIN, Ronald. **O Império do Direito**. São Paulo: Martins Fontes, 2014, 3rd ed. (original text in Portuguese)

FERGUSON, Niall. **A Lógica do Dinheiro: Riqueza e Poder no Mundo Moderno 1700 - 2000**. Rio de Janeiro: Record, 2007. (original text in Portuguese)

GILISSEN, John. **Introdução Histórica ao Direito**. 4th ed. Lisboa: Fundação Calouste Gulbenkian, 2003. (original text in Portuguese)

GRECO, Marco Aurélio. Comentário ao artigo 150, § 5°. In: CANOTILHO, J.J. Gomes; MENDES, Gilmar F.; SARLET, Ingo W.; STRECK, Lenio L. (Coords.). **Comentários à Constituição do Brasil**. São Paulo: Saraiva/Almedina, 2013. (original text in Portuguese)

HENSEL, Albert. **Derecho Tributario**. Madrid: Marcial Pons, 2005. (Translation of the reprint of 1986, the 3rd edition of the original work "Steuerrecht". Berlin/Heidelberg, 1933.)

JARACH, Dino. **O Fato Imponível**. (Translated by: Dejalma de Campos). São Paulo: Revista dos Tribunais, 2004, 2nd ed.

MACHADO, Hugo de Brito. **Curso de Direito Constitucional Tributário**. 1st ed. São Paulo: Malheiros, 2012. (original text in Portuguese)

MONTESQUIEU, Charles de Secondat, Baron de. **O Espírito das Leis**. São Paulo: Martins Fontes, 2000. (original text in Portuguese)

MORAES, Guilherme Peña de. **Constituição da República Federativa do Brasil e Legislação Correlata**. 6th ed. São Paulo: Atlas, 2013. (original text in Portuguese)

NABAIS, José Casalta. **O Dever Fundamental de Pagar Impostos**. Coimbra: Almedina, 2012. (original text in Portuguese)

PINKER, Steven. **Como a Mente Funciona**. São Paulo: Companhia das Letras, 2009. (original text in Portuguese)

RAWLS, John. **Justiça e Democracia**. São Paulo: Martins Fontes, 2000. (original text in Portuguese)

TIPKE, Klaus; LANG Joachim. **Direito Tributário (Steuerrecht)** - Vol. I. Translation.18th ed. German – Luiz Dória Furquim. Porto Alegre: Sergio Antonio Fabris Editor, 2008.

TIPKE, Klaus; YAMASHITA, Douglas. **Justiça Fiscal e Princípio da Capacidade Contributiva**. São Paulo: Malheiros, 2002. (original text in Portuguese)

TIPKE, Klaus. **Moral Tributária do Estado e dos Contribuintes (Besteuerungsmoral und Steuermoral)**. Translated by: Luiz Dória Furquim. Porto Alegre: Sergio Antonio Fabris, 2012.

TORRES, Ricardo Lobo. **Planejamento Tributário – Elisão Abusiva e Evasão Fiscal**. São Paulo: Campus, 2012, p. 123. (original text in Portuguese)

VALADÃO, Marcos Aurélio Pereira. **Direitos Humanos e Tributação: Uma Concepção Integradora**. Direito em Ação (UCB/DF), Brasília – DF, Vol.2, n.1. (original text in Portuguese)

VALADÃO, Marcos Aurélio Pereira. **Limitações Constitucionais ao Poder de Tributar e Tratados Internacionais**. Belo Horizonte: Del Rey, 2000. (original text in Portuguese)

VELLOSO, Andrei Pitten. **Constituição Tributária Interpretada**. Porto Alegre: Livraria do Advogado, 2012. (original text in Portuguese)

XAVIER, Alberto. **Direito Tributário Internacional**. Coimbra: Almedina, 2009, 2nd ed. (original text in Portuguese)

www.ingramcontent.com/pod-product-compliance
Lightning Source LLC
Chambersburg PA
CBHW071534200326
41519CB00021BB/6482